GETTING TO BE
MARK TWAIN

GETTING TO BE
MARK TWAIN

JEFFREY STEINBRINK

UNIVERSITY OF CALIFORNIA PRESS
BERKELEY   LOS ANGELES   OXFORD

University of California Press
Berkeley and Los Angeles, California

University of California Press, Ltd.
Oxford, England

© 1991 by
The Regents of the University of California

Library of Congress Cataloging-in-Publication Data

Steinbrink, Jeffrey.
    Getting to be Mark Twain / Jeffrey Steinbrink.
        p.   cm.
    Includes bibliographical references and index.
    ISBN 0-520-07059-3 (alk. paper)
        1. Twain, Mark, 1835–1910—Biography.   2. Authors,
    American—19th century—Biography.   I. Title.
    PS1331.S75   1991
    818'.409—dc20
    [B]   90-26280
                                                                    CIP

Printed in the United States of America
9 8 7 6 5 4 3 2 1

The paper used in this publication meets the minimum
requirements of American National Standard for Information
Sciences—Permanence of Paper for Printed Library Materials,
ANSI Z39.48-1984. ⊚

For
Virginia and Darwin Hollister
and
Dorothy and James McCarthy

Contents

List of Illustrations ix

Acknowledgments xi

Preface: Getting Home xiii

Abbreviations xix

1. Surviving the Reformation 1

2. Getting to Buffalo 23

3. Coming to Anchor 44

4. An End to Wandering 61

5. Honeymoon 77

6. Nesting 94

7. A Father's Dying 113

8. Writing *Roughing It* 131

9. Lighting Out 151

10. Coming of Age in Elmira 167

Afterword: Getting To Be Mark Twain   188

Notes   193

Bibliography   211

Index   217

Illustrations

Samuel Clemens in 1868   frontispiece

Mary Mason Fairbanks   3

Olivia Langdon, c. 1869   8

Olivia Lewis Langdon   13

The Langdons' home in Elmira   24

The Langdons' parlor   26

Abel W. Fairbanks   36

Jervis Langdon   39

The Wedding Invitation   71

The Newlyweds' Home in Buffalo   73

Elisha Bliss, Jr.   134

The Map of Paris   137

Langdon Clemens   143

Orion Clemens   145

Quarry Farm   168

Acknowledgments

Because it took some time for this book to make clear to me just what it meant to be about, my first thanks are to those who helped make that time available. A generous program of sabbaticals and grants at Franklin and Marshall College, my home institution, made it possible for me to step away from teaching occasionally in order to read Mark Twain's mail and plunder his archives. A fellowship from the National Endowment for the Humanities likewise supported a year of research and writing. I am much indebted to F&M and to NEH for the opportunities these grants opened to me.

For a project like this one, the richest plundering is done among the Mark Twain Papers at the University of California, Berkeley. I thank Robert H. Hirst, General Editor of the papers, James D. Hart, of the Bancroft Library, and all members of the Mark Twain Project staff for their friendship, hospitality, and help. There is no better way to get behind Mark Twain's scenes than to work at the papers, and no better place to do it. For a similar hospitality I thank Darryl Baskin, Director of the Center for Mark Twain Studies at Quarry Farm, his predecessor, Herbert A. Wisbey, Jr., and his staff and associates at Elmira College in Elmira, New York. The center is now doing for Samuel Clemens's Elmira connections what the Mark Twain Memorial has for some time done for his associations with Hartford. In Hartford, I thank the memorial's director, John Vincent Boyer, and Wynn Lee, who held that position before him.

My appreciation also goes to the memorial's staff and to that of its neighbor, the Stowe-Day Foundation, headed by Joseph Van Why. I began to work on Mark Twain fully expecting to enjoy the pleasure of his company; at the time I couldn't have anticipated the extent to which the company of kindred spirits at these collections would deepen that pleasure.

I have also enjoyed getting to know the community of teachers, scholars, and writers who share an interest in Mark Twain. Against the droning of much contemporary academic and critical discourse, they have managed to carry on an intelligent, accessible conversation informed by humane good sense and warmed by persistent good humor. For the generous and continuing interest they have taken in my work I particularly thank Hamlin Hill, Louis J. Budd, Jr., Alan Gribben, Victor Doyno, and Thomas Tenney. It may strike some readers as paradoxical that my deepest debt of gratitude to these distinguished Twain scholars has nothing to do with conventional scholarship: their shared confidence in the power of vernacular values and the vitality of vernacular language bolstered my own determination that this be not a book for scholars only, but one intended for readers of many dispositions who have an abiding curiosity about Mark Twain.

I thank my students, who continue to give me reason and opportunity to become a better reader of books and people. I thank my colleagues in Franklin and Marshall's English Department, who make my work from day to day an adventure and a collaboration. At the University of California Press I thank William J. McClung and Mark Jacobs, who guided this work, and often its author, through the process of publication. And finally I thank three friendly critics, Ken Sanderson, Joe Voelker, and Joanne Sheaffer, who read the early manuscript, claimed to find it good, and helped to make it better. Among my best hopes for the book is that its later readers will discover in it some of the qualities of the fine people who helped bring it into being.

Preface

Getting Home

In the fall of 1870, when Samuel Clemens was struggling with the manuscript of what eventually became *Roughing It*, he told his friend Mary Fairbanks, "My book is not named yet. Have to write it first—you wouldn't make a garment for an animal till you had seen the animal, would you?" (13 October 1870).[1] Just about eight years earlier, though, in the early days of 1863, he had done that very thing in naming Mark Twain. To use Clemens's analogy, "Mark Twain" was at the time a garment in search of an animal, a label rather than an identity. In many respects the invention of that identity was the work of a lifetime, an ongoing effort at self-discovery, self-fashioning, and self-promotion that Clemens managed with inexhaustible dexterity. But the animal assumed its essential shape—grew to its adult, if not mature, proportions—between 1868 and 1871, the period treated in the following chapters.

Although the two were never entirely differentiable from one another, both Clemens and Twain were strikingly unfinished characters in June 1867, when the steamship *Quaker City* set out on the first large-scale pleasure voyage of its kind in American history, a voyage that later gave rise to *The Innocents Abroad*. Clemens, then thirty-one, had managed to parlay the mostly western popularity of Mark Twain, then and thereafter of somewhat indeterminate age, into passage aboard the steamer. The majority of his fellow excursionists turned out to be well-established people with substantial incomes and fixed addresses, whereas the predominating characteristics of his life since he left home at seventeen had been its chanciness and mobility. A week before the ship departed he wrote his mother and sister from New York, stressing as he often had in his letters to them his obsession not to stay put. "All I know or feel," he said,

is, that I am wild with impatience to move—move—*Move!* Half a dozen times I have wished I had sailed long ago in some ship that wasn't going to keep me chained here to chafe for lagging ages while she got ready to go. Curse the endless delays! They always kill me—they make me neglect every duty & then I have a conscience that tears me like a wild beast. I wish I never had to stop *any*where a month. I do more mean things, the moment I get the chance to fold my hands & sit down than ever I can get forgiveness for. (1 June 1867)

In other places Clemens would describe himself as a vagabond or wanderer, but his passion to be on the move amounted to something stronger than wanderlust. "I am so worthless," he wrote his family the day before the *Quaker City* left port, "that it seems to me I never do anything or accomplish anything that lingers in my mind as a pleasant memory. My mind is stored full of unworthy conduct . . . & an accusing conscience gives me peace only in excitement & restless moving from place to place" (7 June 1867).

The newspaper letters he wrote during the voyage of the *Quaker City* extended Mark Twain's reputation and broadened his appeal, but the trip itself did little to relieve that chronic restlessness or, apparently, the feelings that occasioned it. When Clemens stepped off the ship on 19 November 1867 he paused in New York only long enough to publish his dissatisfaction with the expedition—"a funeral excursion without a corpse," he called it—in that city's *Herald* before moving on to Washington, D.C., to serve as secretary to Nevada Senator William M. Stewart. Having passed less than three weeks in the capital, however, he was writing Frank Fuller, another western acquaintance, "I am already dead tired of being in one place so long" (13 December 1867). A few days later he wrote Emily Severance, who like Mary Fairbanks had befriended him aboard the *Quaker City*, "I wish I were in the [Sandwich] Islands now—or in California. . . . I am in a fidget to move. It isn't a novel sensation, though—I never was any other way" (24 December 1867). For much of the next two years he remained in motion, until fully half his life had been spent on the road—untrammeled, if not untormented. When Fairbanks informed him that she had named a pet dog Mark Twain in his honor, he quickly responded, "Don't *chain* him. It makes me restive to think of it" (17 June 1868).

This obsession to be "free" was the prototype of a similar impulse in Huck Finn. Like Huck, Clemens was driven not only by a need to be unconfined but also by the naggings of a guilty conscience and a sense of personal unworthiness. For all the merriment and conviviality he showed the world, particularly in the guise of Mark Twain, Clemens was burdened throughout his life by self-doubts that sometimes gave way to self-loathing. As it did for Huck, motion proved a comfort, if not a cure, for the worst of these feelings. Just before embarking on the *Quaker City* Clemens confided in his mother and sister, "You observe that under a cheerful exterior I have got a spirit that is angry with me & gives me freely its contempt. I can get away from that at sea" (7 June 1867). He seems to have been as little inclined as Huck to believe that this condition would change, and he imagined, rightly, that he would be as restive upon his return from the pleasure trip as he had been at the outset. "If I don't like to land when we get back," he wrote his Hannibal friend Will Bowen, "I will just shift on to some other ship & go away again" (7 June 1867). Like Ishmael, Clemens prepared himself to return to the sea for escape; driven by the same impulse, his own voyage at an end, Huck would resolve to light out for the Territory.

So in a sense this book begins where Huck's ends, with its protagonist—still an adolescent, for all his thirty-three years—restlessly measuring himself against the demands of an establishment culture that seems poised either to embrace or to smother him, or both. Clemens did in fact light out when the *Quaker City* docked— first for Washington, then for San Francisco, then for the western lecture circuit—but his flight was tethered by his having taken on an obligation that tugged at him all the while. Not long after disembarking he had contracted with Elisha Bliss of the American Publishing Company in Hartford to make a book of his *Quaker City* experiences. In doing so, he initiated a series of decisions and commitments that would lead him to find, or to make, his place in the dominant culture rather than seek to perpetuate strategies of escape.

This book tells the story, whenever possible in Clemens's own words and in the words of his correspondents, of the formative changes in his life. Other moments were perhaps more dramatic, more catastrophic, or more dominated by triumph or despair, but between 1868 and 1871 his life took the shape it was essentially to hold from then until its close. During this period Clemens came East—for good, as it turned out—acquired international renown and the beginnings of a considerable fortune with the best-seller *Innocents Abroad,* courted and married Olivia Langdon, and determined to *settle,* first as a newspaper editor in Buffalo and then, and more lastingly, as a professional writer of books in Hartford. Each of these accomplishments represented a profound change of circumstance and, potentially, of outlook in the former Wild Humorist of the Pacific Slope. Even in a life as charged with fortuity and calamity as Clemens's, this span of just three years is remarkable for its compression of crucial choices and turns of fate. By the time it drew to a close in the fall of 1871, with the move to Hartford, the most fundamental of his lifelong evolutions had run its course, providing, in place of the volatility and incoherence of his extended adolescence, the relative stability that informed the great middle period of his career.

This is also, and centrally, the story of the coming of age of Mark Twain. From our vantage point in the late twentieth century, given his status not just as a writer but as a folk character, it is easy to make the mistake of supposing that Mark Twain sprang into being, essentially as we know him, the first time Clemens used the byline in 1863. In fact, although certain characteristic traits were evident from the beginning, it took some time for Mark Twain to assume the dimensions, prerogatives, quirks, and qualities that audiences have since associated with him. Comparing the early Twain with the later, "finished," more familiar persona is in many ways like comparing the first cartoon appearances of Mickey Mouse or Superman, or, for that matter, the early public appearances of John Kennedy or Muhammad Ali or Martin Luther King, Jr., with their later, fully realized images. The basic silhouettes and raw ingredients are there, but before the winnowing, distilling, and refining that produce and intensify their charismatic power.

Mark Twain is one of the very few figures from our history with whom virtually every American, and many others, identifies and feels familiar; he is among the most accessible of our cultural icons. Particularly given that extraordinary familiarity, we need to remind ourselves that in 1868 no one knew Mark Twain as we do, including Samuel Clemens. He was still very much in the works, more a gathering of postures, attitudes, and voices than a unified, fully dimensional, more or less consistent personality. During the years that immediately followed Clemens's stepping off the *Quaker City*, Mark Twain underwent a fundamental sorting out. Certain of his incipient, adolescent qualities would persist and predominate; others would be sloughed off or adapted to integrate, or at least not to compete with, the adult mix. This book sketches the terms of that sorting out, many of them arising from the circumstances of Clemens's personal as well as his professional life. The story it tells should help a reader understand how the Mark Twain we know emerged from among all the Mark Twains that might have been.

That story weaves among three cities: Elmira, Buffalo, and Hartford. In the first of these places, Clemens courted the woman he would marry and came under the influence of her family and her social circle, personified most emphatically by her father. In the second, he assumed his first "permanent" job, ended his wandering, and tried to settle down as a newlywed. In the third, he transacted much of the crucial business of his early career and eventually found the home that had so long eluded him. The book naturally organizes itself around these three places, each with its own attractions and pitfalls for the developing writer. Together they provide not simply a geographical but a circumstantial grid against which to plot the stages of that development.

The earliest of the stages treated here finds Clemens in a frame of mind that anticipates Huck's, fearing that his inherent depravity and worthlessness, his conviction of being ignorant and low-down and ornery, would—and should—forever keep him from the serious regard of decent people. He was determined to make a try at bettering himself, although he displayed a Huck-like skepticism that in his case such an effort would bear fruit. On 31 January 1868 he wrote *Quaker City* shipmate Emeline Beach, "I know I never, never, never shall get reformed up to the regulation standard. Every time I reform in one direction I go overboard in another." A few days later he wrote Mary Fairbanks, "I believe I have a genuinely bad heart anyhow—but in the course of time I will get some of the badness out of it or break it" (9 February 1868). In striving to reform his "bad heart," he would jeopardize not only his own integrity but also the very existence of his alter ego. Weathering that crisis was a crucial part of the evolution depicted in the following pages, an evolution that saw the Mark Twain of the late 1860s become the Mark Twain of all time.

Abbreviations

The following abbreviations appear in the text:

MMF   Mary Mason Fairbanks

MTM   Mark Twain Memorial, Hartford, Connecticut

MTP   Mark Twain Project, Bancroft Library, University of California, Berkeley

OL, OLC   Olivia Langdon, Olivia Langdon Clemens

SLC   Samuel Langhorne Clemens

Chapter One

Surviving the Reformation

By his own reckoning, the most important accomplishment in Samuel Clemens's life was his successful courtship of Olivia Langdon. In many ways he seems to have regarded it as his most surprising accomplishment as well. More than a year before he met her, and more than two years before it occurred to him to fall in love with her, he wrote his old Hannibal friend Will Bowen about his persistent bachelorhood. "Marry be d——d," he said. "I am too old to marry. I am nearly 31. I have got gray hairs in my head. Women appear to like me, but d——m them, they don't *love* me" (25 August 1866). He had definite ideas on the subject, however, ideas that in a general way reflected the Victorianism of his time and the latent Calvinism of his upbringing, ideas that were often at odds with the vagabond adventurer's life he had chosen. Marriage was a static, settled condition; it was also expensive, hallowed, and at virtually every turn informed by a bewildering degree of earnestness.[1]

By contrast, Clemens had spent about half of his thirty-one years unfettered and in motion, having left home at seventeen to see the world and take his chances in it. From the West, where he spent five of those vagabond years, he wrote his mother and sister, "I always intend to be so situated (*unless* I marry,) that I can 'pull up stakes' and clear out whenever I feel like it" (25 October 1861). A few months later he shared with his sister-in-law his notions regarding the contrast between his behavior as a bachelor and his expectations as a husband. "I never *will* marry," he told her, "until I can afford to have servants enough to leave my wife in the position for which I designed her, viz:—as a *companion*. I don't want to sleep with a three-fold Being who is cook, chambermaid and washer-woman all in one. I don't mind sleeping with female servants as long as I am a bachelor—by *no* means—but *after* I marry, that sort of thing will be 'played out,' you know" (29–31 January 1862). Such a view contributed powerfully to the likelihood that under almost any circumstances courtship and marriage would require major changes in Clemens's outlook, habits, deportment, and, he was quite sure, in his character. By ultimately pinning his hopes on Olivia Langdon, a woman whom he took few pains to distinguish from the angels, he raised the ante on change considerably, at least in his own mind, and in so doing sentenced himself to nothing short of thorough, relentless reformation.

"If I were settled I would quit all nonsense & swindle some girl into marrying me," Clemens wrote Mary Mason Fairbanks. "But I wouldn't expect to be '*worthy*' of her. I wouldn't *have* a girl that *I* was worthy of. *She* wouldn't do. She wouldn't be respectable enough." The letter was written on 12 December 1867, just fifteen days before he met Olivia Langdon, the woman he would in fact marry a little more than two years later. During those two years, at first with Mary Fairbanks's finger wagging at him in their correspondence, and then with his idealization of Olivia to encourage him, Clemens gamely undertook a personal reconstruction that was intended to make him a conventionally "better" individual—more religious, more regular in his habits, more refined, more comprehensively civilized. But if Sam Clemens grew up, got religion, and became respectable, what would become of Mark Twain? How does a man who believes and hopes that he has sown the last of his wild oats preserve the vitality of a character who has risen to national prominence in large part by portraying himself as a heedless and irreverent vagabond?

Clemens was as a matter of fact determined to "improve," to become more conventionally respectable, *before* he met Olivia Langdon in December 1867. During the *Quaker City* voyage that began in June of that year, perhaps at the urging of Mary Fairbanks and others, he resolved that the time had come to purge both his life and his writing of their coarseness. This is not to say, as he himself sometimes implied, that he was at the time merely an ignorant vulgarian, but rather that he became increasingly self-conscious

Mary Mason Fairbanks. (Courtesy Mark Twain Papers, The Bancroft Library)

about what he considered his own limitations and those of the prevailing western humorists as he grew more successful. Because of that self-consciousness, he was perhaps ready, even eager, to come under the jurisdiction of a good-hearted and domineering matron—a more formidable Widow Douglas—by the time the *Quaker City* set sail.[2] With Mary Fairbanks just as eagerly playing the part of "Mother," what might be called the comic phase of Clemens's reformation had begun.

Both mother and "cub" were able to regard their roles in this comedy humorously and even ironically. There was room in the relationship for teasing and posturing, strategies which kept the reforming process alive and made it fun for the players. The mother, at thirty-nine, was neither as venerable nor as officiously censorious as she sometimes pretended to be; the cub, at thirty-one, was not as young, or as uncomprehending, or as hopeless as he let on. But the game, like almost all games in Clemens's life and work, had a serious dimension, and he was determined that the comedy would continue happily, with the elevation of its hero to a higher station in life. His very first letter to Mother Fairbanks, written on 2 December 1867, two weeks after the *Quaker City* voyage had come to an end, illustrates the mix of playful exaggeration and sincerity that characterized his attitude toward the improvement she promoted in him:

I was the worst swearer, & the most reckless, that sailed out of New York in the Quaker City. . . . I shamed the very fo'castle watches, I think. But I am as perfectly & as permanently cured of the habit as I am of chewing tobacco. Your doubts, Madam, cannot shake my faith in this reformation. . . . And while I remember you, my good, kind mother, (whom God preserve!) never believe that tongue or spirit shall forget this priceless lesson that you have taught them.

In much the same spirit Clemens wrote to Emily Severance two years after the voyage, thanking her for assisting Mary Fairbanks in his *Quaker City* tutelage: "I shall always remember both of you gratefully for the training you gave me—you in your mild, pervasive way, & she in her efficient tyrannical, overbearing fashion" (27 October 1869). Typically, he closed his 12 December 1867 letter to Mother Fairbanks with a pledge and a plea: "I am improving all the time. . . . Give me another Sermon."

Clemens spent most of this year-long comic phase on the road. In New York, probably on 27 December 1867, he met Olivia Langdon, whose brother, Charles, had been among his *Quaker City* shipmates, and passed a few days there with her and her family. While he may have been attracted to her at the time, he hardly seems to have been smitten, and he was not even to see her again until August of 1868, when the comic phase dramatically ended with his profession of love for her. Olivia may have been vaguely on his mind during this interim, but there is no evidence to show that he was consciously or deliberately "improving" for her sake.[3] Instead, he was hustling up and down the East Coast, returning to San Francisco and the Nevada lecture circuit, giving speeches, writing for newspapers and magazines, trying to complete the manuscript of *The Innocents Abroad*, and periodically sending off dispatches to Mother Fairbanks regarding her cub's progress. "I *am* going to settle down some day," he assured her, "even if I have to do it in a cemetery" (17 June 1868).

Clemens's letters during this period are communiqués from an exhilaratingly *un*settled writer, one whose ethical-esthetic reformation is much less pressing than the day-to-day demands of editors and lecture sponsors. They indicate, however, that he was mindful of his pledge to improve at a time when he was involved in revising the travel letters he had published in the San Francisco *Alta California* and writing new material for *The Innocents Abroad*, whose manuscript he virtually completed in June.

An examination of these revisions demonstrates that Clemens consistently pruned indelicacies, slang, and vulgarisms as he transformed his *Quaker City* correspondence into the text for the book.[4] Given his ambitions at the time, he was apparently as pleased to make these changes as Mother Fairbanks, for one, was to witness them. Improving as he was, Clemens seems also to have been determined to soften his attack on European culture in the course of the *Innocents Abroad* revisions. A letter to Emeline Beach emphasizes the parallel he saw at the time between the literary and the personal reformations he was trying to accomplish: "I have joked about the old masters a good deal in my [*Alta California*] letters," he said, "but nearly all of that will have to come out. I cannot afford to expose my want of cultivation too much. Neither can I afford to remain so uncultivated—& shall not, if I am capable of rising above it" (10 February 1868). While in the West in the early summer of 1868, Clemens submitted a draft of the manuscript to Bret Harte, who, he later claimed, "told me what passages, paragraphs & *chapters* to leave out." Harte, a more experienced and sophisticated editor than Mary Fairbanks, contributed dramatically to the clipping and polishing not only of *The Innocents Abroad* but also of Mark Twain. He "trimmed & trained & schooled me patiently," Clemens said, "until he changed me from an awkward utterer of coarse grotesquenesses to a writer of paragraphs & chapters that have found a certain favor in the eyes of some of the very decentest people in the land."[5] Like a kind of palimpsest, the evolving manuscript itself bore a record of the writer's reformation.

Clemens's attitude toward the revision of both his book and his character reflected the mixture of play and seriousness that typified the comic phase of his reformation. He was able to regard himself, his work, and his persona with a bemused detachment that allowed him to maintain his balance as he anticipated and adjusted to his rising fortunes. The restraints under which he operated, most of them self-imposed, were mild, and his response to them ironic and tolerant. He seems at the time to have been neither threatened nor impaired by his ambition to become conventionally "better" because he himself was aware of its comic dimension and so remained in control of it. This ambition required no violent disjunction between his present and past selves, no repudiation of his earlier life or work for the sake of radical reform. There was no need to cut Samuel Clemens free of Mark Twain; the two could continue to stumble along together. Clemens was candid about his faults and shortcomings, but he was largely self-accepting during the comic phase. "I am not as lazy as I was," he teased Mother Fairbanks, "but I am lazy enough yet, for two people" (12 December 1867). His stance was that of a meliorist and, at that, a meliorist whose attention to reform was easily distracted.

That posture changed drastically in late August 1868, when Clemens paid a long-postponed visit to Elmira and fell thoroughly in love with Olivia Langdon. By the time he departed from the Langdon household in early September he left behind a letter to his would-be sweetheart that reflected the changes in tone and attitude he had begun to undergo. "It is better to have loved & lost you," he wrote Olivia, who had of course turned aside his first advances, "than that my life should have remained forever the blank it was before. For once, at least, in the idle years that have drifted over me, I have seen the world all beautiful, & known what it was to hope. For once I have known what it was to feel my sluggish pulses stir with a living ambition" (7 September 1868). We look in vain for the wink or "snapper" that typically accompanies such a piece of florid writing from Mark Twain. But no wink is forthcoming; the letter continues in the same earnest, superheated fashion and then concludes with a revealing instance of revision: "Write me *something*," Clemens pleads. "If it be a suggestion, I will entertain it; if it be an injunction, I will honor it; if it be a command I will obey it or ~~break my royal neck~~ exhaust my energies trying." The flippant "break my royal neck" has no place here and is virtually obliterated in the manuscript of the letter by a close-looped cross-out.[6] The phrase is appropriate to Mark Twain, of course, as well as to the cub Sam Clemens, but it is clearly inappropriate in the discourse of a man who hopes to establish himself as a suitor worthy of Olivia Langdon. The gap had dramatically widened between what the writer of this letter had been and what he wished to become.

Clemens wanted to be taken seriously by Olivia and her parents—that is, to be taken as a serious *man*—and in the process he seems to have come to believe that he ought to take himself seriously as well. Thus began a phase of his reformation that might be termed melodramatic, a phase during which he sought more fervently than ever before to embrace conventional values and to prove himself according to conventional standards. It would be reductive and unfair to hold Olivia, the Langdons, or the East accountable for these accommodations on Clemens's part; his preconceived notions of respectability had more to do than they with the transformation of the ironist to the zealot.[7] His courtship of Olivia, however, lent urgency to his reformist intentions and encouraged him to believe that his change for the better could and should be radical rather than ameliorative. He seems, in fact, to have caught himself in a snare he set for her. The more emphatically he pledged himself to improve, the more feverishly he came to believe in the necessity and desirability of a sweeping reformation.

In his early letters he petitioned Olivia—as he had Mary Fairbanks, whose name he freely invoked by way of precedent—to help him mend his heedless ways by assuming the "sisterly" role of ministering angel. "Give me a little room in that great heart of yours," he wrote, "& if I fail to deserve it may I remain forever the homeless vagabond I am! If you & mother Fairbanks will only scold me & upbraid me now & then, I shall fight my way through the world, never fear" (7 September 1868). In a letter of 18 October 1868, he again linked Olivia to Mother Fairbanks, maintaining that "between you you have made me turn some of my thoughts into

Olivia Langdon, c. 1869. (Courtesy Mark Twain Memorial, Hartford, Conn.)

worthier channels than they were wont to pursue, & benefits like that, the worst of us cannot forget." While Olivia was no doubt susceptible to these appeals, it was Clemens himself who ultimately took their message most to heart.[8] What was needed, he came to believe, was a thorough overhaul of his character and at least a tacit repudiation of his earlier, unregenerate self.

That conclusion, however resolute, was not reached without a good deal of wrenching and ambivalence on his part. During the fall of 1868, while trying to convince Olivia, the Langdons, and himself that he would be settled, serious, and responsible, he seems instinctively to have sought release from the very respectability he was rushing to embrace. While visiting the Fairbankses' Cleveland home during the fall lecture tour, he wrote a piece entitled "A Mystery," which appeared in Abel Fairbanks's Cleveland *Herald* on 16 November.[9] In "A Mystery" Mark Twain complains that "one of those enigmas which we call a Double" has been marauding around the country, using his name "to borrow money, get rum for nothing, and procure credit at hotels." The double abuses whatever privileges it can wring from the unwary, gives but a single lecture ("in Satan's Delight, Idaho"), and then lapses into full-scale dissipation: "It advertised Itself to lecture and didn't; It got supernaturally drunk at other people's expense; It continued Its relentless war upon helpless and unoffending boarding-houses, and," complains the long-suffering writer, "It was leaving Its bills unsettled, and thereby ruining Its own good name and mine too." The double is last seen riding a stolen horse north from Cleveland, itself a mysterious undertaking.

Clemens has fun on several levels in "A Mystery" and may be revealing a mix of personal feelings as well. Most obviously there is the fun of Mark Twain's trying to pass himself off as a teetotaling pillar of virtue, protesting that his reputation will be devastated by the outrages of the double: "It gets intoxicated—I do not. It steals horses—I do not. It imposes on theatre managers—I never do. It lies—I never do. It swindles landlords—I never get a chance." The reader chuckles along even before he gets to the snapper about swindling landlords because of what he knows of Mark Twain's self-confessed and well-established history as a drinker and liar of western proportions. So the snapper serves more importantly to direct the reader's attention back through the long paragraph which it concludes, a paragraph of Mark Twain's deadpan assertions about the unsuitability of this particular double:

Now to my mind there is something exceedingly strange about this Double of mine. No double was ever like it before, that I have heard of. Doubles usually have the same instincts, and act the same way as their originals—but this one don't. This one has struck out on an entirely new plan. It does according to its own notions entirely, without stopping to consider whether they are likely to be consistent with mine or not. It is an independent Double. It is a careless, free-and-easy Double. It is a Double which don't care whether school keeps or not, if I may use such an expression. If it would only do as I do. But it don't, and there is the mystery of it.

Superficially the paragraph extends (and even belabors) Mark Twain's lament that the double misrepresents him, the joke again arising from the reader's recognition that the traits the writer regards as "new" and "inconsistent" in the double are among those which (the reader has long since come to believe) typify the original. That is, he knows him to be "independent . . . , careless, free-and-easy," just as he knows him to be a tippler and a truth stretcher. The language of the paragraph reinforces the joke by reminding the reader of Mark Twain's rough edges even as he proclaims his respectability.

But on another level the contrast between double and original, between carelessness and responsibility, could not have been entirely a laughing matter for Clemens in November of 1868. His courtship of Olivia, which reinforced and in part depended upon his determination to reform, was driving him more and more sincerely to espouse the very respectability that Mark Twain fraudulently assumes in "A Mystery." Ten days after the piece appeared in the Cleveland *Herald*, he and Olivia became provisionally engaged, a circumstance which bears witness to his own and the Langdons' faith in his potential to develop settled and responsible habits. However eager he may have been to enter into such a commitment, "A Mystery" imaginatively suggests his ambivalences about the prospect, ambivalances that he was very likely unable to express in any other way. The double, most notably, is "careless" not only of Mark Twain's supposed good example, but also of social proprieties generally. He is "independent" and "free-and-easy" in ways that respectable people are not. Through this early and rather rudimentary use of the other self, which was to figure so importantly in his work, Clemens betrayed confusion about the relationship between respectability and unregeneracy in his own makeup. Because the humor of the piece depends upon the implication that, despite his complaints, Mark Twain shares many of the double's lamentable habits, "A Mystery" serves ultimately to reaffirm his bad-boy reputation. Moreover, it does so virtually on the eve of Clemens's engagement, at a time when he was consciously doing all he could to put such a reputation behind him. Unless Mark Twain, too, were to undergo a reformation, it seems that the distinction between him and his creator, a distinction which had become increasingly blurred since Clemens introduced the pseudonym in 1863, would inevitably sharpen and the distance between them dramatically widen.

This process of dissociation may have been at the back of Clemens's mind as he wrote "A Mystery." The piece closes with Mark Twain's discovery that his double is no double after all, but "only a very ordinary flesh and blood young man, given to idleness, dissipation and villainy, and entirely unknown to me or any of my friends." One can almost hear erstwhile suitor Clemens, at this moment wishing that his own character were so genuinely undivided, enthusiastically disowning his earlier, unregenerate self and hoping that "his friends" the Langdons would be willing to overlook the resemblances between the two. The disfranchised doppelgänger, who in his penchant for idleness, dissipation, and villainy bears a likeness to the other, or disreputable, Clemens/Twain, is roundly denounced as "a rascal by nature, instinct, and education, and a very poor sort of rascal at that." But at the last moment, his righteous indignation spent, the writer admits a grudging sympathy for the impostor: "I ought to hate him, and yet the fact that he has been able to borrow money and get board on credit by representing himself to be me, is so comfortably flattering that I own to a sort of sneaking fondness for the outcast for demonstrating that such a thing was possible." The joke, serviceable in its own right, allows Mark Twain to soften his denunciation of the heedless young charlatan just as "A Mystery" ends, adding a final wrinkle of complexity to a piece already noteworthy for its overlapping layers of conscious and semiconscious irony. As we work through these layers, we find writer, persona, and double caught in tangles of imperfectly understood feelings, sometimes attracting, sometimes repelling or rejecting, one another. Whatever else it may suggest, "A Mystery" demonstrates that just ten days before his provisional engagement, and probably while he was a guest in Mother Fairbanks's home, Clemens traded upon Mark Twain's reputation as a rough-and-tumble man of the world even as he insinuated a mild protest against the respectability to which he had pledged himself.

That pledge assumed the weight of a holy vow when he and Olivia became conditionally engaged on Thanksgiving 1868. The conditions, he wrote to Mother Fairbanks, had principally to do with his convincing all involved that his reformation was genuine and consequential. "She must have time to *prove* her heart & make *sure* that her love is permanent," he said of Olivia. "And I must have time to *settle*, & create a new & better character, & prove myself in it & *I* desire these things, too" (26–27 November 1868). Earlier in the letter, in somber and stately language, he spoke of his intentions:

I touch no more spiritous liquors after this day (though I have made no promises)—I shall do no act which you or Livy might be pained to hear of—I shall seek the society of the good—I shall be a *Christian*. I shall climb—climb—climb—toward this bright sun that is shining in the heaven of my happiness until all that is gross & unworthy is hidden in the mists & the darkness of that lower earth whence *you* first lifted my aspiring feet.

There is no intentional humor here, none of the irony of "A Mystery," nor any of the teasing that characterized the cub's earlier correspondence with his mother. Clemens writes as the Rake Reformed, his grandiloquence and almost palpable earnestness emphasizing his melodramatic self-regard. In his fiction he had ridiculed and would continue to ridicule the self-proclaimed born-again sinner, but for a while, at least, in the fall of 1868, he seems with all sincerity to have wanted to play the part. His anxiety to improve, first substantially stirred by his own ambition and the proddings of Mary Fairbanks, threatened now to alienate him from his past and in so doing to open a chasm between writer and persona that not even Clemens's invention could bridge.

Olivia's mother, Olivia Lewis Langdon. (Courtesy Mark Twain Papers, The Bancroft Library)

No doubt with the best intentions, the Langdons initially promoted the widening of this chasm by accepting with gratitude the
notion that their would-be son-in-law *had* undergone a radical
transformation. On 1 December 1868 Olivia's mother wrote Mary
Fairbanks, "I have learned from . . . your conversation, or writing
or both,—that a great change had taken place in Mr Clemens, that
he seemed to have entered upon a new manner of life, with higher
& better purposes actuating his conduct."[10] When Clemens learned
that Fairbanks had responded to Mrs. Langdon with what he called
a "cordial, whole-hearted endorsement," he gratefully declared,
"When I prove unworthy of the service you have done me in this
matter, & the generous trust you have placed in me, even in the
slightest degree, I shall be *glad* to know that that day is the last appointed me to live" (24–25 December 1868). Reform had become
a serious matter, and the past a source of embarrassment and chagrin. But Clemens was determined that his better self would prevail. "Though conditions & obstructions were piled as high as
Chimborazo," he wrote Olivia, "I would climb over them all!" (4
December 1868). By way of promoting a good example of tolerance for her family to follow, Clemens ingenuously quoted his new
Hartford friend, Reverend Joseph Twichell, who had written him,
"I don't know anything about your past. . . . I don't care very
much about your past, but I do care very much about your future"
(4 December 1868). Over the next two months Clemens wrote frequently in this vein as his probation continued, even going so far
as to admit to Jervis Langdon, "I think that much of my conduct
on the Pacific Coast was not of a character to recommend me to
the respectful regard of a high eastern civilization" (29 December
1868). He argued, however, that he was a changed man and that
Olivia was both the occasion and the instrument of his redemp-
tion. On 19 January 1869 he wrote her—appropriately, from the
Fairbankses' Cleveland home—"You will break up all my irregu-
larities when we are married, & *civilize* me, & make me a model
husband & an ornament to society—*won't* you, you dear matchless
little woman?" Five days later he summarized his case to her: "I
have been, in times past, that which would be hateful in your
eyes. . . . I say that what I have been I am not now; that I am striving & shall still strive to reach the highest altitude of worth, the
highest Christian excellence." The best testimony of the Langdons'

faith in this renunciation of a misspent youth is their approval of the couple's formal engagement on 4 February 1869. In order to gain that faith, and for the sake of a newly defined self-esteem, Clemens believed that he had to ransom his past to his future. What was he now to do with Mark Twain?

His circumstances at the time dictated at least a partial answer to the question. During the fall and winter of 1868–69, Clemens was under obligation to two contracts which would further Mark Twain's national reputation and keep him in the public eye through the following year. The first was his commitment to his publisher, Elisha Bliss, to see *The Innocents Abroad* through the final stages of editing and revision, a process which lasted well into the summer of 1869. The second was his agreement to lecture during the 1868–69 season. One effect of these obligations was to make it impossible for Clemens entirely to set his persona aside during his courtship of Olivia, even had he wanted to. In fact, almost all the letters which make up the early, idealizing phase of their relationship, when his intention to reform was most fervid, were written while he was on the lecture circuit, taking Mark Twain and "The American Vandal Abroad" before the public several nights a week.

This has the look of a remarkably lucky coincidence, one of those biographical circumstances that force apparently irreconcilable aspects of a personality into an accommodation. Had such a circumstance *not* prevailed at the time, it is much more likely that the chasm between Samuel Clemens and Mark Twain would have widened, perhaps irreparably, the latter becoming merely a caricature or mascot of the former. This had, after all, been the fate of most other western humorists, "phunny phellows" who had allowed tricks of dialect and spelling to become their stocks-in-trade. That Clemens may have wanted to repudiate Mark Twain as an avatar of his earlier, unregenerate self is suggested from time to time in his love letters, especially when he stresses the distinction between person and persona. On 4 December 1868, for example, he wrote Olivia, "Your father & mother wanted to see whether I was going to prove that I have a private (& improving) character as well as a public one." By the end of the month he was vilifying his earlier work and, by implication, the earlier self responsible for it: "*Don't* read a word of that Jumping Frog book, Livy—*don't.* I hate to hear that infamous volume mentioned. I would be glad to know that every copy of it was burned, & gone forever. I'll never write another like it" (31 December 1868). But the fact of the matter is that between 17 November 1868 and 3 March 1869 Mark Twain was obligated to give more than forty lectures in cities in the Northeast and Midwest and that Clemens had no choice but to come to terms with his persona while he was most deeply in the throes of reformation, writing Olivia almost nightly of his progress.

The result was an accommodation on both sides. Mark Twain saved Sam Clemens from himself, and the lover saw to it that the lecturer revealed a fuller measure than before of his humanity. If the first of these claims has the ring of overstatement about it, it bears the ring of truth as well. The grueling winter lecture season provided an antidote for Clemens's melodramatic self-absorption by keeping him constantly in touch with qualities in his personality upon which Mark Twain thrived—detachment, irony, self-deprecation, testiness, and of course humor. Such an environment tempered the reformer's zeal and helped him recognize the complex interdependence of both halves of the Clemens/Twain identity. At times he bemoaned the consequences of this interconnection, as when he complained to Mrs. Langdon, "I am in some sense a *public* man, . . . but my private character is hacked, & dissected, & mixed up with my public one, & both suffer the more in consequence" (13 February 1869). However, this intermingling of private and public character seems to have served Clemens well during his probationary period, for if the lecturer helped the lover keep his feet on the ground, the lover was particularly determined that the lecturer come across as more than a bumpkin or a buffoon.

Clemens was concerned about his ability to satisfy the demands of eastern audiences even before he fell in love with Olivia and became all the more mindful of what he considered eastern proprieties. On 5 July 1868 he reported to Mary Fairbanks his satisfaction with a San Francisco lecture he had just given but added, "I do not forget that I am right among personal friends, here, & that a lecture which they would pronounce very fine, would be entirely likely to prove a shameful failure before an unbiased audience such as I would find in an eastern city." By the time he began the winter lecture tour on 17 November 1869—in Cleveland, under Mother Fairbanks's watchful eye—he felt considerable pressure, much of it self-imposed, to demonstrate that Mark Twain was more than a "mere" humorist. So it must have been especially gratifying to him when, in her *Herald* review of the performance the next day, Mother Fairbanks proclaimed her approval: "We congratulate Mr. Twain," she wrote, "upon having . . . conclusively proved that a man may be a humorist without being a clown. He has elevated the profession by his graceful delivery and by recognizing in his audience something higher than merely a desire to laugh."[11] Such a notice, especially at the outset of the tour, could only have helped reassure him that it was unnecessary to cut himself off from his persona in order to secure the regard of the respectable and fashionable people among whom he hoped to further his reputation. He must also have realized that praise of this sort would strike a resonant chord in Olivia. "Poor girl," he later wrote Mary Fairbanks, "anybody who could convince her that I was not a humorist would secure her eternal gratitude! She thinks a humorist is something perfectly awful" (6 January 1869).

The lecture performances of 1868–69 partially solved the problems that Clemens faced at the time in presenting Mark Twain to "proper" eastern audiences without eviscerating him. They were instrumental in allowing him to enlarge and redefine the humorist's prerogatives. Those who attended these performances saw the lecturer shamble across the stage, assume a careless attitude at the lectern, and begin drawling out an anecdote, apparently in the most laconic and indifferent way. Perhaps their worst suspicions about Mark Twain were confirmed: here was an irreverent idler with little to recommend him but his cheek. As he talked, however, a strange upheaval took place, first in isolated spots in the hall, then in waves, then in sweeping explosions of laughter, surprise, and recognition. The uninitiated realized that they had been taken in. The indolence and indifference were part of a pose. Mark Twain proved to be a very funny man, but not simply funny in a broad or oafish way. His humor depended upon drollery, flashes of wit, and bright ironies that challenged an audience and kept it awake. The lecture platform allowed Clemens to *show* that Mark Twain's unrefinement was superficial, that it juxtaposed and so rendered only more powerful the operation of a complex and penetrating intelligence. At a time when being taken seriously was of crucial importance to Clemens, the 1868–69 lectures provided him the opportunity to experiment with the vital tension between humor and seriousness that was to characterize his best work. "Mere" humorists were content simply to make the public laugh; especially when the impulse to reform was strong upon him, he was determined to make it think and feel as well.

However sincere this determination, manifestations of reform in Mark Twain were much more modest, subtle, and ameliorative than those which Clemens himself undertook; Mark Twain remained the conservative partner in the complex equation of identity, while Clemens was, for a time at least, the radical. Both person and persona underwent change that carried them in the direction of increasing moral responsibility, respectability, and even piety, but the persona stayed relatively stable while the person swung through dramatic arcs of regret, resolution, and reformation. Mark Twain's relative stability must have been a source of both comfort and consternation for Clemens as he strove to redefine his own "proper" identity during the year that followed his declarations of love to Olivia in September of 1868. There was a kind of solidity and consistency about Mark Twain—qualities which were reinforced by his audience's expectations—that contrasted sharply with the radical mutability which Clemens and others wished to attribute to his own character at the time. Mark Twain had to remain essentially Mark Twain, notwithstanding the broadening and deepening he was undergoing, but Clemens believed that he himself was to become something quite different from what he had been. Never before had there been such cause for isolating person from persona; never again would the two stand so clearly apart from one another.

It is not surprising, given this tension, that Clemens wrote comparatively little during this year of courtship and contrition. In a letter to his family of 4 June 1869 he acknowledged this drought and offered a partial explanation: "In twelve months (or rather I believe it is fourteen) I have earned just *eighty dollars* by my pen— two little magazine squibs & one newspaper letter—altogether the idlest, laziest, 14 months I ever spent in my life. . . . I feel ashamed of my idleness, & yet I have had really *no* inclination to [do] anything but court Livy. I haven't any other inclination *yet*." Although there is some exaggeration of his inactivity here, perhaps because Clemens was late in sending money home to his mother, it is true that his productivity as a writer fell off sharply between September 1868 and the following August, when he became an editor of the Buffalo *Express*. And while other circumstances undoubtedly contributed to this falling off—among them the winter lecture tour and the burden of reading proof for *The Innocents Abroad* in the spring—the primary cause of Clemens's unproductivity during this year of reform was very likely his alienation from the imaginative resources embodied in Mark Twain. Person and persona had to be reconciled before these resources could again be successfully tapped.

That reconciliation came gradually as Clemens grew confident of Olivia's love and the fever of his passion to reform inevitably cooled. Eventually a new personal equilibrium evolved which integrated the Clemens/Twain identity once again and comfortably blurred distinctions between man and writer. Evidence of this evolution emerges intermittently from Clemens's correspondence and from his rare newspaper and magazine pieces of early 1869, among them an article entitled "Personal Habits of the Siamese Twins," which was written on 14 May and appeared in the August issue of *Packard's Monthly*. Significantly, Clemens treats the famous twins Chang and Eng as two distinct personalities vying for control of a single body. Like "A Mystery," "Personal Habits" is a product of the reformation year with obvious and inviting psychological overtones. Writing about the sketch to Olivia on 14 May, Clemens said, "I put a lot of obscure jokes in it on purpose to tangle my little sweetheart," a teasing reference to her literalmindedness in trying to fathom plays of wit or words. But the more provocative tangle in "Personal Habits" is that involving the identities of Chang and Eng, a tangle which Clemens may have seen as a grotesque and literal embodiment of a "double nature" not unlike his own. "As men," he says in the piece, "the Twins have not always lived in perfect accord; but, still, there has always been a bond between them which made them unwilling to go away from each other and dwell apart."[12] By May of 1869 Clemens may well have felt a similar unwillingness, or recognized a similar inability, in the matter of divorcing himself from his past and from those elements of his character which were most recognizable in Mark Twain.

"Personal Habits" obliquely implies such a recognition while it explores the tension between sharply conflicting impulses trapped within a single identity. Together with "A Mystery," it demonstrates that Clemens's lifelong fascination with doubleness, twinning, and paired consciousnesses first came into focus as the disintegrative fervor of self-reformation gradually gave way to the reconciliation of apparent polarities in his personality.

Even by the beginning of 1869, some of Clemens's zeal to reform was exhausted, and his more characteristic realism had begun to reassert itself. Melodramatic self-recrimination gave way to intervals of candor and whimsy and to more pointed reckonings of his chances to get ahead in Cleveland or Hartford or Buffalo. Evidence of this realistic or restorative phase of his reformation appears in a comparatively early courtship letter, where, in language reminiscent of his correspondence with Mary Fairbanks just a year earlier, he acknowledges his fiancée's imperfections and his own incipient worthiness. "I am grateful to God that you are *not* perfect," he told Olivia. "God forbid that you should be an angel. I am not fit to mate with an angel—I could not *make* myself fit. But I can reach your altitude, in time, & I *will*" (5–7 December 1868). As his confidence in her feelings matured, his declarations of intention grew less shrill. On 20 January 1869 he wrote, "I know that you are satisfied that whatever honest endeavor can do to make my character what it ought to be, I will faithfully do." On 6 March, just a month after they had become formally engaged, he summed up his position: "I know that I am not your ideal of what a husband should be, . . . & so your occasional doubts & misgivings are just & natural—but I *shall* be what you would have me, yet, Livy— never fear. I am improving. I shall do all I possibly can to be worthy of you." Clemens is still the reformer in these representations, but no longer the desperate, sentimental acolyte come to worship at the shrine. Self-condemnation has begun to give way to self-understanding and self-acceptance; the petitioner is still penitent, but no longer abject. By May he could write Olivia, "I think we know each other well enough . . . to bear with weaknesses & foolishnesses, & even wickednesses (of mine)" (19–20 May 1869).

With the formal announcement of his engagement to Olivia Langdon on 4 February 1869, Clemens arrived at a psychological watershed. The ordeal of attainment was substantially behind him; the security of his hard-won position allowed him in exultant moments to relax and enjoy his prospects. "I don't sigh, & groan &

howl so much, now, as I used to," he wrote the Twichells; "No, I feel serene, & arrogant, & stuck up—& I feel such pity for the world & every body in it but just us two" (14 February 1869). These spells of complacency were fleeting, and intermixed with them were periods of doubt and chagrin, but ease was gradully displacing urgency in Clemens's correspondence, and playfulness now vied with piety in his appeals to Olivia. "To tell the truth," he told her, "I love you so well that I *am* capable of misbehaving, just for pleasure of hearing you scold" (12 January 1869). Through the spring and summer of 1869 Clemens wondered at his good fortune and learned to trust it. On 4 June he confessed to Mother Fairbanks, "I had a dreadful time making this conquest, but that is all over, you know, & now I have to set up nights trying to think what I'll do next."

By June of 1869 "what I'll do next" came to be a professional as well as a personal question for Clemens. He was in the last stages of proofreading *The Innocents Abroad*, was obligated to prepare a lecture for the coming season, and had been relatively inactive as a writer of anything but love letters since his declarations to Olivia nearly a year earlier. But the restoration of his equilibrium was readying him to return to work. As Olivia and her family came to accept him, and as he concomitantly came to understand that a radical reformation of his character was unlooked for and unnecessary, he regained access to the sources of his vitality as a writer—his past, his skepticism, even his irreverence. The Langdons themselves stimulated and helped sustain this restoration by remarkably and, it would seem, wholeheartedly accepting their would-be son-in-law in the few months that passed before the engagement was formally announced. Clemens was as proud of this trust as he was grateful for it. In a letter to his sister he described the Langdons' devotion to Olivia and then added, "They think about as much of me as they do of her" (23 June 1869).[13] To their credit, Olivia and her family seem often to have been fairer and more perceptive in appraising her suitor's character than he was himself. While they were no doubt impressed by the sincerity of his pledges to reform, they were also quick to appreciate those qualities in him which required no reformation—honesty, generosity, industry, devotion, good-heartedness—and to give him their confidence. It was of this confiding acceptance that Olivia wrote to her fiancé later in the year: "I am so happy, so perfectly at rest in you, so proud of the true nobility of your nature—it makes the whole world look so bright to me."[14] Clemens had proved "worthy," after all, and he may have come to understand that in many respects he had been worthy all along.

These acts of trust and reinforcement shortened the psychological distance Clemens had to travel before returning to the equilibrium that allowed him once again to function as a professional writer. By the time he deliberately resumed that function in late August 1869, by becoming an editor of the Buffalo *Express*, the strenuous and distortive melodramatic phase of his reformation had subsided, and he was in a position to consolidate the gains and losses it had brought: Mark Twain and Samuel Clemens met just about where they had parted, although both had become more consciously serious and a bit more responsive to the conventions of the eastern middle class. The Clemens/Twain identity was returning to the careless integration which rendered its halves only imperfectly differentiable. And, most important, the bridge between Clemens's past and his future could remain intact, bearing the rich cargo of recollection and reminiscence that was to sustain his major work.

Chapter Two

Getting to Buffalo

Late in his life Mark Twain advised the guests at his own birthday party, "If you can't make seventy by any but an easy road, don't you go." He might have said something similar about making Buffalo. As it happened, the road that led Samuel Clemens to that city in 1869 was hardly an easy one, even though it was in a manner of speaking paved by his soon-to-be father-in-law, Jervis Langdon, a circumstance which has led some commentators to maintain that Clemens paid a high price—a measure of his independence—for his passage.[1] Langdon, in fact, had the means to pave the way from Elmira to Buffalo literally as well as figuratively; although his fortune had been made in coal, he had helped underwrite a substantial paving contract in Memphis earlier that year. If the methods he used with his prospective son-in-law were more subtle than those he financed in Tennessee, they were nevertheless effective in bringing Clemens to nest within the range of Langdon's influence.

Nesting became Clemens's essential preoccupation as his obsession to reform his character subsided in the warmth of the Langdon's acceptance. Even before he and Olivia were formally engaged in February 1869, he began turning his attention, and hers, to an idealization of married life whose predominant qualities were stability, comfort, retreat, and tranquillity. For the itinerant lecturer living out of his valise as he shuttled from one town, and one hotel, to another, the notion of *home* was talismanic. "Make some more pictures of our own wedded happiness," he urged Olivia from Rockford, Illinois, "with the bay window (which you shall have,) & the grate in the living-room—(which you shall have, like-

The Langdons' home in Elmira, New York. (Courtesy Mark Twain Memorial, Hartford, Conn.)

wise,) & flowers, & pictures & books (which we will read together,)—pictures of our future home—a home whose patron saint shall be Love—a home with a tranquil 'home atmosphere' about it—such a home as 'our hearts & our God shall approve' " (6 January 1869). Such pictures were acts of faith in a providential future that stood in sharp contrast to Clemens's past and present, if not to Olivia's. As he imagined it, it was to be a future in which the circumstances of his life dramatically changed while those of hers were perpetuated. That cannot be surprising. By the winter of 1868–69, Clemens was thirty-three years old and had been knocking about the world—paddling his own canoe, as he put it—for about half his life. He had lived on both this country's coasts as well as in its heartland, had traveled to the Sandwich Islands, Europe, and the Holy Land, and had been, he said, everything from a newspaper editor to cowcatcher on a locomotive. What he had never truly experienced as an adult was a sense of home.

He first visited the Langdon family mansion in the heart of Elmira late in the summer of 1868. The building itself must have seemed to the self-styled vagabond a manifestation in brownstone of the solidity and stability of Olivia's upbringing, conditions that her semi-invalidism made even more emphatic. Stasis and security had been the facts of her life; movement and opportunism the facts of his. In asking her to marry him, Clemens believed and hoped that he was bringing his vagabondizing to an end, and he looked to Olivia as both the agent and the embodiment of that hope. On New Year's Eve 1868, he wrote her of the change he had already undergone. "The Old Year," he said, "found me ready to welcome any wind that would blow my vagrant bark abroad, no matter where—it leaves me seeking home & an anchorage, & longing for them. . . . I, the homeless then, have on this last day of the dying year, a home that is priceless, a refuge from all the cares & ills of life, in that warm heart of yours."

The brick-and-mortar home he envisioned himself providing the two of them was likewise to be an anchorage and a refuge. As Clemens imagined that home, it stood in juxtaposition both to his own chaotic past and to the contemporary "outside world" which he tended at such times to portray as nasty, venal, profane, and in-clement. "Let the great world toil & struggle & nurse its pet am-bitions & glorify its poor vanities beyond the boundaries of our royalty," he wrote Olivia. "We will let it lighten & thunder, & blow its gusty wrath about our windows & our doors, but never cross our sacred threshold." Part fortress, part tabernacle, such a home was, like Olivia's warm heart, to offer sanctuary and perhaps even salvation by virtue of a kind of sublime domesticity. "Only Love & Peace shall inhabit there," Clemens wrote, "with you & I, their willing vassals" (12 January 1869). Six weeks later he told her that his own visions of their future home "always take one favorite shape—peace, & quiet—rest, & seclusion from the rush & roar & discord of the world.—You & I apart from the jangling elements of the outside world, reading & studying together when the day's duties are done—in our own castle, by our own fireside" (27 Feb-ruary 1869).

Clemens no doubt pleased and moved Olivia with imaginings of this kind, but he was also beguiling himself, immersing himself ever more deeply in a religion of love whose altar was as truly the hearth as the heart. With a convert's fervor he declared himself for-ever cured of wanderlust, eager to forsake the road in favor of the

The Langdons' parlor. (Courtesy Mark Twain Memorial, Hartford, Conn.)

domestic castle. "I have been a wanderer from necessity, three-fourths of my time—a wanderer from choice only one-fourth," he reassured Olivia—and persuaded himself. "Wandering is not a *habit* with me—for that word implies an enslaved fondness for the thing. And I could most freely take an oath that all fondness for roaming is dead within me" (24 January 1869). Just thirteen months earlier, Clemens had written Emily Severance of being "in a fidget to move," declaring that he "never was any other way" (24 December 1867). Now, as if from the ashes of his former selves—the knockabout, the adventurer, the skeptic, the comedian—a more stable, more mature, more unified self was to emerge. Clemens tended to regard this change in terms of the tension between movement and stasis and, for his own sake as well as the Langdons', to dramatize the sincerity of his commitment to a settled future. "I want to get located in life," he wrote Olivia. "*I want to be married*" (13 May 1869).

So settling down became a precondition of marriage and as such a prospect to be taken seriously, almost reverently—"the solemnest matter that has ever yet come into my calculations," Clemens confided to Mary Fairbanks, adding, "I must not make a mistake in this thing" (15 April 1869). The "thing" in question was not *whether* to settle—that had been a vague intention of his even before he met Olivia, and his dream thereafter—but where to settle and under what circumstances. Ironically for someone who had pursued as many occupations as Clemens had—printer, prospector, pilot, reporter, lecturer, correspondent—a big problem was which one he would follow as an established, married man. As it turned out, the answer was, none of them. He would continue to lecture from season to season, but he determined late in 1868 that he would substantially forego his former pursuits, buy an interest in a newspaper, and devote most of his energies to working as one of its editors. At the time, of course, he could boast a wide and varied experience as a journalist, experience that he might have offered as a credential, but full-time editing of a daily newspaper was something he had had neither the opportunity nor, very likely, the inclination to try.

How Clemens arrived at the determination to edit a newspaper, a determination that eventually carried him to Buffalo, is an uncertain if not entirely mysterious matter. Newly engaged and still an itinerant lecturer-journalist as 1868 drew to a close, he had every reason to want to secure a steady income and little confidence that his writing alone would provide one. Mark Twain was no longer a merely local phenomenon; his *Quaker City* travel letters had earned him national attention, and he lectured during the 1868–69 season throughout New England and the Midwest to packed houses. But *The Innocents Abroad* did not appear until late July 1869, and in the meantime his notoriety, to say nothing of his talent, hardly seemed to him a bankable commodity. Even before he met Olivia, he had expressed doubt to Mary Fairbanks that he could support a wife of any, even the humblest, background solely on what he could earn as a writer. "Where is the wherewithal?" he asked her. "It costs nearly two [newspaper] letters a week to keep *me*. If I doubled it, the firm would come to grief the first time anything happened to the senior partner. . . . I am as good an economist as anybody, but I can't turn an inkstand into Aladdin's lamp" (12 December 1867). Although his fortunes improved and his reputation grew over the course of the intervening months, he hardly seems, during the winter and spring of 1868–69, to have entertained the possibility that he could free-lance a living sufficient to support the kind of home he was at the time urging Olivia to join him in imagining.

Becoming a newspaper editor was a compromise solution to the problem of vocation Clemens faced as he scrambled to position himself at the very end of the 1860s as a candidate for gentility. The decade just coming to a close had seen his wanderings describe a wide arc which carried him west from the Mississippi Valley and was now about to fix him in the East. The decade ahead, seen from the vantage point of the prospective bridegroom, was to be distinguished by a new rootedness and seriousness of purpose. The time had come for putting aside childish things, Clemens resolved; adulthood was upon him. "We are done with the shows & vanities of life," he wrote Olivia, "& are ready to enter upon its realities" (15 February 1869). Together they would become "unpretending, substantial members of society, with no fuss or show or nonsense about us, but with healthful, wholesome duties to perform" (21 January 1869).

Just where those roots were to be sunk and those wholesome duties—including the editing of a daily newspaper—performed was a matter of some perplexity for Clemens virtually from the moment he began seriously to court Olivia in the fall of 1868. His anxieties took on a new urgency when on Thanksgiving Day of that year Olivia's parents provisionally accepted him as her fiancé. That night, after the Langdons retired, he wrote from Elmira to share the good news of his engagement with Mother Fairbanks, his principal confidante during the courtship. Although Olivia had at first insisted that he address her only as "sister," he said, "She isn't my sister any more—but some time in the future she is going to be my wife, & I think we shall live in Cleveland" (26–27 November 1868). With the breathless enthusiasm of a man struck anything but dumb by his own good fortune, he went on to propose a happy-ever-after ending to the romantic drama he had for several months been purveying in letters to Mary Fairbanks, an ending which depended strategically on her husband's position as a major shareholder of the Cleveland *Herald*: "I think you will persuade Mr. Fairbanks to sell me a living interest in the *Herald* on such a credit as will enable me to pay for it by lecturing & other work— for I have no relatives to borrow money of, & wouldn't do it if I had. And then we shall live in the house next to yours. I am in earnest, now, & you must not cease your eloquence until you have made Mr. Fairbanks yield."

This remarkable proposal offered an ingenious, one-swoop solution to Clemens's problems. It not only provided him with a vocation but also located him permanently within the sphere of Mary Fairbanks, whom he regarded as both advocate and architect of the regenerate self upon which he believed his happiness with Olivia so substantially depended. Mother Fairbanks had over the course of their correspondence become an important arbiter of Clemens's future, characteristically offering the kind of reassurance that promised now to minister to the insecurities he anticipated as a newlywed nestling. It may even be that his resolution to become a newspaper owner-editor took shape around the fortuitous possibilities that arose from the Fairbankses' situation in Cleveland, the combination of Mary Fairbanks's psychological support and her husband's ties to the *Herald*.

Whatever motives may have led Clemens to settle on settling in Cleveland, both Mary and Abel Fairbanks were apparently willing to play the part he assigned them in his Thanksgiving proposal. A month after making that proposal, he visited them in Cleveland and sent a complementary letter *back* to Elmira—to Jervis, not Olivia, Langdon—announcing the satisfaction he took in Cleveland as a home. "I like the Herald as an anchorage for me, better than any paper in the Union," he wrote. As for his not-quite-formal negotiations with Abel Fairbanks: "He wants me in very much—wants me to buy an eighth [interest in the newspaper] from the Benedicts [his partners]—price about $25,000. He says if I can get it he will be my security until I pay it all by the labor of my tongue & hands, & that I shall not be hurried. That suits me, just exactly. It couldn't be better" (29 December 1868). The extraordinary luck that Clemens credited with guiding him to Olivia and with enabling him to win her love and her parents' approval gave no evidence of deserting him; the storybook courtship seemed destined for a storybook finish, in Cleveland.

With the turn of the new year, Clemens returned to the road, to the monotonous train rides, uncertain accommodations, and virtual absence of privacy that defined the lecturer's zigzag progress from town to town. "You can't imagine how dreadfully wearing this lecturing is," he wrote Olivia. "I begin to be appalled at the idea of doing it another season. I shall try hard to get into the Herald on such terms as will save me from it" (2 January 1869). But Cleveland would not be hurried. Twice in January, on the 19th and 23d, Clemens registered with Olivia his disappointment at having been prevented by the ill health of *Herald* co-owner George Benedict from pushing his newspaper negotiations ahead. By early February, when he wrote to inform his own family of his final acceptance by the Langdons and his formal engagement to their daughter, he was noticeably cooler about his Cleveland prospects. "I can get an eighth of the Cleveland Herald for $25,000," he said, "& have it so arranged that I can pay for it as I earn the money with my unaided hands. I shall look around a little more, & if I can do no better elsewhere, I shall take it" (5 February 1869). Just five weeks after having written so enthusiastically to Olivia's father, Clemens seemed on the verge of recanting his opinion that prospects for an anchorage "couldn't be better" than those offered in Cleveland.

By mid-February, while still lecturing in the Midwest, Clemens took to writing to Olivia about an alternative nesting site:

I look more & more favorably upon the idea of living in Hartford, & feel less & less inclined to wed my fortunes to a trimming, time serving, policy-shifting, popularity-hunting, money grasping paper like the Cleveland Herald. . . . I would much rather have a mere comfortable living, in a high-principled paper like the [Hartford] *Courant*, than a handsome income from a paper of a lower standard, & so would you, Livy. (13–14 February 1869)

Clemens's correspondence offers no explanation for his abrupt change of heart regarding the Cleveland *Herald*. He had visited the Fairbankses while on the lecture circuit in late January and seems then or shortly thereafter to have become disenchanted with the newspaper, if not the city. Of the *Herald* he wrote Olivia, "It would change its politics in a minute, in order to be on the popular side, I think, & do a great many things for money which I wouldn't do" (13–14 February 1869). On the other hand, Hartford's attractions, even apart from the rectitude of at least one of its newspapers, were manifold. Olivia and her family had personal ties of long standing there, many of them established through the Beecher nexus, which connected the city socially as well as spiritually with Elmira. Clemens would in fact accompany the Langdons to Hartford the following June to attend the wedding of Olivia's friend Alice Hooker to Calvin Day. Hartford served as the headquarters for the American Publishing Company, the subscription house which produced several of Mark Twain's early books and which was then in the process of preparing *The Innocents Abroad*. Because of that association, Clemens had already come to know the city and had made a particular friend there of Joseph Twichell, pastor of the Asylum Hill Congregational church.

As Clemens bewitched himself during the winter and spring of 1869 with visions of perfect domestic contentment, Hartford seems to have fixed itself in his imagination, and perhaps in Olivia's as well, as the likeliest place to live out the dream they were together conjuring. But his negotiations with the *Courant*'s proprietors, General Joseph Hawley and Charles Dudley Warner, proceeded haltingly and were characteristically tainted by condescension and evasiveness on their parts. On 14 February 1869 he wrote Twichell, "I think the General would rather *employ* me than sell me an interest—but that won't *begin* to answer, you know. I can buy into plenty of paying newspapers but my future wife wants me to be surrounded by a good moral & religious atmosphere (for I shall unite with the church as soon as I am located,) & so she likes the idea of living in Hartford." Clemens was probably in earnest here in speaking of Hartford's morality, but at the same time he was plainly eager to motivate Twichell to take his part with the *Courant* owners. He could expect Twichell to be moved by his aspiring to the city's elevating atmosphere, particularly when he coupled that aspiration with an implicit promise to join the Asylum Hill church. Even more important, Twichell was the kind of partisan Clemens needed at the time to persuade solid citizens such as Warner and Hawley that they might without committing apostasy think of Mark Twain as a colleague rather than a clown. In a note to Olivia, he indicated Twichell's willing complicity in these matters by acknowledging "his kind efforts in forwarding our affairs" (15 February 1869).

Even with Twichell for an advocate, however, Clemens was stalled and put off by the reluctant Hartfordians. In describing his *Courant* transactions to Mary Fairbanks on 15 April 1869, he wrote, "I made proposals . . . , & they wrote to one partner to come home from Europe & see about it. He was to have spent the summer or part of it abroad, but they say he will now get back in May. Therefore I am reading proof & waiting." The proof pages he was reading at the same time were of *The Innocents Abroad*, the book that would transform Mark Twain's still somewhat regional fame into genuine international celebrity. The *Courant* owners saw themselves negotiating with the latter-day Wild Humorist of the Pacific Slope, not the figure of wide renown and acclaim Mark Twain soon became. So, apparently, they waffled, and while they waffled Clemens wrote to Olivia of another, subtler, even rather perverse, impulse that fixed his hopes on Hartford. It had been the place to which he had retreated after meeting and falling in love with her in the late summer of 1868, the place in which, that September, he had experienced his intensest, most melancholy, most hopeless pining for her. "How *could* I walk these sombre avenues at night *without* thinking of you?" he asked.

For their very associations would invoke you—every flagstone for many a mile is overlaid thick with an invisible fabric of thoughts of you—longings & yearnings & vain caressings of the empty air for you. . . .

I am in the same house [Elisha Bliss's] . . . where I spent three awful weeks last fall, worshipping you, & writing letters to you. . . . . But I don't like to think of those days, or speak of them. (12 May 1869)

It might have seemed particularly gratifying to Clemens to locate in Hartford and by doing so to transform the scene of his former misery and isolation into that of his domestic ascendancy. But Hartford would not be hurried. And while he endured the *Courant* proprietors' procrastinations, "reading proof & waiting," Clemens tried to interest himself in other berths. On 9 March 1869 he attended a lecture in Hartford given by Petroleum Vesuvius Nasby (David Ross Locke), who was not only a fellow humorist but also the editor of the Toledo *Blade*. Clemens met Nasby after the performance and sat up talking with him until the following morning. Among the topics of conversation, apparently, was Clemens's future, for later that day he wrote to Olivia, "Nasby wants to get me on his paper. Nix" (10 March 1869). The disinclination to join Nasby was much less emphatic just a month later, however, when he wrote his mother and sister confessing his indecisiveness on several fronts: "I don't know whether I am going to California in May—I don't know whether I want to lecture next season or not— I don't know whether I want to yield to Nasby's persuasions & go with him on the Toledo Blade—I don't know *any* thing" (ca. 7–10 April 1869).

He didn't know, further, whether or not to pursue matters in Cleveland while his prospects in Hartford remained uncertain. He wrote Mary Fairbanks on 1 April 1869 about the possibility of his visiting her that spring, together with Olivia and her mother. "If we *do* go," he said, "Fairbanks & I can talk business." By the middle of the month, however, he addressed her, perhaps a bit coyly, as if his chances of buying into the Cleveland *Herald* were not only dead, but long since dead. "Why bless you," he wrote, "I almost 'abandoned all idea' months ago, when Mr. Benedict declined to sell an interest. . . . I didn't want Mr. Fairbanks to take me into the partnership unless the doing it would help us *both*—not make me & partly unmake him. So I began looking around" (15 April 1869). A few weeks later he sounded as if he no longer considered settling in Cleveland a practicable alternative. "I had hoped," he told Mother Fairbanks, "that Livy & I would nestle under your wing, some day & have you teach us how to scratch for worms, but fate seems determined that we shall roost elsewhere. I am sorry. But you know, I want to *start* right—it is the safe way. I want to be permanent. I must feel thoroughly & completely *satisfied* when I anchor 'for good & all'" (10 May 1869). He was, not altogether coincidentally, in Hartford at the time, and two days later he wrote Olivia an encomium to that city's loveliness: "The town is budding out, now . . . & Hartford is becoming the pleasantest city, to the eye, that America can show." More than a year earlier he had expressed the same enthusiasm in a travel letter to the *Alta California*, where he declared Hartford "the best built and the handsomest town I have ever seen."[2]

His heart set on Hartford, Clemens did the best he could to be patient while he awaited the return from Europe of *Courant* co-owner Charles Dudley Warner, occasionally and unenthusiastically entertaining the idea of negotiating with the less attractive Hartford *Post*. "You see," he wrote Olivia, "I can't talk business to the Courant, for Warner is not home yet. I don't want to talk to the Post people till I am done with the Courant" (14 May 1869). When Warner returned in mid-June, matters proceeded swiftly and, for Clemens, unsatisfactorily. "Warner says he wishes he could effect a copartnership with me," he wrote Olivia, "but he doubts the possibility of doing it—will write me if anything turns up. Bromley of the Post says the 5 owners of that paper are so well satisfied with the progress the paper is making that they would be loth [*sic*] to sell" (21 June 1869). There was no place in Hartford for Mark Twain.

The next day, burdened with the job of beginning the arduous hunt anew, Clemens contacted Samuel Bowles, editor of the Springfield, Massachusetts, *Republican*, about the possibility of buying a share in that newspaper. "Since I have some reputation for joking," he wrote Bowles, "it is the part of wisdom to state that I am not joking this time—I am simply in search of a home. I must come to anchor." Nothing, apparently, came of the effort, but its impersonal, almost random quality—Clemens hardly knew Bowles, and his inquiry has about it the air of a form letter—signals the writer's chagrin and, perhaps, his approaching desperation. Ironically, as Clemens discovered a few months later, Bowles had been instrumental in discouraging Hawley and Warner from accepting him as a *Courant* partner.[3]

Within a week of the collapse of his Hartford hopes, Clemens wrote to his mother and sister about the prospect of resuming talk of partnership with Abel Fairbanks and his associates: "I shall probably go to Cleveland to-morrow or next day, but I doubt if I [shall] enter into my arrangement with the Herald, for Livy does not much like the Herald people & rather dislikes the idea of my being associated with them in business—& besides, they will not like to part with as much as a third of the paper, & Mr. Langdon thinks—(as I do,) that a small interest is not just the thing" (26 June 1869). Reopening negotiations with Fairbanks was a doomed exercise from the beginning, particularly because Clemens and Olivia had developed the habit of juxtaposing "the quiet, moral atmosphere of Hartford to the driving, ambitious ways of Cleveland" (SLC to OL, 15 February 1869). They had come to regard "the Herald people" as rather coarse and unseemly—that is, they harbored just the sort of reservations about them that the *Courant* people had about Mark Twain.

Moreover, for all the affection and esteem he had for Mary Fairbanks, Clemens felt little of either for her husband. At one point he even went so far as to compare her plight to that of "a Pegasus harnessed with a dull brute of the field." The Fairbankses were "mated, but not matched," he wrote Olivia, judging that circumstance to be "the direst grief that can befall any poor human creature" (10 January 1870). As they talked again of partnership in July and August of 1869, Abel Fairbanks acted to justify Clemens's darkest opinions of him. Exactly what occurred between the two men may never be entirely clear, but much of what happened can be reconstructed circumstantially. In June Clemens had written to his mother and sister, "I am offered an interest in a Cleveland paper. . . . The salary is fair enough, but the interest is not large enough, & so I must look a little further.— The Cleveland folks . . . urge me to come out & talk business. But it don't strike me— I feel little or no inclination to go" (4 June 1869). That was before his negotiations in Hartford broke down; when they did, Clemens may have felt the need, if not the inclination, to deal with Fairbanks. "I mean to go to Cleveland in a few days," he wrote his

Abel W. Fairbanks. (Courtesy Mark Twain Papers, The Bancroft Library)

sister on 23 June, "to see what sort of arrangement I can make with the Herald people. If they will take sixty thousand dollars for one-third of the paper, I know Mr. Langdon will buy it for me."

The details of the ensuing negotiations between Clemens and Fairbanks have gone largely unrecorded. By his own account, though, Clemens was driven to such anger by those transactions that in his frustration he got off a vitriolic letter to Elisha Bliss accusing him of endlessly putting off the publication of *The Innocents Abroad*. ("All I desire," Clemens sneered, "is to be informed from time to time what future season of the year publication is post-poned to and why" [22 July 1869].) By way of apology he sent another note on 1 August explaining the real cause of his outburst. "I wrote you a wicked letter," he told Bliss. "But . . . I have been out of humor for a week. I had a bargain about concluded for the purchase of an interest in a daily paper & when everything seemed to be going smoothly, the owner *raised* on me. I *think* I have got it all straightened up again, now, & therefore am in a reasonably good humor again." The paper in question was clearly the *Herald*, given the timing of the correspondence, and the owner was just as clearly Abel Fairbanks. These conjectures are substantiated by a second apology Clemens sent Bliss on 12 August 1869. Referring to his sarcastic letter of 22 July, he said, "I was in an awful sweat when I wrote you, for everything seemed going wrong end foremost with me. I had just got mad with the Cleveland Herald folks & broken off all further negotiations for a purchase, & so I let you & some others have the benefit of my ill nature."

What seems to have "got it all straightened up" was a letter Fairbanks wrote Clemens on 27 July reviewing *Herald* income and expenses and continuing, "I should have been glad to had [*sic*] Mr. L & yourself here, and let you examine more closely & I explain more fully, all that you might wish to know." Then, bringing the matter to a point, Fairbanks said, "Let me make a proposition, that I will take $50,000 for one quarter of the office—as it stands, assuring you there are no debts against it, & you become interested in all that is due it."[4] If, as Clemens claimed to Bliss on 22 July, Fairbanks had earlier that month "*raised* on me," Fairbanks's 27 July proposal would seem to have put things right again between them; that is, the offer of a one-fourth share of the newspaper for $50,000 was apparently consistent with proposals that Clemens had earlier entertained. At the very outset of his *Herald* negotiations, he had written Jervis Langdon, "Fairbanks says the concern (with its lot & building,) inventories $212,000. . . . He . . . wants me to buy an eighth from the Benedicts . . .—price about $25,000" (29 December 1868). Six months later he expressed his willingness to close a deal with the *Herald* proprietors "if they will take sixty thousand dollars for one-third of the paper" (SLC to Pamela Moffett, 23 June 1869). Fairbanks's 27 July proposal seems exactly proportional to the one Clemens initially considered ($25,000 for one-eighth of the property) and only a bit more costly than the one he himself considered proposing ($60,000 for a one-third interest) in June. It may be, given these circumstances and the record of his comments about his own and Olivia's reservations, that Clemens's decision not to live in Cleveland was finally based on something other than finances. However, his apologetic letter to Bliss indicates that, his uncertainties about Fairbanks's offer having been "straightened up," Cleveland remained a likely site as late as 1 August 1869. What seems to have brought the *Herald* negotiations to an end is that Fairbanks evidently upped the asking price *again* sometime after that date. When he wrote to Mary Fairbanks on 14 August to explain his decision not to join the *Herald*, Clemens said of her husband, "We came very near being associated in business together, & I went home mighty sorry about that $62,500 raise."[5] There would not be, as there never had been, any talk of a "Father Fairbanks."

While he was learning through the spring and summer of 1869 not to trust Abel Fairbanks, Clemens came increasingly to depend on the counsel of a much more strategic elder, his future father-in-law. Taken together with other evidence of a similar kind, Clemens's 26 June letter to his mother and sister makes clear that Jervis Langdon was actively involved in his prospective son-in-law's business dealings: "Mr. Langdon thinks—(as I do,) that a small interest is not just the thing." The placement of the parenthesis here might lead a person to wonder which of the two was the *more* active. Fairbanks's suggestion that "Mr. L" accompany Clemens in examining the *Herald*'s books further substantiates the impression that Olivia's father was an acknowledged participant in the nesting enterprise.

However involved he may have been during its early phases, Langdon was never more clearly and centrally important to that enterprise than he was in promoting the dramatic turn of events that almost immediately followed the collapse of Clemens's negotiations with the *Herald* people in early August of 1869. As Clemens explained it to Mary Fairbanks later that month, "I . . . received a proposition from one of the owners of the Buffalo Express who had taken a sudden notion to sell" (14 August 1869). There had followed "the bore of wading through the books & getting up balance sheets," he said, but "as soon as Mr. Langdon saw

Olivia's father, Jervis Langdon. (Courtesy
Mark Twain Memorial, Hartford, Conn.)

the books of the concern he was satisfied." Langdon seems to have
discovered this opening, if not to have provoked it, and through
the agency of his chief associate in Buffalo, J. D. F. Slee, to have
played a big part in effecting the transaction. He also advanced
Clemens half of the $25,000 he needed to buy a one-third share of
the newspaper. On 13 February 1869 Clemens had written Olivia's
mother, "I propose to earn money enough some way or other, to
buy a remunerative share in a newspaper of high standing." Almost exactly six months later, on 12 August 1869, he used $12,500
from Langdon in closing his deal with the *Express*.[6] Two days later,
in accounting for his preference for Buffalo over Cleveland, he
wrote to Mary Fairbanks, "I guess it has fallen out mainly as Prov-

idence intended it should." To the extent that he believed in such inevitabilities, Clemens must have understood that his future father-in-law's influence extended even to the province of Providence.

Certainly it extended to Buffalo, where Langdon participated in the Anthracite Coal Association and carried on a considerable business. Buffalo was a relatively convenient five hours from Elmira by rail, closer than any other city large enough to support the kind of newspaper Clemens hoped to join. Despite these connections, however, it was clearly an afterthought, a last-minute alternative proposed by Jervis Langdon in the wake of Clemens's failure to come to terms in either Hartford or Cleveland. "I am grateful to Mr. Langdon," Clemens wrote Olivia, "for thinking of Buffalo with his cool head when we couldn't think of any place but Cleveland with our hot ones" (19 August 1869). He demonstrated that gratitude by leaping at the *Express* offer. Having been involved in negotiations with Abel Fairbanks well into July and quite possibly into August, he was nevertheless installed in Buffalo by 14 August and reporting to Olivia five days later, "It is an easy, pleasant, *delightful* situation, & I never liked anything better."

For all his professed determination to proceed deliberately in the question of where and how to settle—"the solemnest matter," he said, "that has ever yet come into my calculations"—Clemens ultimately jumped at an opportunity that he cannot have had two weeks to consider, and even at that declared his impatience with the "bore of taking a tedious invoice, & getting everything intelligible & ship-shape & according to the canons of business" before the deal could be closed (SLC to MMF, 14 August 1869). A partial explanation for his apparent impulsiveness probably rests in the observation that by mid-July he was recoiling, or rebounding, from disappointments in both Hartford and Cleveland. But the fuller truth may lie in recognizing that the Buffalo solution was proposed by the very man he had sought most to please in the matter from the beginning, Olivia's father.

Jervis Langdon had earned Clemens's gratitude by rather remarkably accepting him as Olivia's fiancé, even in the face of considerable advice to the contrary. And, given his daughter's preference, he had consistently shown his prospective son-in-law an open generosity that now included backing his purchase of a share in a newspaper. Clemens's regard for Langdon was no doubt complex and at times contradictory, but some of its terms are relatively clear: his idealization of the senior Langdons, of their home and homelife, was in part an extension of his idealization of Olivia, and he tended to afford them the same uncritical enthusiasm he did her, at one point writing her father, "You are the splendidest man in the *world!*" (2 December 1868). It is not hard to imagine that he saw in the Langdons a whole and complete family, unlike his own, and that he saw in Jervis Langdon an adumbration of the father he had lost as a boy. Unlike Clemens's real father, though, Langdon was a success in business, a powerful man whose wealth seemed, in the light of Clemens's admiration, a natural consequence of his character. Langdon helped to establish in Clemens's personal mythology the figure of the charismatic captain of industry, a figure which was to appeal to him throughout his life. Fully a generation before Henry H. Rogers stepped in to advise Clemens on matters of business and to put his affairs in order, Jervis Langdon was establishing the paradigm that Rogers and other of Clemens's substantial friends were to mirror.

Langdon's wealth at once reflected and enhanced his power, with his prospective son-in-law as with many people who came within the sphere of his influence. In seeking his "anchorage," however, Clemens was at first determined to pay his own way, thus avoiding a potentially compromising indebtedness to Langdon or to anyone else. "I have no relatives to borrow money of, & wouldn't do it if I had," he had told Mary Fairbanks (26–27 November 1868). To Langdon himself he declared his intention to underwrite his purchase of a newspaper interest exclusively through "the labor of my tongue & hands" (28 December 1868). Once the process of finding an anchorage was underway in earnest, he reasserted that intention in letters to his mother and sister, telling them on 5 February 1869, "I don't want *anybody's* help," and later that month elaborating, "My proposed father-in-law is naturally so liberal that it would be just like him to want to give us a start in life. But I don't want it that way. I can start myself. I don't want any help. I can run the institution without any 'outside assistance'" (27 February 1869). By the time his prospects in Hartford had died and he was trying to rekindle his enthusiasm for Cleveland, however, Clemens had arrived at an altogether different attitude toward his proposed father-in-law's liberality. If the *Herald* people would reasonably part with a one-third share of their paper, he wrote his sister, "I know Mr. Langdon will buy it for me" (23 June 1869). By the time Langdon did finance his purchase of an interest in the Buffalo *Express*, Clemens seems to have accustomed himself to the discovery that there were advantages to paddling his canoe in tandem with a generous backer. On the day he arrived in Buffalo he wrote Olivia, "I owe your father many, very many thanks, . . . & I will ask you to express them for me—for if there is one thing you can do with a happier grace than another, it is to express gratitude to your father" (8 August 1869).

Clemens's deference to Langdon in matters pertaining to the course of his future, though, ultimately arose from a source even more powerful and more characteristic than gratitude, indebtedness, or admiration. He felt guilty at the prospect of breaking that exemplary family circle by stealing Olivia away from it. In a letter to her of 23–24 December 1868, he portrayed his intention to marry her in just those terms:

> I just don't wonder that it makes you sad to think of leaving such a home, Livy, & such household Gods—for there is no other home in all the world like it—no household gods so lovable as yours, anywhere. And I shall feel like a heartless highway robber when I take you away from there—(but I *must* do it, Livy, I *must*—but I shall love you so dearly . . . that some of the bitterness of your exile shall be spared you.)

On 13 February 1869, their formal engagement just announced, he began a letter to Olivia's mother on the same note: "It is not altogether an easy thing for me to write bravely to you, in view of the fact that I am going to bring upon you such a calamity as the taking away from you your daughter, the nearest & dearest of all your household gods." Three weeks later he resumed his confession in another letter to Olivia by depicting, or imagining, the response to news of their engagement by certain friends of the Langdons: "These folks all say, in effect, 'Poor Livy!' I begin to feel like a criminal again. I begin to feel like a 'thief' once more. And I *am*. I have stolen away the brightest jewel that ever adorned an earthly home, the sweetest face that ever made it beautiful, the purest heart that ever pulsed in a sinful world" (5 March 1869). Given his penchant for overdramatization, especially in treating his courtship of

Olivia, it would be easy to take too seriously Clemens's self-indictments at times like these. Still, in so consistently portraying himself as criminal, thief, and robber, he betrays an attitude that seems at least to have colored his early relationship with the Langdons.[7] "I feel like a monstrous sort of highwayman," he confessed to Mary Fairbanks, "when I think of tearing her from the home which has so long been her little world" (24–25 December 1868). Imagining himself the interloper, the plundering outsider, he had reason to seek atonement and accommodation.

That attitude, together with the frustration that followed the collapse of his negotiations in Hartford and Cleveland, may well have left Clemens particularly susceptible to Jervis Langdon's ministrations on his behalf. In large part because of those ministrations, he found himself quite abruptly settling in Buffalo. The road that carried him there in early August 1869, might have seemed an easy one at the time; certainly it was convenient to Elmira. But it had opened to him only after a series of circuitous dead ends had taken their toll on his patience and self-esteem. Now he was determined to use his berth at the *Express* to establish his credentials as a man of steady and industrious habits. "It is an exceedingly thriving newspaper," he wrote Elisha Bliss. "We propose to make it more so. I expect I shall have to buckle right down to it" (12 August 1869). For their part, his new partners brought their own enthusiasm to the transaction, describing Clemens in a 16 August editorial as "an acquisition . . . upon which any newspaper would congratulate itself" and informing their readers that they would "hereafter . . . be regularly and familiarly in the enjoyment of the humor of the most purely humorous pen that is wielded in American journalism."[8] Mark Twain would become a fixture, a staple, in Buffalo. " 'Buffalo Express' is my address hereafter," he wrote Bliss; "shall marry & come to anchor here during the winter" (12 August 1869). Clemens had found his harbor and, he believed, his vocation.

Chapter Three

Coming to Anchor

Samuel Clemens went to Buffalo in August of 1869 resolved to do two things he knew little about: settle down and edit a daily newspaper. Having spent most of his life tossing and being tossed about, he intended now to drop anchor in the safe harbor to which Jervis Langdon had piloted him, assume a desk in the *Express* office at 14 East Swan Street, and apply himself with relentless diligence to whatever duties befell him there. Above all he would stay put—would become, as he later phrased it, a permanency in Buffalo.[1]

He arrived in the city on 8 August 1869 bearing characteristic burdens of guilt and gratitude. That night he apologized in a letter to Olivia for an unnamed offense he blamed himself for committing the day before in Elmira ("I hurt you yesterday") and asked her to thank her father again on his behalf, "for my obligations to him almost overshadow my obligations to Charley, now." Clemens's obligations to Olivia's brother derived from Charles's role in introducing him to her. The prospective bridegroom intended to use his berth in Buffalo as an opportunity to justify the confidence others, particularly Olivia and her parents, had placed in him. He would work hard and wholeheartedly at newspapering. As he took his place at the *Express*, he bragged to Mary Fairbanks about the determination and stamina he brought to the job. "I am capable of slaving over an editorial desk without rest from noon till Midnight," he wrote, "& keep it up without losing a day for 3 years on a stretch, as I am abundantly able to prove" (14 August 1869). Mrs. Fairbanks would very likely have caught the intimation here that but for her husband's treachery in dealing with him, Clemens would at that very time have been exhibiting this tireless dedication in Cleveland. A week later he confided in his sister, Pamela Moffett, "We are not in the Cleveland Herald. We are a hundred thousand times better off. . . . I have partners I have a strong liking & the highest respect for. I am well satisfied" (20–21 August 1869).

Clemens plunged into his duties at the Buffalo *Express* with the kind of frantic enthusiasm he customarily lavished on the beginnings of enterprises he regarded as important. "He 'worked like a horse,' " according to Albert Bigelow Paine, who was very likely guided in his assessment by Clemens's reminiscence. "His hours were not regular, but they were long. Often he was at his desk at eight in the morning, and remained there until ten or eleven at night."[2] Clemens had good reasons for working hard, first among them that he believed he was settling into a permanent position that would provide the security upon which his impending marriage to Olivia depended. That is to say, he regarded his position at the *Express* as affording appropriate scope both for his ambition and for the prerogatives of Mark Twain. His commitment there was to be ongoing, perhaps even lifelong. When a correspondent inquired about his availability as a lecturer, he responded, "I mean to make this newspaper support me hereafter" (SLC to Henry M. Crane, 8 September 1869). Insofar as he indulged himself in imagining it, his future was to be spent contentedly in Buffalo with Olivia, and Mark Twain would become, like Toledo's humorist-lecturer Petroleum V. Nasby, a fixture of a daily metropolitan newspaper.[3]

On Saturday, 14 August 1869, Clemens wrote Elisha Bliss, "I entered upon possession [of a one-third interest in the *Express*] today & made the first payment ($15,000.)" He made his official debut as a columnist the following Saturday, a circumstance heralded both by his own paper and by the Buffalo *Commercial Advertiser*. The blurbs announced that his maiden effort would be entitled "Mark Twain's First Visit to Niagara Falls" and that "similar articles from the pen of the above well-known writer will appear each week hereafter."[4] Even before that debut, however, while the ink was still drying on his *Express* contract, Clemens chose to involve himself anonymously in the newspaper's treatment of a controversy of considerable importance to his future father-in-law, a matter known in Buffalo as "the coal question."

While Jervis Langdon's first impulses in proposing Buffalo as a home no doubt arose from his concern for the welfare and happiness of his daughter and prospective son-in-law, there is no gainsaying that his business interests stood to be well served by his placing a sympathetic editor at a major Buffalo newspaper. At the time, virtually all of Buffalo's coal was supplied by four companies which had united to form the Anthracite Coal Association; one of these companies was Langdon's. Believing that the association amounted to a monopoly and that the monopoly was driving prices artificially high, several Buffalo businessmen had created the cooperative Citizen's Mutual Coal Mining, Purchasing and Sale Company in early August 1869. "The coal question" took the form of a debate between backers of the Citizen's company, which was trying to secure coal on its own and offer it at lower cost, and those of the association, which denied fixing or inflating prices.[5]

Controversy engendered by the coal question warmed the editorial pages of the Buffalo papers, and it was squarely into the middle of this controversy that Clemens inserted himself when he joined the *Express*. On 20 August 1869, the day before his official debut in the paper, he apparently wrote an editorial entitled "The 'Monopoly' Speaks," in which he argued that "up to the present we have heard only the people's side of the coal question, though there could be no doubt that the coal men had a side also." The editorial reproduced a letter from association agent and Langdon affiliate J. D. F. Slee, whom Clemens introduced as "a gentleman of unimpeachable character," defending the coal men and maintaining that the charges brought against them were "utterly groundless." The *Express*, which to this point had generally taken the side of the Citizen's company against the "monopolists," also reprinted, at Slee's urging, a pro-association article from the New York *Evening Post*. The *Express*'s turnabout was doubtless attributable to Clemens's arrival, a circumstance which was not lost on rival newspapermen. Shortly after he began work in Buffalo, he fumed to Olivia about "a sneaking little communication in one of the other papers wondering why the Express had become so docile & quiet about the great coal monopoly question" (3 September 1869). In the same letter, however, he made clear the role he had played in producing that docility by silencing some voices raised in opposition to the association:

Another of those anti-monopoly thieves sent in a long *gratuitous* advertisement to-night, about coal "for the people" at $5.50 a ton—& I have deposited it under the table. The effrontery of these people transcends everything I ever heard of. Do they suppose we print a paper for the fun of it? This man Denther sent in just such a thing the other day, & I left *that* out. The other papers insert both of them for nothing.

It would be easy to make too much of this situation, but the fact is that, having found his way to the *Express* with Jervis Langdon's help and feeling for that reason and many others manifestly beholden to him, Clemens wasted neither time nor opportunity in trying to further Langdon's financial interests in Buffalo. Langdon seems never to have applied the slightest pressure in this direction, but perhaps he comprehended, possibly quite benignly, how important his good opinion had become to his daughter's fiancé and how readily that fiancé was bowed by the weight of gratitude.

When Clemens formally and unanonymously addressed his Buffalo readership for the first time, though, it was not as a hardworking, debt-burdened, well-meaning supplicant for approval, but as Mark Twain, the bad-boy outlander who took the opportunity to apologize in advance for the outrages he would play upon the people of Buffalo. "Being a stranger," he wrote, in his August 21 "Salutatory," "it would be immodest and unbecoming in me to suddenly and violently assume the associate editorship of the BUFFALO EXPRESS without a single explanatory word of comfort or encouragement to the unoffending patrons of the paper, who are about to be exposed to constant attacks of my wisdom and learning." The dominating tone is of ironic and even accidental aggression: given the spaciousness of his wisdom and learning, the fledgling editorialist will mount an unprovoked assault upon his readers that will come largely without premeditation and wholly without malice. "I only wish to assure parties having a friendly interest in the prosperity of the journal," he goes on, "that I am not going to hurt the paper deliberately and intentionally at any time." Such an assurance makes it clear that he is very likely to hurt the paper undeliberately, through his heedlessness, incorrigibility, and brash innocence.

Until it dwindles into a general complaint against the custom of salutatories and valedictories, Mark Twain's greeting to *Express*

readers amounts to a funny and compact distillation of the persona
many of them had already encountered on the lecture stage. He
strikes a pose comprised of complacency, unambition, drollery,
and underscrupulousness—and sets it off with the resonant declaration, "Such is my platform." As it was before a lecture audience,
however, Twain's performance here is so laced with ironies and
transparent hypocrisies that he tacitly invites the audience to join
him in a game that mixes self-presentation with self-parody. He
advises his constituents,

I am simply going to do my plain, unpretending duty, when I cannot get
out of it; I shall work diligently and honestly and faithfully at all times
and upon all occasions, when privation and want shall compel me to do
it; in writing, I shall always confine myself strictly to the truth, except
when it is attended with inconvenience; I shall witheringly rebuke all
forms of crime and misconduct, except when committed by the party in-
habiting my own vest.

The patent "clinchers" in this passage signal a reader that both he
and the author know that humor is being committed here; it makes
the two complicitous, and it keeps them so even when one of them,
the author, provocatively denies that complicity by maintaining a
perfect deadpan. The audience laughs *with* the author, and the author demonstrates his control—over the joke, over the audience,
over himself—by mastering the impulse to laugh with them. This
is a very different thing from laughing *at* a clown, a comedian, or
even a "mere" humorist. It was an important part of the essential
mechanism that allowed the Clemens/Twain twinning to persevere
even at the outset of the Buffalo residency, when the would-be
newlywed was trying earnestly to settle into a profession, a community, and a regimen of stable habits.

     The first article signed by Mark Twain during his editorship at
the *Express*, "A Day at Niagara," appeared concomitantly with his
"Salutatory" on 21 August 1869 and did little to carry him beyond
the bounds of bad-boy burlesque. The tourist-narrator is annoyed
by the thicket of signs around Niagara Falls because, he says, "they
always happened to prohibit exactly the very thing I was just wanting to do. I desired to roll on the grass: the sign prohibited it. I
wished to climb a tree: the sign prohibited it. I longed to smoke: a
sign forbade it." When he is forbidden even the "poor satisfaction"

of pitching a stone over the falls "to astonish and pulverize such parties as might be pickinicking below," his equanimity is strained beyond its limits: "There was no recourse, now, but to seek consolation in the flowing bowl. I drew my flask from my pocket, but it was all in vain. A sign confronted me which said: 'No drinking allowed on these premises.'" He nevertheless manages to justify taking a long pull at the flask by recalling the maxim, "All signs fail in a dry time." The anecdote's chief purpose is obviously to arrive at this play-on-words punchline. It is the kind of comic performance in which Clemens claimed to take little satisfaction—the creation of an elaborate, sometimes creaky structure for the sake of a single flimsy pun—but he brought himself to carry out several such performances during his tenure at the *Express*. Perhaps the more surprising feature of the piece, given his groom-to-be status at the time, was his willingness to hinge the joke on Mark Twain's reputation for drinking.

He continued to draw upon that reputation when he extended his Niagara Falls meditations the following Saturday, 28 August 1869, in an article entitled "English Festivities." There the joke depends on Mark Twain's claiming to be a teetotaler when he is invited by a troop of British fusileers to join in round after round of toasts, beginning with one in honor of the queen's birthday: "I said there was one insuperable drawback—I never drank anything strong upon any occasion whatever, and I did not see how I was going to do proper and ample justice to anybody's birthday with the thin and ungenerous beverages I was accustomed to." The fusileers defer to their guest's temperate habits, permitting him to join in their night-long toasts first with soda water, then lemonade, then ice water, then cider. As the night passes and the hard-drinking fusileers glow with robust health, each of the narrator's thin and ungenerous beverages takes its toll on his constitution until at last he is moved to complain: "I am full of gas and my teeth are loose, and I am wrenched with cramps, and afflicted with scurvy, and toothache, measles, mumps and lockjaw, and the cider last night has given me the cholera." The entire episode turns out to be a dream, a circumstance that accounts for Mark Twain's claiming to be a nondrinker but that hardly diminishes a reader's satisfaction either with the stout-hearted fusileers or with the indignities that befall the abstemious narrator. In the ruddy environment of midnight camaraderie, a world Clemens knew well, temperance comes off as foolish, unmanly, and even unhealthy. Clemens himself was an abstainer at the time, but in "English Festivities" he saved Mark Twain from the taint of teetotaling by allowing him to wake from the dream and wink at his audience: "One avoids much dissipation by being asleep."

Clemens's debut appearances in the *Express*—whether anonymous, as in "The 'Monopoly' Speaks," or under his pseudonym, as in "Salutatory," "A Day at Niagara," and "English Festivities"—reflect the complex pressures he faced at the time, pressures that grew largely out of the tension between his need to establish credentials as a solid citizen and his unwillingness to abandon the anarchic or rebellious side of his character, particularly as it was manifest in Mark Twain. When Mary Fairbanks sought to check that rebelliousness by criticizing some of his early *Express* pieces for their impiety, he responded, "I *will* be more reverential, if you want me to, though I tell you it don't jibe with my principles. There is a fascination about meddling with forbidden things" (26 September 1869). Had his tenure at the *Express* gone uninterrupted, Clemens might have chosen to exploit rather than to resolve this tension by making use of his double identity as editor-celebrity, working with sober earnestness in his unsigned pieces and allowing Mark Twain to cavort among burlesques, hoaxes, tall tales, and other amusements. That is essentially how he operated when as a reporter in Nevada he first appropriated the pseudonym, and that is how his *Express* editorship began, but circumstances conspired to intercept his plans to fashion a coherent, if double, life in Buffalo.

Clemens labored diligently during his initial stint at the *Express*, as if to underscore his commitment to settling down. On 21 August 1869, after little more than a week on the job, he reported to Olivia that he had asked lecture agent James Redpath to excuse him from performing during the coming season. "I would rather scribble, now," he told her, "while I take a genuine interest in it." Should that interest flag, he could look to his co-editor, Josephus N. Larned, as a model of steady self-discipline. "That fellow works straight along all day, day in & day out, like an honest old treadmill horse," he wrote Olivia. "I tell him I wish I had his industry & he had my sense" (8–9 September 1869). The Buffalo press corps welcomed Clemens with comradely warmth, and on 9 October the *Express* ran several columns of "Press Greetings" to its new editor from papers across the country. Nasby's Toledo *Blade* declared Mark Twain "the greatest humorous writer America has ever produced" and concluded, "The Express has always been a good paper—it will henceforth be better." The Leavenworth *Conservative* agreed that "that paper and the press in general will be greatly benefited by so genial, keen and vigorous a writer—at present the first of American humorists." "His paper is the liveliest that has ever been seen in Western New York," chimed the Meriden *Reporter*. "That's what one smart man can do."

By the time these greetings appeared, however, Clemens's plans had already changed in such a way as to jeopardize his fledgling dedication to the *Express*. James Redpath was unable or perhaps unwilling to free him from several lecture commitments which had already been made for the forthcoming season. Clemens consequently authorized Redpath to schedule him for a full season's calendar of performances, maintaining, at least with Olivia, that "it isn't worth the bother of getting well familiarized with a lecture & then deliver it only half a dozen times. . . . When I once start in lecturing I might as well consent to be banged about from town to town while the lecture season lasts, for it would take that shape anyhow." He reasoned that he "ought to have some money to commence married life with" and that lecturing was a ready and proven source of income for him. All of that having been argued, a serious ethical and professional problem lingered. "The distress of it," Clemens wrote Olivia, "is that the paper will suffer by my absence, & at the very time that it ought to keep up its best gait & not lose the start we have just given it & have the long, hard pull of giving it a *new* start after a while. I feel sure that the money I make lecturing, the paper will lose while I am gone—but you see how I am situated" (3 September 1869).

When Clemens wrote Mary Fairbanks three weeks later, he presented the matter quite differently: "I'm not *settled* yet," he said. "My partners want me to lecture some this winter, though, & it seemed necessary anyhow, since I could not get all my engagements canceled" (27 September 1869). According to this version of the story, Clemens's *Express* partners, the very people who should have been looking out most jealously for the paper's wel-

fare, were the active agents urging him back out on the road. Just
what gave rise to this rendition is a matter open to speculation. It
is possible that when they learned of Clemens's "opportunity" to
return to lecturing his partners united in encouraging him to do so,
conjecturally in the belief that his platform performances would
enhance his reputation, something that would in turn benefit the
newspaper he edited. It might even be that after only a few weeks'
association they welcomed the prospect of his leaving town. But
it seems more likely that when he raised the matter of his lecture
obligations with them his partners sought to ease his tender conscience by assuring him that the paper could survive his absence.
That being the case, Clemens's choosing to represent the other *Express* owners—to moral censor Mother Fairbanks, anyway, and
perhaps to the Langdons—as "wanting" him to lecture amounts to
a small manipulation of the facts whose likely purpose was to protect him from charges of dereliction or lingering wanderlust. On
11 September 1869, just three weeks after his "Salutatory," the *Express* ran the following announcement, headed "Personal" and
signed by Mark Twain: "This is to inform lyceums that, after recently withdrawing from the lecture field for next Winter, I have
entered it again . . . because I was not able to cancel all my appointments, it being too late, now, to find lecturers to fill them."

Whatever Mother Fairbanks or the Langdons may have thought
of Clemens's intention to leave Buffalo and the *Express* for a three-
month lecture tour, critics have typically regarded his taking to the
platform as evidence of his frustration with the city and with his
new vocation.[6] It is sometimes adduced quite casually as a demonstration of Mark Twain's mythic untameability. The truth is that
Clemens did grow exquisitely weary of Buffalo and of his circumstances there, but it seems very unlikely that even he could have
managed to do so by the time he decided to lecture during the
1869–70 season. He moved to the city on 8 August 1869; his 3 September letter to Olivia ("Redpath says he *can't* get me free . . .")
shows that by that time—less than a month after arriving—he had
already committed himself to lecturing. Nothing in the extant correspondence indicates that he had begun to sour on Buffalo or the
Express during that month. Had Redpath been able or willing to
release him from his obligations to lecture, there is good reason to
believe that Clemens would have spent the fall and winter of 1869

as he had spent the late summer, working dutifully on the paper through the week and commuting to the Langdon home in Elmira almost every weekend.

Clearly, Clemens's dominant feelings at the time had only indirectly to do with Buffalo or with his new vocation. His heart and most of his attention were fixed on Olivia, a predicament he lightly acknowledged in a note to New York *Tribune* editor Whitelaw Reid. "When you happen to be at Buffalo or Elmira," he wrote Reid, "you must come & see me—half of me is at Mr. Langdon's in Elmira, you know" (7 September 1869). Whatever restiveness and impatience he felt had less to do with his situation in Buffalo than with Buffalo's distance from Elmira. Becoming a lecturer once again was hardly a cure for that frustration, since his itinerary would make Olivia less accessible to him than she was while he was fixed in Buffalo, but he did take leave of his newspaper duties a month before the lecture tour was to begin—in order, he said, to ready himself for the tour—and he spent that month, October 1869, as a guest of the Langdons. When he departed for Elmira in early October he had spent all of six weeks as an *Express* editor. Just before leaving Buffalo, he wrote Elisha Bliss, "I like newspapering very well, as far as I have got—but I adjourn, a week hence, to commence preparing my lecture, & shall not be here again till the middle of February" (27 September 1869). His short initial stint in Buffalo would hardly have given him much of a chance to draw any important conclusions about newspapering even if he hadn't been distracted all the while by the pleasures and pinings of courtship.

Although he went to Buffalo determined to take his new vocation seriously, Clemens produced little memorable copy during his first six-weeks' residence there. After the "Salutatory" of 21 August 1869, a beginning which promised well enough, his *Express* writing was often typified by a kind of forced, uninspired humor that might reflect either his preoccupation with Olivia at the time or his uncertain ability to find an appropriate voice for Mark Twain, given his new audience and station. The most sustained pieces he produced during the period, the signed Saturday articles, were uneven attempts to be funny sometimes characterized by their comparative witlessness and immaturity. At their worst, Clemens's Saturday efforts fall gracelessly, resoundingly flat.

Dixon Wecter saw fit to label "The Last Words of Great Men," which appeared 11 September 1869, "a sophomoric and flippant travesty upon deathbed speeches," and "The Latest Novelty" (2 October 1869), which directs a similar adolescent glibness at the fad of taking "Mental Photographs," is just as much a failure even though its subject matter is light and topical.[7]

The problem with "The Latest Novelty" is not Clemens's irreverence, as Wecter's judgment about "Last Words" might be mistakenly generalized to imply, but the dimensionlessness of his pose as an overaged adolescent ignoramus—a kind of no-frills version of the *Innocents Abroad* narrator. In answering the questions which constitute Mental Photography, Mark Twain comes across as indolent (Favorite hour in the day? "The leisure hour"), unsavory (Favorite tree? "Any that bears forbidden fruit." Occupation? ". . . lying." What do you most dread? "Exposure"), uncultured (Favorite painters? "Sign-painters." Musicians? "Harper & Bros." Character in history? "Jack, the Giant Killer"), itinerant (If not yourself, who would you rather be? "The Wandering Jew, with a nice annuity"), mercenary (Favorite perfume? "Cent. per cent." Book to take up for an hour? "Vanderbilt's pocket-book"), and not altogether respectful of women (Favorite object in nature? "The dumb belle"). In other places, including *The Innocents Abroad*, Clemens was able to make good, sometimes hilarious, use of most of these shortcomings and opacities, but in the *Express* they typically remained unleavened and therefore unfunny.

Many of Clemens's early *Express* pieces reflect his confusion about, or perhaps his inattention to, the problem of reconstituting Mark Twain in such a way as to make him a serviceable feature of a daily newspaper. Taken together, they offer an array of postures and attitudes but no unified personality and no obvious agenda apart from occasional attempts to chronicle and satirize "the Byron scandal."[8] For all their ostensible discontinuity, however, quite a few of these first efforts do concern themselves in one way or another with a matter in which Clemens found himself taking sharp and sudden interest: a criticism of the working press. His comments on the Byron matter, for instance, whether direct or oblique, focus on the public's appetite for gossip and the newspapers' willingness to pander to it. More generally, he pillories the press for its vulgarity, its bias, and especially its sensationalism.

In the third of his Saturday features, "Journalism in Tennessee" (4 September 1869), Mark Twain tells the story of his arrival as a new editor not at the Buffalo *Express* but at the *Morning Glory and Johnson County War-Whoop*. His first assignment is to skim the exchanges and write up the "Spirit of the Tennessee Press," a job that he dispatches in five paragraphs of humdrum and rather genteel prose. Of a competing newspaperman, for instance, he writes, "We are pained to learn that Col. Bascom, chief editor of the *Dying Shriek for Liberty*, fell in the street a few evenings since and broke his leg. He has lately been suffering with debility, caused by overwork and anxiety on account of sickness in his family." When he hands his work over to his own chief editor for improvement, the chief scowls his disapproval, shouts, "Thunder and lightning!" and slashes away at the manuscript contemptuously. "I never saw a pen scrape and scratch its way so viciously," says the bewildered newcomer, "or plough through another man's verbs and adjectives so relentlessly." The result of the chief's ploughing is a bona-fide instance of Tennessee journalism: "That degraded ruffian, Bascom, of the *Dying Shriek for Liberty*, fell down and broke his leg yesterday—pity it wasn't his neck. He says it was 'debility caused by overwork and anxiety!' It was debility caused by trying to lug six gallons of forty-rod whisky around town when his hide is only gauged for four, and anxiety about where he was going to bum another six." While he claims to admire "that sort of energy of expression," the narrator quickly discovers that it "has its inconveniences," the most pressing of which is having to deal with the outraged targets of the libel it routinely practices. His first day on the job begins with someone taking a potshot into the editorial room; then a hand grenade demolishes the stove; next a brick shatters the window. The smoke and glass have hardly settled when a Colonel Blatherskite Tecumseh appears to challenge the chief to a duel and is obliged. As the Colonel totters away toward the undertaker's, the chief excuses himself to prepare for dinner guests and instructs the narrator on tending to business in his absence: "Jones will be here at 3. Cowhide him. Gillespie will call earlier, perhaps—throw him out of the window. Ferguson will be along about 4—kill him. That is all for to-day, I believe."

Backwater Tennessee, where newspapers have names like the *Moral Volcano*, the *Semi-Weekly Earthquake*, the *Thunderbolt and*

Battle-Cry of Freedom, and the *Morning Howl*, turns out to be a place where the excesses of nineteenth-century journalism are practiced with savage enthusiasm and met with savage consequences. "Mush-and-milk journalism," the chief tells the narrator, "gives me the fan-tods." When the narrator quits after his first day—"for my health," he says—he acts, comically, on a principle that Clemens held in earnest: "Tennessee journalism is too stirring for me."

Although he took pains to distance the narrator's circumstances in back-country Tennessee from his own in metropolitan Buffalo, Clemens felt that the *Express* and its competitors were by no means innocent, in their somewhat subtler way, of the kinds of abuses that were the order of the day at the *War-Whoop* and the *Moral Volcano*. In fact, the impulse to satirize newspaper malpractice in "Journalism in Tennessee" may well have grown out of his early experience in Buffalo. Before he had been even a week on the job at the *Express* he wrote Olivia of steps he was taking to curb practices there that would have been encouraged at the *Morning Howl*. "I am simply working late at night in these first days," he told her, "until I get the reporters accustomed & habituated to doing things my way. . . . I simply want to educate them to modify the adjectives, curtail their philosophical reflections & leave out the slang." The newspaper would also be made to *look* less stirring:

I have annihilated all the glaring thunder-&-lightning headings over the telegraphic news & made that department look quiet & respectable. Once in two months, hereafter, when anything astounding *does* happen, a grand display of headings will attract immediate attention to it—but where one uses them *every day*, they soon cease to have any force. We are not astonished to hear a drunken rowdy swear, because he does it on great & trivial occasions alike—but when we hear a staid clergyman rip out an oath, we know it *means* something. (19 August 1869)

It is a telling analogy. In his capacity as editor Clemens promoted the staid clergyman as a kind of personification of journalistic restraint and civility even while, as Mark Twain, he inclined toward the company of the drunken rowdy. That is only to say that Clemens was able to internalize the tension upon which his best humor depended. Mark Twain needed a context of staid sobriety against or within which to function effectively; if his newspaper behaved no better than the *War-Whoop*, where was he to find that sense of decorum he needed for the sake of juxtaposition? And if his readers were bludgeoned by screaming headlines and overemphatic writing, how could he expect them to be alert to the subtle as well as the broad strokes of his humor?

So Clemens had a vested, unhypocritical interest in the civility of the press, not just as the would-be-genteel suitor of Olivia Langdon but as a humorist who played during some of his best moments against the boundaries of civility. Two weeks after the appearance of "Journalism in Tennessee," on 18 September 1869, he again devoted a Saturday feature to indicting fellow newspapermen, this time focusing on their eagerness to capitalize on things tawdry, venal, or scandalous. The piece is entitled "The 'Wild Man' Interviewed," and in it the narrator—Mark Twain, according to the byline—searches out a Yeti-like creature "represented as being hairy, long-armed, and of great strength and stature; ugly and cumbrous." The two meet and talk, the Wild Man revealing himself to be a figure as old as human history, his early augustness and serenity now fallen on hard times. "I have helped to celebrate the triumphs of genius," he tells his interviewer. "Once I was the honored servitor of the noble and the illustrious . . . , but in these degenerate days I am become the slave of quack doctors and newspapers." When the interviewer asks his subject his name, the Wild Man responds, "SENSATION!" and cries that he has just been summoned "To DIG UP THE BYRON FAMILY!"

Clemens inveighed a bit more genially against the press's weakness for gossip the following Saturday in treating the "Private Habits" of prominent preacher Henry Ward Beecher, the gimmick in this case being to cite instances of very ordinary behavior on Beecher's part as if they revealed something shocking or lurid or iconoclastic about him. "The great preacher never sleeps with his clothes on," we are told. "Mr. Beecher never wears his hat at dinner. . . . He always goes to bed promptly between nine and three o'clock, and . . . is just as particular about getting up, which he does the next day, generally." The reader comes to understand the gimmick—that a lot is being made of a little, sometimes of nothing—and in that understanding he or she is made to confront in an exaggerated form the essence of gossip itself. Here as in other September Saturday features the new *Express* editor was wasting no time in lodging a complaint against the press and its patrons. Gently in "Private Habits" and more aggressively in "Wild Man" and "Journalism in Tennessee," he held up to ridicule the press's willingness to exploit sensationalism and, at least tacitly, the public's apparently bottomless capacity for more. Something of dignity was wanting on both sides of this complicity, but Clemens held journalists of the day particularly culpable. His Wild Man, in a poignant moment, broods that he has only recently been dragged down from his former eminence "and all to gratify the whim of a bedlam of crazy newspaper scribblers." Finding himself for the first time in charge of a battery of those scribblers as well as one of them, Clemens began his *Express* tenure with an unsystematic but fairly consistent criticism of his new profession's sins and excesses. Taken in concert these pieces offer, as his "Salutatory" did not, something of the credo or ethic the new editor brought with him, together, perhaps rather surprisingly, with the notoriety and appeal of Mark Twain.

Clemens's early work at the *Express* is that of a man scrambling and often straining to find his creative and professional identity. The writer of these pieces is sometimes the clever self-parodist, sometimes the Wild Humorist, sometimes the ironic critic, sometimes the leering adolescent, and sometimes the hapless innocent— as, for instance, when he is flung over Niagara Falls ("A Day at Niagara") or inadvertently shot full of holes during another man's duel ("Journalism in Tennessee"). The stance or status of the persona can fluctuate befuddlingly. By the end of "A Day at Niagara," for example, "Mark Twain" is a kind of schlemiel, the cartoon victim of a tribe of Irish "Indians" who attack him ("They tore all the clothes off me, they broke my arms and legs, they gave me a thump that dented the top of my head till it would hold coffee like a saucer") and hurl him to perdition. At the beginning of the following week's "English Festivities," however, he is a worldly misanthrope who regards tourists at the falls with the same Olympian scorn that would become a signature of Clemens's meditations three and four decades later:

Any day . . . you may see stately pictures of papa, and mamma, and Johnny, and Bub, and Sis, or a couple of country cousins, all smiling hideously, and . . . all looming up in their grand and awe-inspiring imbecility before the snubbed and diminished presentment of that majestic presence whose ministering spirits are the rainbows, whose voice is the thunder, whose awful front is veiled in clouds—who was monarch here dead and forgotten ages before this hack-full of small reptiles was deemed temporarily necessary to fill a crack in the world's unnoted myriads, and will still be monarch here ages and decades of ages after they shall have gathered themselves to their blood-relations the other worms and been mingled with the unremembering dust.

A Saturday article like that containing "English Festivities," one that begins with a brooding invective directed at the "marvelous insignificance" of the human reptile and ends in broad physical comedy involving drinking bouts with fusileers, compactly demonstrates the jumble of moods and methods that characterized Clemens's initial output as a Buffalo editorialist. Perhaps more than anything else, these uneven performances suggest how unsettled he remained during his first try at settling down. He was, after all, barely installed in Buffalo before he determined to leave it for the lecture circuit, so in effect he came to conduct a kind of holding action there. Real settling would come later, after the wedding, with Olivia to serve as guide and tether. In the meantime his writing understandably mirrored his uncertainty about his present circumstances, his preoccupation with the future, and an eagerness to suspend critical judgment of his work.

However willing Clemens may have been to overlook weaknesses in his newspaper writing, Mother Fairbanks, to whom he had directed an *Express* subscription, was not. Taking in earnest her charge to caution him on matters of taste and literary decorum, she raised questions about the Saturday features, probably because of the unflattering light some of them shed on Mark Twain. While she could be merely censorious or conventional in her criticism, Mary Fairbanks often served Clemens valuably by prodding him to allow his audience the chance to appreciate the seriousness and complexity of his character in his work. When he drifted toward the simpleminded buffoonery of the literary comedian, as he did in some *Express* pieces, she was often there to check him. "I don't wonder you are a trifle uneasy about the Saturday articles," he wrote her toward the end of his initial stay in Buffalo, "for *I* am. You see, I am worried about getting ready to lecture, & so I fidget & fume & sweat, & I can't write serenely. Therefore I don't write Saturday articles that are satisfactory to me" (27 September 1869).

Like his Saturday articles, his initial stint in Buffalo proved less than satisfactory. It had not been a failure, exactly, but neither had it measured up to the hopes he had held for it when he arrived in the city in early August. His expectations, typically, had been spacious. He was to be a model of industry and diligence at the *Express* as well as the newspaper's chief celebrity and drawing card. Self-inflicted responsibilities of this kind inevitably persecuted him, but the demands in this case were particularly maddening because they pitted the editor's work ethic, personified in Clemens's colleague J. N. Larned, against the humorist's pose of lazy indifference. The consequence of these conflicting pressures seems to have been a characteristic mix of fire and ice in Clemens's office demeanor. "He was a man of wonderful charm," Larned recalled four decades later. "His disposition was to be genial and companionable; but the geniality was easily frosted, and he could bristle with repulsions as readily as anybody I have ever known."[9] Earl D. Berry, another *Express* writer at the time, had a similar recollection of his cooler side. "Samuel L. Clemens was not a rollicking soul," he claimed, "not a verbal joke-maker. He was chary of conversation even with personal acquaintances and positively repellent to strangers."[10]

The delightful situation Clemens had spoken of finding upon his arrival at the *Express* proved, as his early days there passed, to be subject to its share of strain and frustration. Buffalo turned out to be not quite the promised land, at least not yet. He could hardly find real satisfaction there, a genuine sense of ease and belonging, while, as he put it, half of him remained in Elmira. His circumstances provided him with another instance of doubleness in his life, in this case of trying emotionally and otherwise to be in two places at once. But the real harbor he had found in Olivia's "great heart" proved far more snug and attractive than the Buffalo breakwater he hoped would eventually provide the two of them an anchorage, and he came naturally to associate the Langdon family home in Elmira rather than his rooming-house on Swan Street with shelter and a sense of well-being. This dividedness or preoccupation on Clemens's part contributed to his uneven presentation of Mark Twain to the Buffalo reading public, but it was not wholly or even chiefly responsible for his deeper confusion about reconciling himself and his persona to the grind of a daily job. The 1869–70 lecture tour forestalled the necessity of that reconciliation and offered a month's vacation at the Langdon mansion in the bargain. He would attend to settling and editing in due time. Now, again, the road beckoned.

Chapter Four

An End to Wandering

When Clemens left Buffalo for Elmira the first week in October 1869, knowing he would be away from the city for four months, he may have carried along a residue of dissatisfaction with the work he had done there, but his attention was drawn in other directions—toward the happiness of spending a month with Olivia, toward the prospect of marrying the following February, and toward the demands and exhilarations of the lecture tour that was to intervene. He had been diverted from finally coming to anchor even though he believed he had found his anchorage and allowed himself a teasing chance to sample it. Having spent all of seven weeks in Buffalo, he determined that anchoring would have to wait until he could return to the city a married man the following February. However unevenly or inconclusively, though, Mark Twain had begun his tenure as a newspaper editor, proving, as he himself might have said, that the thing could be done. Shortly he would return to the more familiar venue of the lecture platform, where he was surer of himself and of his audience's expectations. Lecturing was at best a very mixed blessing for Clemens, but there was about it a clarity in the contract between performer and public that must have come as a relief after weeks of struggling to find an identity as a newspaper proprietor, editor, columnist, and celebrity. As it had the previous year, a schedule of lectures required that Clemens take a flesh-and-blood Mark Twain—a coherent, more or less unified personality, not a pastiche of experimental postures and voices—before audiences night after night. There was a discipline about lecturing that compelled him to resolve some of the contradictions and inconsistencies that were manifest in Mark Twain at the *Express*. By forcing him into certain strategies of simplification, lecturing provided a tonic for the confusion Clemens experienced in finding a voice at the newspaper, but there can be no doubt that it interrupted, perhaps ended altogether, whatever chance he might have had to work through that confusion in Buffalo.

Although he hardly needed another major distraction at the time, one to accompany and augment the intervention of the lecture tour, Clemens was further diverted from settling down peacefully as a Buffalo newspaperman by a circumstance he could not have foreseen: he found that he had written a best-seller. In May of 1869 he had corrected the last galley proofs of *The Innocents Abroad*. By early June Elisha Bliss's American Publishing Company had begun an initial run of 20,000 copies. On 20 July, just as Clemens was failing to connect with newspapers in Hartford and Cleveland and just before Jervis Langdon directed his attention to the *Express*, the first completed copy of the book was delivered.[1] Clemens arrived in Buffalo about the time that the first shipments of *Innocents* were coming into the hands of Bliss's agents and their subscribers. Within a month it was clear that the book was to be enormously popular. "The Cincinnati, Toledo & other western papers speak as highly of the book as do the New York & Philadelphia papers," he told Olivia on 6 September 1869. The next day he wrote Whitelaw Reid, editor of the New York *Tribune*, "The book is selling furiously, & the publisher says he is driving ahead night & day trying to keep up."

The reception of *The Innocents Abroad* did for Clemens what he had intended to accomplish through the move to Buffalo: it changed his status. But where the Buffalo move had as its object his acquiring steady, settled habits, the book promoted and celebrated the popular impression of Mark Twain as an irreverent wanderer with a true innocent's suspicion of civilizing conventions. Ironically, Clemens published what was to be the most successful travel book in this country's literary history just as he was determining to forsake travel forever. *Innocents* also established Mark Twain in the public mind as the writer of a six-hundred-page book, no longer, primarily, as a performer on the lecture platform, and not as a journalist, let alone a newspaper editor. It enlarged the dimension of his fame, in one sense by carrying him to international celebrity, and in another by demonstrating that the appeal and complexity of his persona were sufficient to hold an audience over a long course, something that the literary and stage comedians of his day were unlikely to be able to do. Perhaps this is what Petroleum Nasby, himself one of those comedians, had in mind in welcoming Mark Twain to the *Express* by declaring him "the greatest humorous writer America has ever produced."[2] And perhaps in his milder way this is what William Dean Howells meant to imply by saying of Clemens in his review of *The Innocents Abroad*, "It is no business of ours to fix his rank among the humorists California has given us, but we think he is, in an entirely different way from all the others, quite worthy of the company of the best."[3]

The success of *The Innocents Abroad* helped to divert Clemens's life from the course he—and Olivia, and her father—had been plotting for it over the spring and summer of 1869. In all probability his own temperament and talent would eventually have led him to weary of newspaper editing, even under the permissive circumstances he enjoyed at the *Express*; the book's reception accelerated that disillusionment by enhancing his reputation and, consequently, his prerogatives. Moreover, it did so at the same time that his lecture commitments were in more overt ways carrying him away from the anchorage he had sought so avidly only weeks before.

Clemens's 1869–70 tour, which began in Pittsburgh on 1 November and ended in Jamestown, New York, on 21 January, emphatically interrupted his tenure as a Buffalo newspaperman. Ironically, perhaps revealingly, though, he did his best *Express* writing while he was on the road, away from his desk and his other editorial duties. The 2 October piece on Mental Photographs ("The Latest Novelty") was the last Saturday article he wrote in Buffalo.[4] On 16 October, two Saturdays later, he began a series of "Around the World" letters in the *Express* which ran through the following March. The letters, the first two of which were very probably written in Elmira while Clemens was preparing his lecture, were intended to trace the progress of Olivia's brother Charles and his traveling companion, Professor Darius Ford of Elmira College, as they circumnavigated the globe. Rather than wait for reports from Charles and the professor, however, Clemens began the series on his own, chiefly by recounting some of his experiences in California and Nevada. The result was a relaxed, informed, and entertaining collection of portraits and anecdotes drawn from life and written with the assurance of a seasoned raconteur.

The important difference between the Saturday articles composed in Buffalo and the "Around the World" letters is that the latter offer a substantial body of lore and information in which Clemens took a genuine interest. Their humor arises easily, almost accidentally, out of the storytelling process; it isn't the exclusive purpose of the pieces. Consider, for example, his account in the first letter of discovering sea gulls' eggs on an otherwise desolate island in California's Mono Lake:

Nature has provided an unfailing spring of boiling water on the largest island, and you can put your eggs in there, and in four minutes you can boil them as hard as any statement I have made during the past fifteen years. Within ten feet of the boiling spring is a spring of pure cold water, sweet and wholesome. So, in that island you get your board and washing free of charge—and if nature had gone further and furnished a nice American hotel clerk who was crusty and disobliging, and didn't know any thing about the time tables, or the railroad routes—or—any thing—and was proud of it—I would not wish for a more desirable boarding house.[5]

The ease and confidence of the "Around the World" letters are no doubt largely attributable to Clemens's pleasure in discovering the matter of Nevada and California as a literary resource. But it also seems worth noting that it was while he was in Elmira, luxuriating in Langdon hospitality and mulling his western reminiscences, that he found the comfortable, unstrained voice that had for the most part eluded him in Buffalo.

Clemens's immersion in his western recollections, an immersion perhaps made possible by his sense of well-being in Elmira, seems to have relieved a good bit of the inhibiting self-consciousness he felt as the *Express*'s resident funnyman. Those recollections engaged and stimulated his imagination while much of his other writing at the time simply strained it. What particularly distinguishes the "Around the World" letters from the other writing is that in them Mark Twain is subsumed in the role of teller. He is freed from the burden of exhibiting himself as a comic personality and instead functions mainly as a voice, a sensibility. He remains a presence in the work, but not a performer. At its extremes this difference is like the one that distinguishes Huck Finn from the King, especially the King as he disports himself in the Royal Nonesuch. Mark Twain stopped short of prancing around in stripes at the *Express*, but he clearly felt himself to be under considerable pressure there to make people laugh. He had yet to learn—he would never entirely learn—how to overcome that pressure and its accompanying temptations and pitfalls, but the "Around the World" letters offered a comparatively early lesson of that kind.

The first letter was written on 10 October 1869. The next day Clemens posted another letter from Elmira, this one bearing his good wishes to a society of Forty-Niners then convening in New York. When it appeared in the New York *Tribune* on 14 October and in the *Express* on 19 October, its unforced good humor resembling that which would distinguish the "Around the World" series, his "Greeting to the California Pioneers" amounted to a public handshake from a reformed vagabond to his former cohorts, whom he addressed as "the Returned Prodigals." "I cordially welcome you to your old remembered homes and your long-deserted firesides," Mark Twain tells the pioneers, "and . . . hope that your visit here will be a happy one." Although much of the letter is taken up with a comic rendition of his own California adventures, the "here" to which he welcomes the pioneers is the East, and he speaks as an easterner, albeit a naturalized one, on behalf of other easterners in extending his greeting to those who have yet to make the transcontinental adjustment he has accomplished. From the sanctuary of the Langdon's substantial Elmira home, Clemens wrote with a kind of borrowed serenity, a stability and sense of rootedness that he hoped and expected to achieve in his own right at the close of the coming lecture season. In Buffalo he had as yet experienced little or none of that home feeling, living as he did in yet another boarding house, but he looked forward to establishing himself there unequivocally once he and Olivia were married in February. When he left Elmira and took up the lecture circuit, his idealization of his future married happiness often made him impatient with a mundane present that seemed only to be in the way. By the turn of the new year his bachelorhood seemed simply a burden. Like a man living out a sentence, he wrote to Olivia on 10 January 1870, "One day less to worry through before my rascally pilgrimage is finished."

The exigencies of life on the lecture circuit did little to diminish the rascality of Clemens's pilgrimage. He was then, as he would be later, ambivalent about lecturing, acknowledging it as a ready source of income and attention but knowing that the price of an hour's celebrity was often a day's misery. The itinerant lecturer was inevitably and all but incessantly at the mercy of strangers, many of whom practiced a particularly virulent hospitality. From a chilly New England outpost in mid-November, he complained to Olivia, "I had to submit to the customary & exasperating drive around town in a freezing open buggy this morning (at Norwich [Connecticut]) to see the wonders of the village." Wonders of this kind, he grumbled, are predictable, interchangeable, and insipid. "All towns are alike—all have the same stupid trivialities to show, & all demand an impossible interest at the suffering stranger's hands." These monotonous shrines and scenes would be infliction enough, but they are very likely to be followed by "other inanimate wonders with dull faces, but with legs to them that show them to be human: the mayor; the richest man; the wag of the village (who instantly assails me with old stale jokes & humorous profanity); the village editor—& a lot more of people I take no possible interest in & don't want to see." When his tormenters finally relent and discharge him for the night, the lecturer is left to face a solitude as dismal as the society that preceded it. "Here I am in a hotel," Clemens concludes, "& a villainous one it is—shabby bed, shabby room, shabby furniture, dim lights—everything shabby & disagreeable" (15–16 November 1869). Such circumstances must have made him acutely aware of the distance that lecturing had put between him and the comfortable Elmira mansion to which he addressed his letters.

As the interminable fall of 1869 stretched on, though, Jervis Langdon was seeing to it that he knew how and where Clemens's bachelor pilgrimage would end, and that this ending would be neither shabby nor disagreeable. Even as he had guided his future son-in-law to Buffalo, he now undertook to guide the newlyweds to their first home. Because Clemens was to be away from the city lecturing until after the wedding, he had left it to the ubiquitous

J. D. F. Slee, Langdon's Buffalo business associate, to find lodgings that would be suitable for him and his new bride when they arrived following the ceremony in February. Langdon, however, made a co-conspirator of Slee and with Olivia's happy complicity arranged to surprise the bridegroom by buying, furnishing, and staffing a large, lovely residence on Buffalo's fashionable Delaware Avenue as a wedding gift. Langdon bought the property, in his daughter's name, on 13 November 1869. It was on that day, perhaps only coincidentally, that Olivia wrote Clemens, "I am so happy, so perfectly at rest in you, so proud of the true nobility of your nature—it makes the whole world look so bright to me."[6] Like Olivia's letter, the Delaware Avenue house offered both a testimonial of confidence in Clemens's character and an incentive to live up to an implied standard. In its own way, too, the gift offered yet another demonstration of the enormous power of money, and particularly of Langdon money. Throughout their courtship Clemens and Olivia beguiled one another by picturing the perfect domestic castle. Olivia's father bought the castle for them.

As these maneuvers were going forward, Clemens was out on the lecture circuit, his duties at the *Express* having been curtailed but not altogether suspended, writing Olivia from town after town as he had the year before. Just as Jervis Langdon was closing the deal on the Buffalo house in mid-November, Clemens's schedule carried him to Hartford, where he had the satisfaction of discovering that the owners of the Hartford *Courant*, who had been offish and evasive toward him only months earlier, were now nothing short of eager, thanks to the popularity of *The Innocents Abroad*, to secure Mark Twain as a partner. The book was, after all, the product of a Hartford firm; neither its success nor the consequent fame of its author would have been lost on the *Courant* proprietors. Having spent an evening in the company of one of those proprietors, Charles Dudley Warner, Clemens wrote Olivia that "Warner soon talked himself into such a glow with the prospect of what we could do with the Courant now that I have achieved such a sudden & sweeping popularity in New England, that he forgot we had not yet come to any terms" (24 November 1869). Six months earlier, when he was far more enthusiastic about Hartford than Hartford was about him, Clemens had looked forward to the publication of *The Innocents Abroad* and expressed his hope to Olivia that "the book will possibly make me better known in New England & so consequently more valuable to a newspaper" (14 May 1869); that hope proved prophetic. Now, however, he reasoned with Warner—and, in the letter, with Olivia—that to sever his connections in Buffalo for the sake of joining the *Courant* would be to incur a further debt: "$9,000 altogether to get hold of an interest far less valuable & lucrative than my Express interest." Even at that, he allowed, the idea was not without appeal: "All I should get for it would be, the pleasure of living in Hartford among a most delightful society, & one in which you & I both would be supremely satisfied."

The letter must have caused something of a stir in the Langdon household, arriving as it did within two weeks of the family's secret purchase of the house in Buffalo and bearing the clear intention of reopening the possibility of the newlyweds' settling in Hartford. For his part, Clemens had by this time grown accustomed to addressing himself indirectly to Jervis Langdon through his letters to Olivia, sometimes asking advice and sometimes exploring the prospect of more tangible support. In the November 24 letter, he made that appeal overtly. Referring to Warner's proposals on behalf of the *Courant* owners, he wrote her, "I said if I were absolutely worth $35,000 I would pay $9,000 in a moment for the sake of getting ourselves comfortably situated, but unfortunately I wasn't worth any such sum. I said I would do nothing till I talked with you. He wanted me to talk with Mr. Langdon & write the result, & I said I would." There seems to be no record of Langdon's response to this line of inquiry, assuming that Olivia brought the letter to his attention or that Clemens himself later raised the Hartford offer with him. At the very least, though, the matter emphasizes how important and influential Langdon had become in Clemens's life and the extent to which Clemens had come to depend on him for counsel and a sense of stability as well as for financial backing. Langdon, complementarily, demonstrated a characteristic knack for using that dependency, whether emotional or material, as a means of conditioning and occasionally of manipulating his future son-in-law.

The letter gives rise to two further observations: first, that despite an earlier claim that he "never liked anything better" than his "easy, pleasant, *delightful* situation" at the *Express* (SLC to OL, 19

August 1869), Clemens was, toward the end of 1869, hardly devoted to Buffalo or the newspaper; and second, that Hartford continued to exert an attraction for him and, he implies, for Olivia as
well, just as it had from the very outset of their seriously considering places to live. For the time, though, perhaps recognizing that
his vacillation might strike the Langdons as evidence of undepend-
ability, he ended the letter by resigning himself to staying put.
"Livy darling," he wrote, "I guess we couldn't pull loose all the
Buffalo anchors easily, & so we may as well give up Hartford."
Acknowledging with just a hint of chagrin the drag of those substantial anchors, Clemens set aside his Hartford aspirations once
again and settled for Buffalo.

Knowing nothing about the wedding gift waiting for him on
Delaware Avenue, he had no idea how settled he was soon to be.
Within a month of his writing Olivia about the beguilements of
Hartford, he heard from Langdon associate Slee, who pretended to
be on the lookout for a suitable boarding house for the newlyweds,
about the supposed realities of Buffalo. Slee took an insider's satisfaction in keeping Clemens in the dark about the Delaware Avenue surprise. "Boarding *anyhow* is miserable business," he wrote,
with the hand-wringing solicitousness of the amateur hoaxer. "It
may answer for the *unsophisticated* and *unmarried* but for the *learned*
and *wedded* it is horrible." "However," Slee went on, "in this instance I think we are peculiarly fortunate—I have found you a place
on one of our most pleasant streets. . . . The family a small one,
and choice spirits—: with no predelictions for takeing *Boarders*, and
consenting to the present arrangement only because of the anticipated pleasure and profit of your company." Slee played his part
enthusiastically, describing the two rooms the newlyweds would
occupy, one of them "a delightful cozy nest," advising that the
privilege of boarding with a family of choice spirits would cost $20
a week and concluding, "The whole thing pleases me so well, that
I have closed the arrangement least they (these people I mean)
should grow sick of the idea."[7]

Ironically, on the very day Slee sent his hoaxing letter, Clemens
was once again in Hartford, enjoying a warm reception by some
of its leading citizens. "They all assailed me violently on the Courant matter," he reported to Olivia, "& said that it had ceased to be
a private desire that we take on ownership in that paper, & had be-

come a public demand." *Courant* co-owners Warner and Hawley, he was told, "would do anything to get me in there," and longtime Langdon family friend Isabella Hooker "said she had been writing to Mr. Langdon to make us sell out in Buffalo & come here." Bearing in mind his earlier humiliation in Hartford, he savored the moment even more deeply and candidly than he had savored one like it a month before: "It afforded me malicious satisfaction to hear all this," he told Olivia, "& contrast it with the insultingly contemptuous indifference with which the very same matter was treated last June, (by *every one of them*)" (27 December 1869). Unlike the letter Clemens wrote a month earlier, this one makes no explicit mention of trying to pull loose the Buffalo anchors. Slee's letter of the same day, for all its eager and innocent subterfuge, makes it clear that the prospective bridegroom had little idea just where those anchors were being set, or how deep.

With the turn of the new year Olivia's parents dispatched wedding invitations: "Mr & Mrs J Langdon request the pleasure of your presence at the Marriage Ceremony of Saml L Clemens and their Daughter on Wednesday evening Feby 2."[8] The two clergymen who officiated at the ceremony, held in the Langdon parlor, were Thomas K. Beecher, the family's Elmira minister, and Joseph Twichell, Clemens's particular friend in Hartford. They represented two points of the triangle which would establish the essential environmental geometry of Clemens's life during the early years of the decade just beginning. The third point in that figure, Buffalo, was largely unrepresented, either by clergy or guests, at the wedding.

Olivia and her parents had managed to keep the Delaware Avenue house a secret from Clemens over the course of the two-and-a-half months that had passed since its purchase, much of the time attending to furnishing, decorating, staffing, and provisioning it. The house was Jervis Langdon's trump, and he played it with a high style that would have won the admiration of Tom Sawyer. When the newlyweds were deposited at its front door the evening after the day of the ceremony, Langdon was there to bid them welcome and to hand his dumbstruck son-in-law a gift box containing the deed. Behind him the reassembled wedding party was arrayed, no doubt in attitudes of admiration and expectancy. It is just possible that even as he stammered out his thanks, Clemens dimly sus-

Elmira Jany 1870

Mr & Mrs J Langdon request
the Pleasure of Your Presence
at the Marriage Ceremony of
Saml L Clemens and their
Daughter on Wednesday evening
Feby 2d.

The Langdons' wedding invitation to Clemens's sister, Pamela, and her daughter, Annie. (Courtesy Mark Twain Papers, The Bancroft Library)

pected the deed of amounting to a "paper of indenture," as Justin Kaplan has characterized it.[9] Perhaps the gift is better understood as reflecting the complexity of Langdon's attitude toward Clemens, an attitude that included a worldly man's ungrudging admiration for one of his own kind as well as a father's jealous anxiety over his daughter's happiness.

While it was quite foreign to his own experience, Clemens had ample opportunity during their courtship to appreciate how protected and even coddled Olivia had been by her family. He might therefore have felt more than a little uneasy when, about a year before their wedding, he found himself on the receiving end of a joking reference to that protectiveness. "It was just like Mr. Langdon in his most facetious mood," he had written her, "to say he would kill me if I wasn't good to you" (16 January 1869). During the intervening year, Olivia's father had apparently been persuaded to "put up his tomahawk," as Clemens phrased it, if not entirely to allay his apprehensions. On the day of the wedding, in fact, Langdon is said to have confided in Annie Moffett, Clemens's seventeen-year-old niece, "My only fear is that Livy will not be equal to what lies before her. Sam will go far, and Livy has been brought up so quietly and so simply that I sometimes wonder if she will be able to hold him."[10]

Whatever the mix of regard and reservation, of openhanded generosity and coercive protectiveness, behind his actions, Jervis Langdon very largely determined the circumstances of the Clemenses' early life together. He had accepted Clemens as his daughter's fiancé—even, according to legend, when the suitor's supposed partisans argued against him; he had "discovered" Buffalo as a potential home, had at the very least advised Clemens during his *Express* negotiations, and had financed the deal; and he had provided the castle, complete with servants, furnishings, and a check to defray operating costs, that the newlyweds had spent much of their courtship imagining.[11]

Clemens's overt response—perhaps it is fair to say his conscious response—to Langdon's benevolent machinations was that of a grateful protégé, one who had not come under the influence of so powerful and effective a man since he completed his apprenticeship to Horace Bixby more than a decade earlier. Beneath the surface of his gratitude, amplifying it, Clemens's guilt at "robbing" Olivia

The newlyweds' home in Buffalo. (Courtesy Mark Twain Papers, The
Bancroft Library)

from her parents no doubt contributed to the deference he paid
Langdon. Early in their courtship he had tried to mitigate Olivia's
likely unhappiness at being stolen away from her family by suggesting that they would "model [their new] home after the old
home" (23 December 1868). Later he wrote his sister, Pamela, of
proposing an even more radical cure for the Langdons' devastation
at losing their daughter: "I will engage that they *follow* that daugh-

ter within twelve months. They couldn't stay away from her" (23 June 1869). Still further beneath that surface Clemens may well have harbored some resentment at the way in which the Langdons' manifest generosity was fixing his circumstances and defining his prerogatives. Late in his life, in the *Autobiography*, he observed that "gratitude is a debt which usually goes on accumulating like blackmail"; in 1869, before his ambivalence about the benevolence of others had darkened to cynicism, he could scarcely express his frustration so directly.[12] But during that year he did publish "The Legend of the Capitoline Venus," a story that crudely reflected not only his situation but also, perhaps, his attitudes.

The story, which appeared in the *Express* on Saturday, 23 October 1869, was almost certainly written while Clemens was the Langdons' guest in Elmira for the month of October. In it a poor American sculptor, George Arnold, falls in love with a young American woman, Mary, while he is working and she is visiting in Rome. Mary's family is quite well-off, and her father, "a money making, bowelless grocer," decrees that the two can wed only if George manages to acquire $50,000 before six months pass. George despairs: "If I had six centuries what good would it do?" Enter John Smithe, yet another American and George's friend since boyhood. John berates George for shrinking from a challenge—"Idiot! Coward! Baby!"—and pledges to take matters in his own hands. John accomplishes the $50,000 miracle by taking a hammer to George's latest creation, a statue of "America," burying the mutilated result on land deeded to George, and then excavating it, "sadly stained by the soil and the mould of ages," almost six months later. A committee of "art critics, antiquaries and cardinal princes of the church" determines that the statue is a Venus, more than two-thousand years old, and declares it "the most faultless work of art the world has any knowledge of." The Roman government pays George five million francs in gold, and the world, most notably represented by Mary's father, beats a path to his door. "My noble boy, she is yours!" says the bowelless grocer. "Take her—marry her—love her—be happy!—God bless you both!"

"Capitoline Venus" spends most of its energy spoofing Old World art and the authorities who purvey it, in the familiar *Innocents Abroad* manner. It also capitalizes on the sensation that at the time surrounded the alleged discovery of a "gigantic Petrified

Man" in upstate New York, as the author acknowledges in an end-note. All along the way, though, it caricatures circumstances that were powerful sources of anxiety and frustration for Clemens in 1869. Mary's mercenary father is a dime-novel rendition of Jervis Langdon, not simply in his having met with success in business but also in his demand that his daughter's suitor somehow prove himself worthy of her hand. The test of worthiness he proposes, that George produce $50,000 by the end of six months, is a good deal less subjective than the Langdons' inquiries about Clemens's character, although in both cases the probationer must remain in limbo until he is judged to have *earned* the daughter. That the grocer couches his test in blatantly financial terms, moreover, very likely reflects Clemens's apprehensions about being able to provide for Olivia on anything approaching the scale of living to which her upbringing had accustomed her.

But the most provocative comparison that can be drawn between George's plight and Clemens's has to do with the questions each might harbor about the value of the work he does. When Mary's father accuses George of offering her nothing but "a hash of love, art and starvation," George counters that "The Hon. Bellamy Foodle, of Arkansas, says that my new statue of America is a clever piece of sculpture," a defense so lame and so transparently ridiculous as to substantiate rather than refute the charge. Not very strictly speaking, a piece of George's art *is* responsible for making his fortune (and therefore for his gaining Mary), but only because his friend Smitthe mutilates and misrepresents it. Smitthe's chicanery may win the day for George, but in doing so it ultimately reinforces the bowelless grocer's position that George's work— and perhaps art in general—is essentially worthless. Nothing in the story effectively undercuts its basic philistinism, and Smitthe's justifiable indignation at George's simpering helplessness inclines the reader to sympathize with the philistines. The uncertainties George is forced to confront in the story—about his talent, about his vocation, about the artist's ability to function in a hostile American environment—were hardly unfamiliar to Clemens in 1869. The story exacerbates rather than resolves these uncertainties. George is delivered from his most pressing problem, earning Mary, but only at the cost of becoming part of a hoax that calls the value of his work sharply into question. The story may even suggest that some charlatanism is involved in the positive reception of most works of art, a suspicion that was alternately to amuse and to trouble Clemens throughout his career, although in this case, interestingly, the artist himself is spared the role of charlatan.

In "The Legend of the Capitoline Venus," John Smitthe solves George Arnold's problem, the artist's perennial problem of making a living in an aggressively materialistic culture, by exploiting the entrepreneurial immorality of that culture on his behalf—specifically, by converting George's work to a valued commodity through the familiar agency of creative misrepresentation. In his own way Clemens faced the same problem in 1869 as he sought a way to parlay his gifts as a writer, predominantly as a journalist, into a regular, remunerative position that would enable him, like George Arnold, to deserve and provide for the woman he loved. In Clemens's real-life drama, however, Jervis Langdom came to play the two parts represented in the story by the bowelless grocer and by John Smitthe. More subtly than Mary's father (and in concert with Olivia's mother), he established the standards, both moral and material, that Clemens would have to meet in order to secure Olivia. More conventionally and more scrupulously than Smitthe, he worked behind the scenes to make it possible for Clemens to meet those material standards.

The confluence of these roles was emphatically dramatized in Langdon's stunning Clemens the day after his wedding by presenting him the key to the house at 472 Delaware Avenue in Buffalo. The gift reflected the scope both of Langdon's generosity and of his expectations. Pinioned between the two, perfectly bewildered with gratitude and a sense of booming good fortune, Clemens had ample reason to believe that he was about to live out in Buffalo the dreams of domestic contentment and professional stability he and Olivia had spent the interminable months conjuring. He was, he thought, at last, at home.

Chapter Five

Honeymoon

Olivia Langdon could hardly marry Samuel Clemens without running the risk of becoming Mrs. Mark Twain. She faced the prospect not simply of seeing her own identity eclipsed by her husband's more formidable personality but of becoming a kind of public figurine, the little lady who had cast her lot in with that of the Wild Humorist. The danger, though, was not all on one side. Mark Twain had survived the reformist zeal of Clemens's courtship and the rigors of the 1869–70 lecture season, but there had not been time, between the two, for him to accomplish the one thing that had led him to Buffalo in the first place: finding a stable role for himself at the Buffalo *Express*. Now, as the newlyweds took possession of their elegant little palace on Delaware Avenue, the novelty and the pleasures of married life threatened to join the roster of distractions that contributed to prolonging a period of imperfect adjustment in the city. As a writer for the *Express* Mark Twain remained, at the beginning of 1870, a catalog of stances, postures, and voices rather than a unified sensibility.

Clemens's failure either to establish himself as a practicing newspaper editor or to find a coherent voice for Mark Twain as a newspaper contributor during his early tenure at the *Express* was perhaps inevitable, given, among other obstacles, the brevity of his stay and the tug of Elmira on his attention. For all his determination and enthusiasm, he had not come to anchor. But marrying Olivia Langdon on 2 February 1870 changed the circumstances that had kept him adrift and promised to make Buffalo the fixed center of his life, a place for staying put. About a month before the wedding, he had written Mary Fairbanks that once married he and Olivia would "not be likely to stir from that town for several months, for neither of us are fond of traveling. I doubt if we *ever* stir again," he added, "except to visit home & you" (6 January 1870). "Home" in this case meant the Langdons' brownstone mansion in the heart of Elmira. A few weeks after the wedding he informed his lecture agent, James Redpath, "I am not going to lecture any more forever" (22 March 1870). Clemens's dream of domestic contentment, of settled, steady habits and abiding, impregnable security, seemed about to come true. Olivia wrote her parents, "We are as happy as two mortals can well be" (9 February 1870).

The wedding itself, relatively small and private, took place in the Langdon home. That privacy was substantially abridged by the fastidious Mary Fairbanks herself, who excused her apparent lapse of taste in reporting the event in her husband's Cleveland *Herald* by reasoning that while "the quiet, impressive ceremony with all its beautiful appointments is sacred to the few who witnessed it . . . , 'Mark Twain' belongs to the public which has a right to know."[1] Clemens wrote her that he appreciated her "graceful account" of the event but pointed out that he had "made a special request (for Livy's sake) of all the other writers present at the wedding, that they put all they had to say into one stickfull [of set type], & leave out the adjectives" (13 February 1870). Mother Fairbanks's rendition of the ceremony promoted the image of a mannerly, genteel Mark Twain who "filled the role of bridegroom with charming grace and dignity" and whose "moistened eyes spoke deeper thanks than words" when his new father-in-law presented him with the deed to the house on Delaware Avenue. Many months earlier, within about a week of Clemens's arrival in Buffalo, the *Express* had noted that "Delaware street, from the number of its costly residences, may be styled the 'Street of Palaces.' "[2] With the newlyweds now installed there in their own modest palace, it remained only for Mary Fairbanks to publish a fairy godmother's benediction upon them:

> Nothing that love or wealth could suggest or supply was wanting to make the scene the fulfillment of the poet's dream, from the delicate blue satin drawing room to the little sanctum quite apart, with its scarlet upholstery, amid the pretty adornments of which inspiration must often come to its happy occupant.
>
> Long life and happy days to our young friends, whose morning sky gives such rosy promise.

It is hard to imagine that at the time of the wedding anyone would have been more alive to that sense of promise than Clemens himself. He had finally married the woman he idolized; had been transfixed by the Langdons' gift of house, furnishings, and staff; had returned to the secure and remunerative editorial post he had left to fulfill his lecture obligations. Should the combination of these circumstances somehow fail to bewilder him with happiness, he had only to reflect that *The Innocents Abroad* was a booming best-seller, the New York *Tribune* citing sales of 45,000 copies as of January 1870 and reporting that the book's publisher was "running six presses to keep up with the demand."[3] Within a few days of the wedding, an Elmira newspaper retailed the rumor "that Mark Twain will realize more than $100,000 from 'Innocents Abroad.'"[4] The figure was extravagantly exaggerated—about a year after the book's publication Clemens wrote his mother and sister that "The 'Innocents Abroad' paid me 12 to $1500 a month" (27 July 1870)—but its apparent plausibility is an indication both of the book's popularity and of Twain's growing celebrity as a successful writer.

The almost palpable satisfaction newlywed Clemens took in his good fortune, both domestic and professional, shone warmly through his correspondence at the time, as for instance in his 6 February letter to boyhood friend Will Bowen. The letter is widely known as an early instance of Clemens's extraordinary responsiveness to the "Matter of Hannibal," since in it he claims that upon reading a note from Bowen he "rained reminiscences for four & twenty hours." Those reminiscences, however, powerful and significant as they are, serve finally to bring him up sharply in the *present.* "Heavens what eternities have swung their hoary cycles about us since those days were new!" he writes Bowen, "since Laura Hawkins was my sweetheart." That remark "fetches" him: "Hold! *That* rouses me out of my dream, & brings me violently back unto this day & this generation. For behold I have at this moment the only sweetheart I ever *loved,* & bless her old heart she is lying asleep upstairs in a bed that I sleep in every night, & for four whole days she has been *Mrs. Samuel L. Clemens!*" There follows a paean to his new life, beginning with a worshipful encomium to Olivia ("Before the gentle majesty of her purity all evil things & evil ways & evil deeds stand abashed. . . . She is the very most perfect gem of womankind that ever I saw in my life"), including an account of the Langdons' surprise wedding gift ("the daintiest darlingest, loveliest little palace in America"), and concluding with a boast about his professional success ("My book gives me an income like a small lord, & my paper is a good profitable concern").

Clemens's letter to Will Bowen is the dispatch of a happy man, albeit one who is above neither Victorian chauvinism nor a certain amount of aggressive self-promotion. It sounds the notes that would play through much of his correspondence and much of his experience during the first few months of his married life. At least as fervently as Olivia, he had earlier conjured a vision of a life whose essential terms were retirement and refuge from a hostile world. The dainty palace—whose reigning totem was a statuette of Peace, a further gift of the Langdons—made a reality of that vision, and Clemens was appropriately proud and protective in his regard for it. After Joseph and Harmony Twichell came to visit less than a week after the wedding, he wrote Olivia's parents of his pleasure in showing them "elaborately" through the house, adding that he "made Twichell wipe his feet & blow his nose before entering each apartment (so as to keep his respect up to an impressive altitude)." The Clemenses were particularly gratified to find that their first houseguests shared their appreciation of their home. "We listened to their raptures," Clemens reported, "& enjoyed the same" (9 February 1870).

No visitor's rapture, though, could match his own. The depth of his commitment to an idealization of home and hearth reflected Clemens's inexperience, as an adult, of anything approaching domestic stability. Olivia made inevitable comparisons between her present circumstances and those she had known all her life, confiding, for instance, in a letter to her parents, "I am perfectly happy in this new home. Still I do not yet love the rooms in it as well as I do those in the maiden home" (12 February 1870). Her new husband, on the other hand, was nothing short of florid in his uncritical enthusiasm, writing to Mrs. Langdon,

Our home . . . is the daintiest, & the most exquisite & enchanting that can be found in all America—& the longer we know it the more fascinating it grows & the firmer the hold it fastens upon each fettered sense.— It is perfect. Perfect in all its dimensions, proportions & appointments. It is filled with that nameless grace which faultless harmony gives. . . . Our home is a ceaseless, unsurfeiting feast for the eye & the soul, & the whole being. It is a constant delight. It is a poem, it is music—& it speaks & it sings to us, all the day long. (20 February 1870)

The house was simply the most massive and tangible embodiment of the domestic ideal in which Clemens, at thirty-five, was making an enormous emotional investment. He had been resigned, at the time of the wedding, to boarding for a year or so until he and Olivia could afford a home of their own. The Langdons' gift had eliminated that last bit of transience and fully enfranchised him as a settler. Ironically, but not surprisingly, there was for him a feeling of unreality about this combination of stability and good fortune. He described himself as "Little Sammy in Fairy Land" in recounting to Olivia's parents his amazement at being presented the deed to the house on Delaware Avenue (9 February 1870). As that astonishment ebbed, its place was taken by his day-to-day wonderment at the storybook life he found himself leading. "We are settled down & comfortable," he wrote Mother Fairbanks, "& the days swing by with a whir & a flash, & are gone, we know not where & scarcely care. To me passing time is a dream" (13 February 1870). The dream was essentially the one he had summoned while he was courting Olivia, especially in his letters. Its genesis was literary as well as psychological and had a great deal in common with the sentimental melodrama that Mark Twain characteristically ridiculed. "We are about as happy in our Aladdin's Palace," Clemens wrote Joel Benton, editor of the Amenia, New York, *Times*, "as if we were roosting in the closing chapter of a popular novel" (20 February 1870).

Leaving such a roost for any destination would very likely have taken considerable effort, but leaving it for the editorial offices of the Buffalo *Express* evidently required a power of will Clemens could seldom muster. In his letter to Benton he confided, "I don't go to the office once a week." Six months earlier, when he was new to the job and to Buffalo, he had written to Olivia of the long hours and diligent energy he was devoting to the *Express*; now, ensconced with her in the dainty palace, he was tempted to boast to others of his ease and complacency. A week after the wedding, he wrote Francis P. Church, joint editor of the *Galaxy*, that the *Express* "pays me an ample livelihood, & does it without my having to go near it. I write sketches for it, & occasional squibs & editorials—

that is all. I don't go to the office" (9 February 1870). The next day
he joked with another editor, Charles C. Hine of the *Insurance Monitor and Wall Street Review*, that his inactivity was a matter of principle, a principle deriving from his new status. "But now I am *married*," he wrote Hine, "I renounce my former life & all its
belongings. I have begun a new life & a new system, a new dis-
pensation. And the bottom rule of this latter is, To Work No More
than is Absolutely Necessary. I've got plenty of money & plenty
of credit." By the end of the month he informed Elisha Bliss, perhaps a little defensively, "I don't go near the Express office more
than twice a week—& then only for an hour. I am just as good as
other men—& other men take honeymoons I reckon" (23 February
1870).

Clemens was of course entitled to a honeymoon, as even he was
willing to allow, his anxieties, insecurities, and guilts notwithstanding. And no doubt the month or so following the wedding
did amount to a honeymoon in Buffalo, particularly given his
dreamy idealization of Olivia and his sense of storybook well-
being in their new home. But in facing the adjustment that sooner
or later confronts all honeymooners—making the transition from
romantic reverie to the practical demands of day-to-day living—
he was peculiarly at a disadvantage, especially when it came to re-
establishing himself as a working writer and editor. Having never
really found his niche or his voice as a newspaperman during his
initial stay in Buffalo, he had little residual experience to draw upon
in resuming his place at the *Express*. From the beginning, moreover, that place had been only nebulously defined, his "roving
commission" amounting to a very mixed blessing for a writer
trying to fashion a stable persona. Clemens was a self-confessed
vagabond before he landed in Buffalo, and Mark Twain had been
a vagabond's creation, an evolving, unsystematic concatenation of
masks and postures rather than a fixed and well-integrated personality. Even on the lecture stage, Twain remained something of an
enigma to those who paid attention; for all the shambling and
drawling and apparent carelessness—behaviors that for some simply confirmed his reputation as a drinker—his performances, particularly in 1869–70, were typically freighted with serious and
even moralizing sentiments. His early stint at the *Express* reflected
the conflicting mix of impulses Clemens experienced in offering

Mark Twain to the public but hardly allowed him time to resolve them.

His tenure at the *Express* having been interrupted first by the lecture tour, then by preparations for the wedding, then by honeymooning, he was, in February 1870, practically in the position of having to start all over again in finding his way as a Buffalo newspaperman. By that time, however, both his *Express* partners and his *Express* readers had outlived the first blush of enthusiasm for the novelty if not the pleasure of Mark Twain's company. His advent had not transformed the paper or very substantially increased its circulation, and his contributions, rendered infrequent by months on the road and uneven by his conflicting ambitions, had failed to galvanize an audience in Buffalo.[5] Returning to the *Express* after that equivocal start, Clemens was at bottom anything but the easy, complacent lounger he claimed to be in letters to distant editors. For all the good fortune that had befallen him, perhaps in part *because* of that good fortune, he was every bit as anxious and uncertain in February 1870 about making a success of himself at the *Express* as he had been when he arrived in Buffalo six months earlier. Not long after the wedding, in fact, while he was boasting to others of his deliberate, abundant leisure, he provided Mary Fairbanks a very different, and no doubt a truer, account of his circumstances and state of mind. "Every day," he wrote her, "I nerve myself, & seize my pen & dispose my paper, & prepare to buckle on the harness & *work*! And then I pace the floor—back & forth, back & forth, with vacuous mind—& finally I lay down the pen & confess that my time is not come—that I am utterly empty. But I must work, & I *will* work. I will go straight at it & *force* it" (13 February 1870). Shaping the public perception of Mark Twain had given Clemens ample experience in playing the loafer, in masking effort and even earnestness behind a pose of torpor. Now he resorted to a similar strategy in seeking to disguise his confusion as he returned to the bewildering and ill-defined business of newspaper editing.

Having created no stable or ongoing role for himself at the *Express*, Clemens had none to resume when his hiatus and his honeymoon ended. As a writer, particularly, he had no momentum to pick up or draw upon as he nerved himself, seized his pen, and disposed his paper. The single notable exception to this observation was the "Around the World" series. The first "Around the World" letter, probably written while Clemens was the Langdons' house-guest in Elmira, had appeared in the *Express* on 16 October 1869. The eighth letter in the series, which was also very likely written under the Langdon roof, this time while Clemens was awaiting the wedding, appeared on 29 January 1870, meaning that to that point he had managed to turn out an average of one letter every other week, even when he was on the lecture circuit. This hardly amounted to a prodigious output, but it did establish a certain rhythm, and apparently Clemens planned at least to keep to that pace when he returned to full-time newspapering. On 22 January 1870 he explained to Elisha Bliss his decision not to copyright the "Around the World" letters, a decision that meant other papers were free to copy them from the *Express* without penalty. "It don't hurt anything to be well advertised," Clemens wrote Bliss—who, as the publisher of *The Innocents Abroad*, had reason to be jealous of Mark Twain's byline—"but you see out of fifty letters not more than six or ten will be copied into any *one* newspaper—and *that* don't hurt." Clemens's marketing strategy aside, his assurances to Bliss indicate that he saw the "Around the World" series running to something like fifty letters, a circumstance implying that at the time he imagined himself embarked on a long and continuing proj-ect which would provide at least intermittent continuity to his work in Buffalo. On the day he wrote Bliss, the seventh "Around the World" letter appeared in the *Express*; he envisioned at least forty more such letters ahead of him, some of them, presumably, assembled from the raw material provided by his collaborator, Pro-fessor Darius R. Ford, Charles Langdon's traveling companion.

As it turned out, Clemens's participation in the "Around the World" series ended the very next week, with the publication of the eighth letter on 29 January. That is to say that—although he could not have known it at the time, and despite his plans to the contrary—he had in fact written his last "Around the World" letter *before* he returned to Buffalo and tried to resume his *Express* duties. While a number of circumstances contributed to the demise of the series, the most telling consequence of its failure was to isolate Clemens further from whatever beginnings he may have made on the newspaper. The dwindling of the series resulted from a coin-cidence of bad judgment and bad timing, which served finally to make the task of his finding a role or place at the *Express* even more uncertain. His bad judgment was manifest principally in his choice of a co-correspondent. Professor Ford, a friend of the Langdons and a member of the faculty of Elmira College, may have been, as Clemens wrote in introducing him to his *Express* audience on 16 October 1869, "a scholarly man . . . whose attainments cover a vast field of knowledge," but he proved to be anything but a prolific source of grist for the Mark Twain mill. Insofar as he gave it any very deliberate thought at all, Clemens seems to have envisioned his "dual correspondence" with Ford in much the same way that he subsequently imagined other projects of a similar nature. A friend or acquaintance was deputized to visit some exotic locale and to send back copious details, observations, and anecdotes which Clemens would then transform into the further adventures of Mark Twain, thus capitalizing on and extending the strategy of *The Innocents Abroad* without jeopardizing the newlywed's determination to settle down by requiring him to leave home.

However appealing this scheme may have been to Clemens's developing entrepreneurial side, it was, like its successors, destined to fail. The ostensible reason—or the reason he pointed to, at any rate—was Ford's reserve as a correspondent: the professor was a long time writing a few letters. The more telling explanation of the series' failure, however, probably rests with Clemens himself, and particularly with the brevity of his attention span. The idea for the series must have come to him in September or early October of 1869, when he was still very new at the *Express* and frequently a guest at the Langdons', where the globe-trotting expedition about to be undertaken by Charles and Professor Ford naturally occupied the family. Given his own appetite for travel, curbed for the time by the onset of domesticity, Clemens no doubt took a lively interest in the trip. In his eagerness for the project, he published the first "Around the World" letter in mid-October, knowing that the professor's earliest correspondence, from Japan, would be unlikely to arrive until the following January. That eagerness enabled him to carry the series on his own through that January, when preparations for the wedding intervened and when he expected help from Ford.

That help, in the form of a letter from the professor, seems not to have arrived until February, at which point Clemens chose simply to publish it without alteration as the ninth letter in the "Around the World" series (12 February 1870). At the time he may simply have been too busy honeymooning to care to embellish or sport about with Ford's writing as he had originally proposed. Or it may be that after months of waiting he found his collaborator's first effort disappointing. Entitled "The Pacific," Ford's contribution amounted to eight hundred words—about half Clemens's usual output—beginning with a remarkable compression of the trip west ("First the tree belt, next the prairie belt, then the desert belt, beyond the Rocky Mountains"), pausing briefly to glance at some of the social issues a western traveler encounters ("the 'Indian Question,' . . . the 'Mormon Question,' . . . the 'Chinese Labor Question' . . ."), and concluding with an enthusiast's inventory of the American steamship he and Olivia's brother were taking to the Orient ("386 feet long, 50 feet wide, three masted, of 4454 tons burden, and requiring 1200 tons of coal for a single voyage"). Ford's letter was hardly effusive or deeply evocative, but Clemens could have made something of it if he had the inclination. The professor's second letter, which appeared in the *Express* on 5 March 1870 under the title "Japan," was considerably richer in detail and observation than his first, particularly because it included an emotional account of the catastrophic collision between a merchant steamship and the United States Navy ship *Oneida*. Again, however, Clemens simply allowed the letter to pass into print without comment, signing it with Ford's initials, "D. R. F." The "dual correspondence" had dwindled to a discrete tandem. Later that month he wrote the Langdons that he had soured on the enterprise altogether, citing as his reason Ford's failure to hold up his end of the bargain. "I have given up Prof. Ford," he wrote, "& shall discontinue the 'Round the World' letters—*have* done it. The Prof. has now been 6 months writing 2 little letters. . . ." Of Ford and Charles Langdon he said, "If they continue their trip 18 months, as they propose, the Prof. will succeed in grinding out a grand total of 6 letters, if he keeps up his present vigor" (26 March 1870).

Ford *was* a poor, or at best a diffident, correspondent, but during his tenure at the *Express* Clemens probably lacked the combination of patience, judgment, and self-assurance to be a good collaborator regardless of his partner. Mark Twain was still too volatile a personality, given the manifold transitions he was undergoing at the time, to stand securely on his own feet, let alone to play off someone else. The best thing about the "Around the World" letters was the incentive or excuse they gave Clemens to delve into his own western experience in beginning the series independently of the professor. Perhaps the major strategic reason behind their coming to an end was that even before the first piece of Ford's correspondence arrived Clemens had written his way through that western material and, having done so, had little inclination to trail along after the professor to Japan. His treatment of the American West had ended with his publication of the seventh letter in the series, entitled, "Pacific Coast—Concluded," on 22 January 1870. Like its predecessors, it introduced topics that he would later develop more fully in *Roughing It*, in this case the Chinese population and the notoriety of Nevada desperadoes.

His eighth and last letter, "Dining with a Cannibal," appeared in the *Express* on 29 January and is by contrast a windy tall tale that merely plays predictably on popular superstitions concerning Pacific islanders. It is in all likelihood a letter Clemens never intended to write, owing to his expectation that something from Ford would be forthcoming in January, his preoccupation at the time with the wedding, and his having come to a natural stopping or transitional point with the close of his western accounts in letter seven. Following in the wake of those accounts, it also marked a regression in the series itself. They had been vivid, first-hand evocations of a territory located somewhere between the boundaries of history, geography, and myth; it amounted only to the playing out of an elaborate, trivial hoax. Clemens's enthusiasm for the "Around the World" project, like his enthusiasm for the Buffalo *Express*, seems to have exhausted itself before Ford's letters began to arrive, which meant that the professor had little real opportunity either to gratify or to disappoint his co-correspondent. In telling the Langdons of his intention to "drop the 'Round the World' business," Clemens indicated a vague intention to pursue some vestige of the original plan by periodically using Charles Langdon's journals of the trip to concoct "a vagrant correspondence" to the *Express* from a fictitious traveler (26 March 1870). It was an intention he never acted upon. With the publication of Ford's second letter, therefore, the "Around the World" series, already moribund despite its notable earlier vitality, died of its own inertia.

For all the emotional contentment and expectancy with which he returned to Buffalo in February 1870, Clemens was professionally adrift. The frustration he expressed to Mary Fairbanks on 13 February ("I must work, & I *will* work. I will go straight at it & *force* it") reflected the directionlessness he felt at the time as a writer and betrayed the professional anxiety that troubled his domestic paradise. Not surprisingly, he gave a great deal of his attention to that domesticity, trying above all to fathom and carry off his role as master of an elegant and expensive home while assuring his new wife that she showed an uncanny knack in fulfilling hers. "Livy makes a most excellent little housekeeper, & I always knew she would," he wrote the Langdons a few days after the wedding. "Everything goes on as smoothly as if it were worked by hidden machinery" (9 February 1870).

In fact, both newlyweds tended to regard housekeeping as if there were something mysterious or hidden about it, or something slightly unreal. On 16 February, Olivia wrote her parents, "Two weeks tonight since we were married, it all seems like a dream— It seems as if we must be playing keep house—but I assure you that we are thankful that we do not have to board—*dear, dear* Father how happy he has made us by his great magnificent gift to us."[6] The Clemenses were more comfortably situated in their own home on Delaware Avenue than they would have been as boarders, but that situation forced upon them the responsibility of supervising the operation of an elaborately appointed, fully-staffed, Victorian household. For Olivia, who unlike her husband was not surprised by the Langdons' gift of the house, it was a responsibility to be greeted apprehensively, particularly because it required the management of servants. "I cannot but expect that the clouds will come some time," she wrote her parents after her first two days of dealing with the household staff, "but I pray that when they do I may be woman enough to meet them."[7] Three weeks later she was still bracing for catastrophe. "I have, as yet had none of the troubles that ladies groan over," she told her father. "Hattie Marsh Tyler was here yesterday and was telling me about how much trouble the Buffalo Ladies have with their girls, I hope it will not come to me."[8] Clemens sometimes sent comic dispatches from the domestic front, as for instance in writing Mother Fairbanks that Olivia "goes around with her bunch of housekeeper's keys (which she don't know how to unlock anything with them because they are mixed,) & is overbearing & perfectly happy," or that he was afraid of being outdressed by his coachman (13 February 1870), but because his own insecurities to a large extent mirrored his wife's, he was only occasionally more capable than she of treating housekeeping as a laughing matter.

For all the pleasure they claimed to take in it, the newlyweds were often as much daunted as delighted by the dainty palace. The sudden onset of gentility sometimes led Clemens to adopt a reverent fastidiousness that reflected his deference to the dominant formality of the house. "He has grown wonderfully care taking," Olivia reported to her mother after an incident in which he drove fellow humorist Petroleum Nasby from a room for tracking snow into it. "Who would have ever *dreamed* of seeing Mr Clemens so carefull."[9] For Olivia herself the burdens of domesticity were even more intimidating. The object of her family's zealous care for much of her life, she was, like other daughters of privilege, still in many respects a child at the age of twenty-five. Given the peculiarities of the Victorian code to which both she and her husband innocently subscribed, she found herself abruptly unprepared to meet the domestic and social obligations that she regarded as a measure of her "womanliness." Clemens accepted and for that matter prized the impracticality of his wife's upbringing—"*You* know anything about cookery!" he once wrote her. "I would as soon think of your knowing the science of sawing wood" (6 January 1869). But the pairing of her ignorance with his own often consigned the two of them to a self-conscious timidity that contributed to their isolation in Buffalo. While the newlyweds looked forward to receiving callers and friends, for instance, Olivia confided in Mrs. Fairbanks her anxiety that their guests "may have some things to excuse in our way of doing, owing to our both being rather inexperienced in all these matters."[10]

Clemens could, gingerly, make private jokes at the expense of that inexperience, as for example when he wrote Olivia's parents about her inquiring of him "whether they sell sirloin steaks by the pound or by the yard" (9 February 1870), but he was unable in at least two early attempts to convert his domestic insecurities to public humor. He twice set out, all but certainly during those first days or weeks of marriage in Buffalo, to write a sketch on the tribula-

tions of housekeeping. His pose—conjecturally as Mark Twain—
is the same in each and quite familiar: that of the hapless innocent
thrown into bewildering circumstances but trying at all costs to
disguise his ignorance and unease. "If I stick to this novel outrage
they call 'keeping house,' three weeks longer," he confides to his
reader, "I shall be a dead man. I do not know anything at all about
it (for I have boarded all my life,) & yet I have to keep up a solemn
farce of being perfectly acquainted with everything connected
with it."[11] The immediate danger is that he will expose himself to
the derision of his servants, but of course he only makes himself
ridiculous, in the reader's eyes and his own, by maintaining a coun-
terfeit swagger in their presence. "And my wife is no better off than
I," he continues, with particular reference to her ordering up a
yard-and-a-half of beefsteak for dinner. "She was not certain that
steaks were sold by the yard, but it would not do to appear ignorant
before the cook, & so she gave that order with an impressive assurance that almost convinced even me that she knew what she was
talking about." The gambit would have played resonantly before
any reader of *The Innocents Abroad*, with the single difference that
in this case the narrator is accompanied in his silly posturing not
by one or another of "the boys"—as in the *Innocent*'s kid-glove episode in Gibraltar, for instance—but by a wife.

The first fragment breaks off at the point where the narrator is
almost fooled into thinking his wife knows what she is talking
about. The second makes no mention of a wife, thus rendering the
narrator alone the butt of its ridicule. It begins with his acknowledging the unexpected pleasure he takes in maintaining a home,
given that he has known nothing but boarding since the age of thirteen, a pleasure he largely attributes to his intuition for housekeeping. "I seem to know all about it by a sort of instinct," he muses.
"I can see that I surprise the servants every day, & they are old,
experienced domestics."[12] The narrator is clearly being set up for a
fall here, as he himself intimates when he confesses that "there are
times when you give an order with some little lack of confidence,
some little consciousness that you are not entirely certain that you
know what you are about." His strategy, once again, is to mask or
deny that uncertainty, especially in the presence of the old, experienced domestics. "As soon as you have taught your servants to
respect your knowledge & your judgment, they respect you," he

advises, "& beware how you betray ignorance of anything in presence of a dependant! [*sic*]" The second fragment ends here.

Clemens evidently made no more of his intention to work up a humorous sketch about housekeeping. Perhaps only coincidentally, he began his 9 February 1870 letter to the Langdons, the letter in which he jokes about Olivia's ordering sirloins by the yard, by confessing his inability to write anything suitable for the *Express*. "A man cannot do a thing well which his heart is not in," he tells them, "& so I have dropped the newspaper scribbling for to-day." In this letter, too, and in all sincerity, he praises Olivia's intuition for housekeeping and observes, "The servants are willing & entirely respectful toward her (which they had *better* be.)" Whether or not the newspaper scribbling he attempted that day included the two fragments on housekeeping, Clemens was plainly preoccupied at the time with the very concerns they exploited, especially those touching on the insecurities of new householders and the potential tyranny or derision of servants. That the sketches remained fragmentary and unpublished is very likely owing to their striking too close to home. Clemens took the burdens and coercions of genteel housekeeping too much in earnest to treat it as a game. He sought to acquire the domestic self-possession that his narrator fakes, to be the steady and accomplished master of his castle, not a bumbling or scornful poseur. No similar aspirations stymied his satiric impulses in *The Innocents Abroad*, where his aim was to pillory rather than to aspire to the egregious piety of the *Quaker City* pilgrims or the venality of traveling Americans. He could of course make fun of himself, or of "himself" as Mark Twain; to do so was one of his chief stocks-in-trade. But in those first weeks and months of marriage, too much of his tenuous self-esteem rested on his fathoming the mysteries of housekeeping to allow him to regard it with a humorist's detachment.

He may also have had a problem in imagining a domesticated Mark Twain or in presenting such a paradox to the public. Samuel Clemens had fallen in love, married, and pledged himself to settling responsibly in Buffalo, but did it inevitably follow that Mark Twain had done so as well? There may have been reason to suppose so, but there was also reason for doubt. The two did not in fact share an identical biography. Twain, for instance, claimed at times to be an orphan, or, as in the case of his essays on housekeeping, to have been a vagabond, a boarder, virtually from the outset. Neither of these circumstances applied to Clemens, although he had lost one parent, his father, as a boy, and although he had spent a little more than half his life on the road. Generally, and often as the exigencies of a given piece of writing required, Twain was revealed to be more undisciplined, more outrageous, more unpolished, and in strategic ways more "innocent" than Clemens. He was a better comic property, a rendition of the prototype that emphasized the ironic and unconventional. With their differences, many of which seem to have registered with him just below the level of full consciousness, Clemens may have instinctively balked at identifying Mark Twain as a married man or at the prospect of arraying him among household gods. The two aborted sketches on housekeeping were his only attempts to treat the experience of ordinary domestic life through a first-person narrator who might be construed to be Mark Twain. When he later wrote a series of three stories dealing with comic episodes in the home of a young married couple, he named his main characters George and Mary McWilliams, not Sam and Olivia Clemens—and certainly not Mark and Mrs. Twain.[13]

Clemens's sensitivity to Olivia's feelings may also have played a part in his abandoning the housekeeping sketches and, more generally, in his writing very little during the first months of their marriage. Her fear that she might not measure up to the demands of homemaking would have rendered it cruel on his part to publish a piece, however joking or fictive, which begins with a confession of his own clumsiness at keeping house, goes on to admit that "my wife is no better off than I," and includes a ludicrous instance of her failing to fool the servants into believing "that she knew what she was talking about." To publish such a piece in the Buffalo *Express*, moreover, at just the time when he and Olivia were trying to establish themselves in the city would have required either an indifference or a self-confidence that Clemens lacked. His dominant feelings at the time combined his own anxieties about the mysteries of settling down with a solicitousness for Olivia's misgivings that bordered, at least, on the paternal. His insistent preoccupation with her girlishness and inexperience, two of the qualities that had most drawn him to her, disadvantaged both of them in coming to terms with one another and with their new circumstances. The early imaginings of married life that he had conveyed to her in his letters pictured a mature, reposeful couple reading or talking quietly within the confines of a secure domestic haven that held an uncertain, tumultuous world at bay. In reality, domesticity itself proved a source of uncertainty, and the newlyweds the victims of their own expectations.

Under the circumstances Clemens was much of the time simply too distracted by the novelty of married life to pay any more than perfunctory attention to his work, his responsibilities, or his persona. More subtly, but also more formidably, he was also very likely to have been troubled by the tension between the terms of his own domestication and the characteristic rootlessness and irreverence of his alter ego. There would not be a Mrs. Twain. As Clemens sought to become intensely married, Mark Twain remained essentially unattached—not free, by any means, but unaccompanied in the process of discovering and playing out his more public role. In time this distinction, more the result of Clemens's instinct for privacy than any deliberation on his part, would provide him an escape from the torments and frustrations that beset his home life. But in the early months of 1870 that life amounted to a beguiling if somewhat bewildering idyll from which Mark Twain was accidentally but effectively banished.

Chapter Six

Nesting

Not long after he and Olivia were married, Clemens wrote Mary Fairbanks, "I feel that we shall get along well here in Buffalo, & with its people, & that we shall be happy & content" (13 February 1870). But contentment with life in Buffalo beyond the walls of the Delaware Avenue palace was more a hope than a certainty for the newlyweds, who sometimes found themselves puzzled not only by their new responsibilities as householders but also by their new and unfamiliar environment. "Three or four days ago I felt somewhat like a stranger in a strange land," Olivia wrote Mary Fairbanks, "and I thought now if we lived in Cleveland I should have Mrs. Fairbanks to mother me." The immediate cause of her chagrin was the obligatory ritual of receiving callers, or the cards of callers, and of returning those calls. Olivia spoke impatiently of her own "stupid blunders in trying to find the houses of callers" in Buffalo and of her need of a guiding hand. "Mr. Clemens is splendid to laugh it off with," she wrote, "but when it comes to his giving me any practical advice in these matters I find him a little incompetent."[1] About a week earlier she had written Alice Day, a friend who had grown up, married, and settled in Hartford, of "the experience I have been having that did not come to you, the going into a strange city and meeting strange faces." Perhaps a little enviously she observed, "There is some thing pleasant and some things not so pleasant about it," admitting, "I felt a little desire to see familiar home faces the first day that I went out to make formal calls."[2]

In many respects the Clemenses were simply undergoing a period of adjustment like that experienced by many newlywed newcomers in a first home in an unfamiliar city. Predictably, Olivia was sometimes reticent or self-conscious about the "womanly" responsibilities her new circumstances forced upon her, particularly those involving the management of a home and domestic staff. And predictably, although he had long been accustomed to making his own way among strangers, Clemens knew almost nothing about accompanying his wife into the enclaves of polite society. These were, the two at least indirectly reassured one another, the kinds of difficulties people overcame. But circumstances conspired to exacerbate Clemens's insecurities, particularly those involving his already unsteady association with the *Express*. Within a month of the wedding, for example, he was troubled by the suspicion that the newspaper's finances had been misrepresented to him at the time of his purchase and that he had been cheated. Suspicions of this kind would bedevil him throughout his career, in part because his own frustration and bewilderment with all things relating to accounting led him to regard it as a dark science and its practitioners as born opportunists and manipulators. When friends led him through an exonerating audit of its books, he wrote to Jervis Langdon of his relief at determining "that the Express is not a swindle," but revealed in the same letter that a rumor "of my intending to leave Buffalo" had begun circulating in the city (2 March 1870). Within a few days that rumor had grown sufficiently virulent to warrant his posting the following notice prominently on the newspaper's editorial page:

PERSONAL

The paragraph now going the rounds of the press to the effect that I am going to withdraw from Buffalo and the Buffalo EXPRESS is entirely foundationless. I am a permanency here. I am prospering well enough to please my friends and distress my enemies, and consequently am in a state of tranquil satisfaction. I will regard it as a favor if those journals that printed the item referred to will also mention this correction.

SAMUEL L. CLEMENS
"Mark Twain."

The notice ran in the *Express* for four successive days, from 8 March to 11 March 1870, and might be said in retrospect to have the sound of a man protesting too much.[3] In fact, at the same time that he was proclaiming his permanency in Buffalo and publishing this daily declaration of his tranquil satisfaction with his circumstances there, Clemens was involved in a series of other gestures betraying his growing disaffection with the *Express*.

One of these gestures took the form of yet another abandoned sketch, this one entitled "A Wail" and apparently drafted early in March 1870, about the time the above notice was appearing in the *Express*.[4] Its narrator begins by identifying himself as "part proprietor of a certain daily newspaper, & . . . also one of its editors" and goes on to describe not the tranquil satisfaction but the misery that his position has brought him. "There are other editors & other proprietors in the establishment," he complains, "but I appear to get all the cuffs & but few of the compliments earned by the combined strength of the concern." Because he is blamed for most of the newspaper's failings, whether in reporting, advertising, or typesetting, he is "always getting waylaid, & bruised, & knocked down, & shot at," or abused in "anonymous letters [that] inquire feelingly if I was drunk or merely crazy when I printed my last issue." The result is to make him regret assuming the position of editor in the first place and to convince him that he was better off before he did so. "When I was an obscure miscreant," he says, "I did not even have to suffer for my own sins more than half the time, but now I have to take the consequences of my own & many other people's too."

In many respects "A Wail" recycles the ploy Clemens used in "Journalism in Tennessee" (*Express*, 4 September 1869), with the obvious difference that the narrator in this later piece has suffered for some time as an editor while his Tennessee counterpart had the good sense to quit for the sake of his health after a single day.[5] To an extent, that difference mirrors the circumstances of Clemens's tenure with the *Express*. When he published "Journalism in Tennessee," he was himself just coming to the end of his second week as a newspaper editor. By the time he began "A Wail" six months later, he was no longer a newcomer, and the editorship that had once seemed a novelty now threatened to degenerate into a chore, a routine, and a burden. Strategically, "Journalism in Tennessee" assumes the perspective of the tenderfoot or innocent who wanders into the world of adult and altogether savage responsibility, is singed by the encounter, and instinctively withdraws. "A Wail" shows what happens when the innocent fails to act on those preserving instincts and tries instead to behave like a grown-up: he is made "to take the consequences" not only of his own actions but also of those of his associates, and to suffer accordingly. The outlook here, like that in much of Clemens's writing, including much of his best, is profoundly adolescent—not the sort of thing he could afford to broadcast in March of 1870, when he was supposedly rededicating himself to his duties at the *Express*. He could, however, privately utter a wail, an expression of resistance typically offered up not by adults, but by innocents who find themselves in torment.

If in its juvenile way "A Wail" registers Clemens's resentment at the abuse that newspapermen suffer, it also calls attention to a form of abuse that newspapers themselves promote. It holds up to ridicule the sappy, melodramatic "literary" material, much of it poetry, with which dailies like the *Express* routinely sugared their pages. Clemens often fumed about this treacle in his private correspondence; "A Wail" would have paraded his scorn before the public. "All the dreary blank verse that appears in the paper," his narrator complains, "I am generally supposed to write, &, what is still harder to bear, I am praised for doing it. I am looked upon as the author of all the sentimental rhymes we print, & so my compulsory correspondence with young people who admire that sort of thing & desire to help do it, is large." These attributions clearly pain the narrator, who nevertheless declares himself "content" to be held accountable for his paper's excesses, "provided they remain within the bounds of a fair & reasonable degree of depravity." So "A Wail," which begins by lamenting one kind of indiscrimination on the part of the newspaper's readers, their eagerness to blame the hapless narrator for offenses committed by others, includes at its heart an attack on their indiscrimination of another kind, their enthusiasm for the cloying drivel which the newspaper, in its depravity, publishes in pandering deference to their sentimentality.

This performance would hardly seem calculated to win over an audience, but it does offer a glimpse at Clemens's withering estimation of some newspaper writing and some newspaper readers at just the time when he was supposedly trying to work his way back into newspapering. Those estimations were even more clearly, if also more comically, at the center of a second sketch that Clemens apparently drafted at the same time as "A Wail," perhaps as a revision. Entitled "A Protest," it opens more pointedly than "A Wail" and makes no effort to mask Mark Twain—and behind him Samuel Clemens—as its writer.[6] "I wish to protest, mildly but firmly," it begins, "against being called upon to bear all & single, the promiscuous, manifold & miscellaneous sins of the BUFFALO EXPRESS." While it touches upon one of the paper's other sins—the "brashness" of its local items, a matter called to his attention by a reader Clemens refers to as "this sensitive vermin"—"A Protest" spends five of its seven manuscript pages on the iniquity of publishing sentimental verse. To speak for those who make such sinning profitable, Clemens concocts an admirer named Almira Roberts, who sends an approving letter to "*Mr. Mark Twain . . . from a town away down in Arkansas.*" "Those poems of yourn are sweet," Almira begins, allowing that her discernment in such matters is the natural consequence of her having been "sensitive & delikit from a child." She praises his authorship of the popular pieces "Shoo-Fly, Don't Bodder Me" and "Wearin' of the Green" and, surprisingly, of Emerson's "Brahma," confessing, "I *never* can git through it dry." Almira Roberts is one entirely satisfied subscriber. "Mr. Twain," she says, "I jest dote on poetry, & the more of it you can jam into your paper the better you'll suit me, I can tell you."

Mark Twain's response to Almira Roberts breaks off after a single paragraph. "I am not the author of 'Wearin' of the Green,' " he says. "There are many troubles on my mind, but that is not one of them." Like "A Wail," "A Protest" remained unpublished, perhaps because each in its way too openly exposed Clemens's frustration with newspaper writing, particularly as that frustration was brought on by the limited appetites and capacities of newspaper readers. The two pieces, at any rate, can hardly be thought of as arbitrary or theoretical exercises. At the time of their composition, Clemens had been honeymooning about a month—extending a separation from the *Express* that had already lasted four months—and was taking a hard look at the prospect of writing for and editing a daily newspaper for the rest of his professional career. The notion evidently struck him much less favorably than it had the preceding August, when Jervis Langdon had led him to the *Express* and he himself had proclaimed it a "delightful situation." *Then* he had sought the security and stability of a permanent life's work; *now* he chafed at the restrictions imposed upon him by that work and spoke increasingly of his intention to avoid it whenever he could.

If "A Wail" and "A Protest" were expressions of resistance on Clemens's part to the limitations of newspapering, they immediately preceded a more telling gesture of the same kind. On 11 March 1870, he agreed with Francis P. Church, co-founder and co-editor of the magazine *Galaxy*, to produce a monthly humorous column that came to be called "Memoranda." "If I can have entire ownership and disposal of what I write for the *Galaxy*," he told Church, "I will edit your humorous department for two thousand ($2,000) a year—and I give you my word that I can start out tomorrow or any day that I choose and make that money in two weeks, lecturing." He wrote Elisha Bliss the same day, announcing that "a first-class New York magazine wants me to edit a humorous department in it" and indicating what particularly attracted him to the idea: "I consider the magazine because it will give an opening for higher-class writing—stuff which I hate to shovel into a daily newspaper." About two weeks later he explained his choice at greater length to Mary Fairbanks:

I just came to the conclusion that I would quit turning my attention to making money especially, & go to writing for enjoyment as well as profit. I needed a *Magazine* wherein to shovel any fine-spun stuff that I might accumulate in my head, & which isn't entirely suited to either a daily, Weekly, or *any* kind of newspaper. You see I often feel like writing something, & before I set down the first word I think, "No, it isn't worth while to write it—might do for a magazine, but not a newspaper." (22–24 March 1870)

Clemens's attitudes toward his *Galaxy* commitment demonstrate how disenchanted he had become with his position at the *Express* by the time he should have been resuming his duties there in March of 1870. Although he had actually been on hand in Buffalo and at work on the paper for only six weeks, in August and September 1869, and although he had left his editorial duties in October of that year with the manifest intention of returning to them full-throttle after his lecture tour was completed and he and Olivia were married, he regarded those duties with something approaching repugnance when the time came to face them. "I shall still write for the Express, of course," he assured Mary Fairbanks, "but not every week, perhaps. People who write every week *write themselves out*, and tire the public, too, before very long" (22–24 March 1870).

Given how little he produced during his tenure as editor, the work he did for the *Express* cannot have exhausted either Clemens or the interest of his readers. By its nature, however, some of it was burdensome, and much of what awaited him upon his return to the paper—exchanges to be scanned, local items to be written up, readers' correspondence to be attended to—had the look of dreary routine. In response to this prospect, he somehow managed not so much to withdraw from the *Express* as simply to refuse to become any more deeply associated with it. The financial success of *The Innocents Abroad* relieved the urgency of his commitment to the newspaper, and without entirely meaning to he was acting out the ironic promise he had made in his *Express* "Salutatory": to "work diligently and honestly and faithfully at all times and upon all occasions, when privation and want shall compel me to do it" (21 August 1869). Having been secured from privation and want by his success as a book writer, he had the opportunity to relax his diligence as a newspaperman. When he wrote to inform the Langdons of his *Galaxy* engagement, he said, matter of factly, "I shall write one or two sketches a month for the Express, & I have an idea that for a good while I shall do nothing else on the paper" (27 March 1870). Perhaps Clemens's co-editors at the newspaper had grown so accustomed to operating in his absence that no one saw fit to try very hard to press him back into service. In any case, no signs of struggle surround his decision to maintain a low profile at the *Express*. Whatever dreams his partners may once have entertained about the benefits of securing Mark Twain as a daily feature were apparently allowed simply to atrophy and die.

Accordingly, no one at the *Express* appears to have objected when Clemens published a notice there on 12 April 1870 addressed to "*Mr. F. P. Church, Editor of the Galaxy.*" It read, "My own paper, the Buffalo Express, does not occupy my entire time, and therefore I accept your offer, and from the present time forward will edit and conduct a 'department of Agriculture' in *The Galaxy* Magazine." The *Express*, of course, *could* have occupied his entire time; according to the intentions that brought him to Buffalo in the first place, it was supposed to. But during his absence from the city, his

outlook had changed, and by the time he should have been returning wholeheartedly to his post at the newspaper, he found himself
marshaling arguments against it. Newspaper writing was writing
for profit rather than enjoyment; it was humdrum or vulgar rather
than "fine-spun"; it pandered to the tastes and prejudices of a semi-
literate audience; its practitioners suffered from burnout and overexposure. It came to be associated in Clemens's mind with drudg-
ery and confinement, with a shackling he found intolerable. "Do
you know, Madam," he asked Mary Fairbanks, "that I would
rather write for a Magazine for $2 a page than for a newspaper at
$10? I *would*. One takes more pains, the 'truck' looks nicer in print,
& one has a pleasanter audience" (29 May 1870). In explaining his
acceptance of the *Galaxy* offer to Olivia's parents he said, "If I
hadn't taken it I would have been tied hand & foot here & forever
& ever" (1 April 1870). Eight months earlier he had shared with
them his anxiety to find a secure anchorage; now he wriggled
against the threat of becoming entangled in his anchor lines.

Clemens's decision to write for the *Galaxy* did not so much fos-
ter as confirm his determination to keep his distance from the Buffalo *Express* and, at least indirectly, from Buffalo itself. In his estimation the magazine offered not only a wider scope for his talents
than the newspaper but also a more literate and cosmopolitan readership, a national—or at least an eastern—audience far different
from the one he associated with the narrow, parochial demands of
the *Express*. The *Galaxy*, he told the Langdons, "gives me a chance
to write what I please, not what I *must*" (1 April 1870). The celebrity he was gaining as the author of *The Innocents Abroad* no doubt
contributed to his desire for greater freedom as well as for a wider,
more literary forum than Buffalo could provide. He apparently had
no intention of leaving the city or the newspaper but tended to
look beyond both as he negotiated his future. In his correspondence during the early spring of 1870, he increasingly entertained
the possibility of going to Europe for several months with Olivia,
or of spending an extended vacation in the Adirondacks with the
Twichells, or of joining the Langdons for the summer in Elmira.
When he first addressed his *Galaxy* audience in the magazine's May
1870 issue, he appended the following postscript to his introduction: "I have not sold out of the 'Buffalo Express,' and shall not;

neither shall I stop writing for it. This remark seems necessary in a business point of view."[7] The people of Buffalo were left to draw what satisfaction they could from such cold comfort.

Although Clemens claimed to take the *Galaxy* post as an outlet for "fine-spun" writing, it would be hard to demonstrate that the work he did for the magazine was markedly different from that he published in the Buffalo *Express*. During that time, as it turned out, he wrote even less for the newspaper than he had forecast, and after those first few months virtually everything of his that appeared in the *Express* was merely drawn from a contemporaneous or upcoming "Memoranda" column. So within a very short time his decision to accept the *Galaxy* offer resulted in his all but entirely ceasing to write original material in his own paper. And when he took simply to culling his "Memoranda" for pieces to place in the *Express*, whatever distinction he had meant to observe between magazine writing and newspaper writing was blurred beyond recognition.

Even his first *Galaxy* column, appearing in the May 1870 issue, bore no features dramatically distinguishing it from the writing he had been doing for some time in Buffalo. His "Introductory" was genial, spoofing, and ironic, as had been his *Express* "Salutatory" eight months earlier. Of the four longer pieces included in that first column, two were reminiscent of sketches he had written for newspapers: "The Facts in the Case of the Great Beef Contract" in the May *Galaxy* echoed "The Facts in the Great Land Slide Case," which appeared in the 2 April 1870 edition of the *Express*, chiefly in its title, but Clemens himself introduced "The Story of the Good Little Boy Who Did Not Prosper" to his *Galaxy* audience as "a fair and unprejudiced companion-piece" to an earlier newspaper effort, "The Bad Little Boy Who Did Not Come to Grief."[8] The most vitriolic of these first "Memoranda," "About Smells," an indictment of the Reverend T. De Witt Talmage for fussing over the smell of working men in church, occasioned a long follow-up in the 9 May 1870 *Express*. The fourth of Clemens's principal *Galaxy* features for May, "Disgraceful Persecution of a Boy," rails against the mistreatment of the Chinese in San Francisco, much of that mistreatment condoned and even furthered by municipal policy and the abject truckling of newspaper editors, among others. It is a characteristic instance of Mark Twain's social criticism, full of fiery and contagious outrage, but it is hardly the kind of writing that could be described as "higher-class," and nothing really separates it from the similar social invectives he published in newspapers, invectives such as his attacks on the insanity plea in "The New Crime: Legislation Needed" (*Express*, 16 April 1870) and "Our Precious Lunatic" (*Express*, 14 May 1870).

If any quality typifies his early *Galaxy* pieces, in fact, it is their anger rather than their gentility. Of the May "Memoranda," for example, "About Smells" and "Disgraceful Persecutions of a Boy" attack particular class or racial prejudices by exposing the individual or groups that promote them to scathing ridicule. "The Story of the Good Little Boy Who Did Not Prosper" literally blows a sanctimonious little prig to bits, and with him the smug pieties that motivate his behavior. Even "The Facts in the Case of the Great Beef Contract," for all its burlesquing, decries a Washington bureaucracy so choked in red tape and habituated to featherbedding as to have abandoned both common sense and common courtesy. While these pieces may not be fine-spun, they have in common an impatience with and a skepticism about conventional, established, or accepted values. They were followed in the *Galaxy*'s June issue by another, even more unified, set of complaints, this time focusing on matters of literary discernment and taste.

Mark Twain's June 1870 "Memoranda" entries, prepared by early May, open with a piece which sets both the tone and the topic of those to follow.[9] Entitled "A Couple of Sad Experiences," it expresses his dismay in discovering that some readers failed to fathom the humor in a notice announcing his intention to write for the *Galaxy*.[10] "When . . . I said I was going to edit an Agricultural Department in this magazine," he begins, "I certainly did not desire to deceive anybody." Finding to his chagrin that he was nevertheless taken seriously in some quarters, he protests that he "purposely wrote the thing as absurdly and as extravagantly as it could be written," believing that its "manifest lunacy" would "protect the reader." That in many cases it did not leads him to acknowledge that "to write a burlesque so wild that its pretended facts will not be accepted in perfect good faith by somebody, is very nearly an impossible thing to do." It is an admission that comes as no revelation. "I have had a deal of experience in burlesques and their unfortunate aptness to deceive the public," he says, and then goes on to describe two of his own making in pieces entitled "The Petrified

Man" and "My Famous 'Bloody Massacre.' "[11] By his own account
the first amounted to "a string of roaring absurdities" and the second to a melodrama so patently outrageous that "the very pickled
oysters that came to our tables" could have seen through its "sat-
ire." Like some of those oysters, though, both were swallowed
whole by a heedless, sensation-happy audience "in innocent good
faith," a response which leaves him marveling "how really hard it
is to foist a moral truth upon an unsuspecting public through a burlesque without entirely and absurdly missing one's mark." Recounting these episodes allows Clemens to make confidants-in-
criticism of *Galaxy* subscribers, to share with them a chuckle at the
expense of those gullible or careless readers—those *newspaper* readers—who were taken in by his travesties. While anecdotes of this
kind might also serve indirectly to prod them to be more alert
themselves, Clemens's tone here is that of a literary man confessing
to sympathetic listeners his frustration with audiences less
sophisticated.

That impulse to invite commiseration in lamenting literary offenses dominates Clemens's June "Memoranda," giving the column coherence and providing him an outlet for his own unsystematic aesthetic opinions, many of them aimed at excesses
commonly practiced in newspapers. In an entry entitled "Hogwash," for instance, he places before his *Galaxy* readers an item
from a California paper which he introduces as a "miracle of point-
less imbecility and bathos," claiming to have preserved it for five
years, "waiting to see if I could find anything in literature that was
worse." Having failed to do so, he offers up the excerpt, an over-
wrought description of a "beautiful lady" breaking suddenly and
inexplicably into "hot tears," as "the sickliest specimen of sham
sentimentality that exists." In "Post-Mortem Poetry," similarly, he
pays sarcastic tribute to a Philadelphia paper's "custom . . . of ap-
pending to published death-notices a little verse of two of com-
forting poetry." These "plaintive tributes" turn out to be boiler-
plates of "solacing poesy" which routinely and repetitiously
accompany obituaries. After two columns of saccharine, inept,
and redundant examples, he observes, "There is an element about
some poetry which is able to make even physical suffering and
death cheerful things to contemplate and consummations to be desired."[12] The last long piece among the June "Memoranda," "Wit-

Inspirations of the 'Two-Year-Olds,' " bemoans the practice common to newspapers and magazines of the day of printing clever comments attributed to small children. "Judging by the average published specimens of smart sayings," Twain reckons, "the rising generation of children are little better than idiots." He registers his contempt for the sentimental fawning behind "the sunbursts of infantile imbecility which dazzle us from the pages of our periodicals" before veering into an account of his own parents responding quite differently to the "brilliant remarks" he himself made as a child: "They snubbed me sometimes and spanked me the rest."

Readers of *The Innocents Abroad* would have recognized familiar Mark Twain signatures in these pieces, especially in their impatience with "sham sentimentality" and with the insipid, degenerate romanticism that lay behind it. That attack continued, although more diffusely, in the July "Memoranda," which Clemens would have prepared by early June. He picks up the joke he initiated in his *Galaxy* "Introductory" by opening the July column with "How I Edited an Agricultural Paper Once." The piece makes its fun by parading his ignorance of all things agricultural. He claims, for instance, to have editorialized that "The guano is a fine bird, but great care is necessary in rearing it." The fun takes on an edge when he boasts of that ignorance as his chief journalistic credential. "It is the first time I ever heard of a man's having to know anything in order to edit a newspaper," he exclaims when the paper's regular editor returns, hurriedly, to relieve him of his post. He then conducts an inventory of the particular kinds of ignorance that typically outfit writers for particular kinds of newspaper work and concludes that in "the newspaper business . . . , the less a man knows the bigger noise he makes and the higher the salary he commands." For all its bluster about editorial ignoramuses, "How I Edited an Agricultural Paper Once" is saved from mean-spiritedness by its comic exaggeration and its narrator's unflappable self-incrimination.

In another of the July "Memoranda," "The Editorial Office Bore," however, Clemens removes the gloves—and, very nearly, the mask—in describing the drones who infest newspaper offices with their loitering and their gossip. "The bore and his comrades," he says, "hold noisy talks among themselves about politics in particular, and all other subjects in general . . . ; they smoke, and sweat, and sigh, and scratch, . . . and never seem to comprehend that they are robbing the editors of their time, and the public of journalistic excellence in next day's paper." His grudge against the bore—"a person who can consent to loaf his useless life away in ignominious indolence"—is so fervent and enthusiastic as to seem to have been drawn, still smoking, from Clemens's own experience, perhaps his experience at the *Express*.[13] "To have to sit and endure the presence of a bore day after day," he concludes, "is an affliction that transcends any other that men suffer."

Clemens's early *Galaxy* columns, those for May, June, and July of 1870, indicate subtle changes in his own course and in his still-evolving understanding of Mark Twain. Professionally and personally, he was more and more openly disaffected with the work, the life, and the prerogatives of the newspaper writer and editor. His declarations to the contrary notwithstanding, his ties to the Buffalo *Express* were increasingly strained and tenuous. He had taken few pains to reestablish them after his initial break from the paper in October 1869. The anchorage that he had been so grateful to discover a few months earlier now seemed more a backwater than a safe harbor. With the success of *The Innocents Abroad* filling his sails, moreover, an anchorage was hardly what he needed. As his celebrity and his reputation grew, so did his suspicion that the newspaper trivialized his talent, provided no outlet for the "better" writing he imagined himself doing, tethered him to the limits of its audience, and guaranteed his overexposure. As the spring of 1870 passed, it became increasingly clear that he had come to regard the *Express* as an investment, not a calling. He would maintain and tend to it by submitting an obligatory feature now and then, but it was never, as he had once supposed, to occupy the center of his professional life.

Mark Twain's was still anything but a unified sensibility. By undertaking to edit a department in a New York literary magazine, however, Clemens acted on ambitions that aligned him more nearly with the eastern cultural establishment that supposedly provided him a discriminating, literate audience and that extended his credentials as a professional writer rather than a journalist. The Wild Humorist had become the Resident Humorist, a sign not so much that he had been tamed or traduced as that he himself was willing to exchange a measure of his touted "notoriety" for recognition as a writer of stature and substance. He was much more likely now to voice elements of his own rather undisciplined social or aesthetic criticism in his pieces than he was simply to offer up comic renditions of Mark Twain's transgressions against decorum or custom. The humor in his early *Express* writing—"A Day at Niagara," for example, or "English Festivities," or "The Latest Novelty"—often arose from Mark Twain's bad-boy behavior or reputation. There was nothing really nasty about him in these squibs and sketches, but in them he typically exhibited an adolescent's impatience with rules and responsibilities, and by narrow reckoning he may have fallen short of thoroughgoing respectability. In his early work for the *Galaxy* and in the contemporaneous writing he did for the *Express*, he could still play the innocent, the butt of his own jokes, but the cast of naughtiness, even boyish naughtiness, was gone.

The *Galaxy* and *Express* writing he did during the spring of 1870 shows Clemens becoming more clearly and coherently a moralist. Defining right behavior and impeaching bad had of course been a part of his satiric agenda from the beginning, but now, as he sought more and more deliberately to make his way as a professional writer, social criticism emerged unambiguously as a focus of his work. It was not so much a change as a clarification in his ongoing effort at self-fashioning, an effort most consciously manifest in his presentation of Mark Twain in print. Early in his *Express* tenure, when Twain gave a thumbnail character sketch of himself in his article on "Mental Photographs" (2 October 1869), he played up, or with, his notoriety by casting his answers to leading questions in such a way as to exploit his reputation for laziness, drinking, gambling, lying, greed, and perhaps even womanizing.[14] While he obviously had little intention of being taken seriously in the sketch, it shows how willing he was at the time to do a little bad-boy posturing for the sake of a laugh. It was a familiar mask, and, during those first weeks in Buffalo, one that was still useful to him.

That was clearly not the case by the time he resumed his *Express* duties five months later and prepared to take on his new responsibilities with the *Galaxy*. On 28 February 1870, for instance, in an unsigned *Express* article entitled "The Blondes," he assumed a tone of high moral dudgeon in training editorial fire upon a burlesque company led by a performer named Lydia Thompson. His outrage

at Thompson and her troupe was touched off by their ambushing
and assaulting a newspaper editor they thought had slandered
them, but it quickly spread to encompass their performance, their
sensibilities, and their characters. "Now who would suppose those
Lydia Thompson Blondes could be insulted?" he asks. "The idea
seems grotesque, and yet those people are as dainty in their feelings
. . . as if they really had a reminiscence of decency still lingering
in some out-of-the-way corner of their systems." On stage, he
says, the Blondes are "coarsely, vulgarly voluptuous. . . . They
dance dismal dances, assisted by a melancholy rabble of painted,
tinselled, gamey old skeletons, who spin on one toe and display
their relics beseechingly to dull pitlings who refuse to hunger for
them and will not applaud." During fifteen minutes of such enter-
tainment, an audience is exposed to "more . . . vulgarity, slang and
obscenity . . . than ought to be distributed over the female utter-
ances of fifteen years of all the she-rowdies that be upon the stage."

It is only fair to recognize that Clemens is writing anonymously
here, as an unnamed *Express* editorialist and not as Mark Twain,
but the tone and attitude of the piece are in keeping with those of
sketches that appeared under Twain's signature in the spring of
1870 and very unlike those of the preceding fall's "Latest Novelty,"
where Twain listed as his favorite tree "Any that bears forbidden
fruit" and as his favorite object in nature "A dumb belle." For that
matter, they also differ strikingly from the outlook of the *Innocents
Abroad* narrator, who can be found watching the Parisian can-can
through his fingers. The writer of "The Blondes" is a censorious
Victorian in full plumage, a very senior cousin to that unfledged
adolescent sneaking a forbidden peek at naughty pleasure.

Under the aegis of his own byline, Mark Twain was not about
to degenerate into a Victorian prude, even as he came during the
spring of 1870 to think more and more deliberately about deepening his reputation and furthering his credentials as a writer. He
was, however, much more likely than he had been to turn his
"nonsense" to serious ethical purposes. "A Mysterious Visit,"
which appeared in the *Express* on 19 March 1870, for example, has
a familiar look and feel to it for the first three of its four columns.
Its guileless narrator, who not only signs himself "Mark Twain"
but also speaks of his experience as a lecturer, an editor of the Buffalo *Express*, and the author of *The Innocents Abroad*, welcomes to

his home an agent of the Internal Revenue Department. Wholly in the dark about the agent's business or motives, but of course never wishing to seem so, he allows himself to be coaxed into disclosing his various incomes for the preceding year. In his boyish eagerness to impress the agent, in fact, he substantially magnifies those incomes. The sketch's "snapper" arrives when, too late, it breaks upon the narrator that his guest is none other than a tax man and he finds himself facing an assessment for "the appalling sum of ten thousand six hundred and fifty dollars, income tax."

Ordinarily the sketch might end here or briefly take flight toward some comic resolution. Instead it turns abruptly serious. The narrator seeks the advice of "a very opulent man" of his acquaintance, a person who "stands away up among the very best of the solid men of Buffalo—the men of moral weight, of commercial integrity, of unimpeachable social spotlessness." The experience of this moral pillar enables him to "manipulate" and falsify the narrator's records until his taxable income amounts to $250. "I bowed to his example," the narrator says,

I went down to the revenue office, and under the accusing eyes of my old visitor I stood up and swore to lie after lie, fraud after fraud, villainy after villainy, till my immortal soul was coated inches and inches thick with perjury and my self-respect was gone forever and ever.

But what of it? It is nothing more than thousands of the highest, and richest, and proudest, and most respected, honored and courted men in America do every year. And so I don't care. I am not ashamed.

Often in the course of his earlier sketches, Mark Twain's bewildered innocence would lead him to suffer a series of physical calamities so dire, so undeserved, and so exaggerated as to place him in the vanguard of the tradition of slapstick humor. In "A Mysterious Visit," however, the catastrophe is financial and its consequences are moral and quite deliberately unfunny. Readers find themselves in the presence not of a schlemiel, underdog, or victim, but of an unsavory cheat who entombs his conscience after the fashion of the "best" men of his town and time. This is moral fiction, to use Twain's own idiom, with the bark left on.

Almost five years earlier, Clemens had written his brother, Orion, that becoming "a preacher of the gospel" had been one of the *"powerful* ambitions of my life" (19–20 October 1865). No rendition of his career to this point could demonstrate that he had ever pursued this alleged ambition in earnest, but the impulse to judge, to chastise, and to exhort was an abiding quality of his character. In much of the writing he did during the spring of 1870, he acted on that impulse more directly and unambiguously than he had before. The sketches that he produced at the time may not have been "better" or more "fine-spun" than their predecessors in the belletristic sense, but they were more pointedly exercises in social and, relatedly, aesthetic criticism. Most of the few remaining *Express* pieces he wrote during this period followed this predilection. They included such Saturday features as "The New Crime" (16 April 1870) and "Our Precious Lunatic" (14 May 1870), both complaints against the insanity plea, and "Curious Dream" (30 April and 7 May 1870), a two-part nightmare story lamenting the neglect of cemeteries.

Clemens's work for the *Express* and the *Galaxy* during the spring of 1870 reflects an important stage in the evolution of his craft, his ambition, and his personality. It brought into at least approximate resolution the divergent, mercurial, and sometimes contradictory tendencies that constituted Mark Twain, particularly in seeking to enfranchise him as a social critic. For the time, his adolescent posturing went into abeyance, as did all mention of the drinking, lying, loafing, and gambling that were associated largely with his wild-west reputation. Especially in the *Galaxy* pieces, Clemens experimented with letting the mask slip or even fall as he sought to confide a writer's frustrations to a sympathetic readership. Each of these gestures signaled a maturity that he was, however unconsciously, in the process of learning to reconcile with his conception and presentation of Mark Twain. This is not to say that Twain would simply "grow up," but rather that the line between Clemens's private and public sides might remain as fluid and indefinite as it had always been, even as he accustomed himself to the myriad respectabilities he faced as married man, newspaper proprietor, best-selling author, and *Galaxy* mainstay. Increasingly, evidences of unrefinement, notoriety, and even of childish or adolescent innocence were to be associated with an earlier Mark Twain, or with Mark Twain's earlier life. He would write retrospectively about that innocence; as he grew more worldly and reflective, it would be less and less a quality of his contemporaneous

character, as it had been in *The Innocents Abroad*. As 1870 continued, in fact, he would begin *Roughing It*, the first of his books to
be organized around this initiation into the world of adult experience and in many senses the most revealingly autobiographical.
Roughing It treats "the transformation of a tenderfoot."[15] During
his time in Buffalo Clemens was undergoing just such a transformation, if under very different circumstances.

That transformation was made easier and more likely in the
spring of 1870 as the not-quite-so-newlyweds began to relax and
find their way in Buffalo. They were particularly pleased to make
the acquaintance of David Gray, an associate editor of the Buffalo
Courier, and of his wife, Martha. Gray, who was himself a minor
poet, had published an intelligent and enthusiastic review of *The
Innocents Abroad* in the *Courier*, which observed that "the secret of
the humorist is [that] there must be no visible effort in the work
we are to be amused by or amazed at." "Mark Twain's art," he said,
rests in the capacity of his humor "to flow as water does, simply
because it respects the law of gravitation."[16] Olivia described the
Grays as "attractive people" in a letter to her mother and said they
"seem as if they might be friends" (27 March 1870).[17] Two months
later Clemens wrote Olivia's father of having "spent yesterday
evening most pleasantly with the Grays" and of inviting them to
join the Adirondacks excursion which was then scheduled for August or September (22 May 1870).[18] As the newlyweds' anxiety and
self-consciousness subsided, Buffalo began to seem more welcoming and their prospects cheerful, after all. "We are so happy," Olivia wrote her sister, Susan Crane, "that nothing seems able to mar
our joy" (16 April 1870). Her husband chimed his agreement, telling her father, "We are burdened & bent with happiness, almost"
(22 May 1870).

Clemens's experience would eventually condition him to shud-
der in response to such unguarded expressions of contentment.
The events that followed these happy declarations in the late spring
of 1870 doubtless contributed to that conditioning. After a period
of anxious adjustment, he and Olivia had begun to make their
peace with their new circumstances and environment. His reputation and his finances buoyed by the success of *The Innocents
Abroad*, he was able to sidestep the burden of routine newspaper
work in order to experiment with a regular magazine assignment

and, generally, to feel in more control of his professional life. The eager, singleminded, almost desperate tenderfoot whom Jervis Langdon had guided to the Buffalo *Express* the preceding August now kept the *Express* at arm's length and looked to other prospects. His transformation to maturity was provisional and incomplete, but its terms were sharply reflected in work whose humor was increasingly critical and occasionally angry—a moral humor. To this point the matter of becoming Mark Twain, of arriving at the posture and personality that would be recognizable behind the great works of the 1870s and 1880s, had amounted to a fairly easy transition, the qualities of Clemens's professional life evolving for the most part according to his erratic good fortune, as yet to be tested or tempered by calamity.

Chapter Seven

A Father's Dying

When the Fates smiled upon Samuel Clemens, they tended to show their teeth; when they frowned, their fangs. Basking in one of those broad smiles in the late spring of 1870, he inventoried his good fortune in a letter to his lecture agent, James Redpath. "I have got a lovely wife," he said, "a lovely house bewitchingly furnished, a lovely carriage & a coachman whose style and dignity are simply awe-inspiring—nothing less. And I am making more money than necessary, by considerable" (10 May 1870). About two years later, he received a note from Bret Harte that cast that same good fortune in a different and more ominous light. "You ought to be very happy with that sweet wife of yours," Harte wrote, "and I suppose you are. It is not every man that can cap a hard, thorny, restless youth with so graceful a crown." Having himself come to know something about the awful precariousness of states of grace, Harte closed with the brooding observation, "You are so lucky that . . . I almost tremble for you."[1] Perhaps because they had been separated during that two-year period—separated for most of it by a continent and for some of it by a good deal of mutual petulance—Harte may not have known that by the time he expressed this apprehension Clemens had already been driven from his fragile, fated Eden. In fact, even as Clemens was crowing contentedly to Redpath in May of 1870 about his lovely wife, bewitching house, and imposing coachman, there gathered on the Buffalo horizon a thunderhead of calamities about to break upon him in furious and bewildering succession. When Olivia Clemens reflected that spring on her own happiness, writing her sister on 16 April 1870 that "nothing seems able to mar our joy," she cannot have foreseen that she was about to be visited by the first of those calamities, by the one calamity surest to mar her joy and mar it deeply: her father was about to die.

For all his activity and apparent vigor, Jervis Langdon had for some time been troubled by an insidious digestive disorder which was eventually—but only eventually—diagnosed as cancer of the stomach. The onset of the disease appears to have coincided with the entrance of Samuel Clemens into the life of his family in the fall of 1868. Family correspondence of the period makes reference to Langdon's illness, which his doctors, after the fashion of the nineteenth century, termed "nervous dyspepsia," and for which they prescribed various combinations of rest and changes of climate.[2] From late March to late April of 1870, accordingly, Jervis and Olivia Lewis Langdon traveled for the sake of his health through Virginia, the Carolinas, and Georgia in the company of the family physician, Dr. Henry Sayles. In a letter from Richmond to his daughter and his new son-in-law, Langdon candidly described his condition, admitting that "all my organs seem to have susbended [*sic*] their functions." Still, characteristically, he remained upbeat about his chances for recovery. "I look now for rapid improvement," he said; "for 4 days I have not thrown up my food & my liver seems to have assumed its function. . . . I think I shall return [to Elmira] entirely restored."[3]

Langdon's optimism, however, more aptly reflected his psychological than his physical makeup. Despite his sunny prediction of imminent recovery, he came back from the south on 29 April "having gained nothing," according to his daughter Susan, "unless it be that [he] learned more fully the importance of taking care of himself."[4] One significant instance of that caretaking was his 1 May restructuring of J. Langdon & Company, the firm he had run singlehandedly in amassing his fortune. From that time forward, he would share its management with his son, Charles, his son-in-law Theodore Crane, and his Buffalo associate J. D. F. Slee.[5] When Langdon's illness reasserted itself later in the season, at just about the time that Olivia Clemens was proclaiming her unmarrable domestic joy to her sister, the family's caretaking took the form of a volley of plans for trips or longer excursions, at least one of which involved recruiting their pastor, Thomas K. Beecher, as a traveling companion. One measure of Langdon's standing in the community is that Beecher readily agreed, even to a six-months sojourn, declaring to his friend and parishioner, "I am ready to do as much to save you as I would to save a church."[6]

The Clemenses themselves entertained the notion of accompanying the Langdons abroad on a trip that might have nicely dovetailed filial responsibility and professional opportunity. Clemens told his in-laws in a letter of 1 April 1870 that his publisher was already pressing him to make a European expedition in order to gather material for a sequel to the hot-selling *Innocents Abroad.* "Bliss is *very* anxious that I go abroad during the summer & get a book written for next spring," he said, "but I shan't unless you find that you will have to go." The clear hope here is that Langdon would not "have to go"—that is, that his condition would improve and make the therapeutic European tour unnecessary. By the end of the month, however, Langdon's health had so deteriorated that the question was no longer whether he was well enough to stay home but whether he was too weak to go. On 23 April 1870 Clemens wrote Bliss, "We shall soon know, now, whether Mr. Langdon will try Europe or not." By early May his father-in-law's failing strength put such an exertion out of the question. "Mr. Langdon has been dangerously ill for some days," Clemens wrote Bliss, "& it is plain that he cannot travel a mile this year. So we shall not move out of reach of sudden call. That closes out all notion of crossing the ocean" (7 May 1870).

Clemens was writing from Elmira, where he and Olivia spent two weeks in early May attending to her father's convalescence. Their plans had been somewhat altered by his illness, but they remained basically sanguine that he would recover, as indeed he had, if never quite completely, in the past. Clemens was gradually being habituated to the rhythms of chronic illness, to the alternation of "good days" and "bad days," and to the family's struggle to maintain emotional equilibrium in the face of despair. "We are constantly vacillating between hope and fear," Susan Crane wrote of the anxious watchers around her father's sickbed. "We are hopeful when for several days he retains his food . . . ; then we are cast down and fearful, when for three successive days he retains nothing. He is about the house and yard much of the time, but suffers constantly from pain and weariness."[7] For Olivia, her sister, and

her mother, Jervis Langdon's agonizing deterioration was the
sternest kind of tragedy. In their letters they frequently spoke of
his failure in terms of the sun going out of their lives. Clemens,
too, fell under the pall of these somber shadows, not simply out of
sympathy for his wife and her family but because of the complex
and genuine, if somewhat ambivalent, regard in which he held
Langdon. It was Clemens who had referred to him some months
earlier in a letter to Olivia's mother as "our loved father, our precious father" (20 February 1870).

During the spring and summer of 1870 Jervis Langdon's illness
became the central fact of Clemens's life and an inescapable influence on his work. It often determined where he could write, and
when, and under what circumstances; it conditioned his moods and
the moods of those around him; it could peremptorily command
his attention, and frequently his presence, at any time; and it could
exhaust him, emotionally and physically, by drawing him through
its gamut of false hopes and causeless, apparently gratuitous, set-
backs. Under this duress he withdrew almost entirely as a contributor to the Buffalo *Express*. Even before Langdon's condition began to deteriorate, Clemens's position at the *Express* had been
problematic. He had simply never "taken hold" there after the
wedding, finding that he could get by with very little work and
that his partners were remarkably unwilling to press his obligations
upon him. Langdon's illness provided him the occasion for practically severing his active connection with the newspaper. Between
May 1870 and the time he sold his interest in it about a year later,
he published virtually no original material in the *Express*. Pieces of
his that did appear there were almost without exception reprinted
from his *Galaxy* "Memoranda." And so, ironically, the newspaper
berth that Clemens had coveted, found, and purchased with the
prompting and encouragement of his father-in-law became in a
way an early victim of his father-in-law's failure. It is very likely,
given the history of Langdon's anxious involvement in the matter,
that Clemens found it far easier to abdicate his *Express* responsibilities while Langdon was ailing than he would have if Langdon
had remained able to monitor his dedication to the paper with his
customary paternal interest. Mark Twain had come into being in a
newspaper, but during the spring and summer of 1870 it became
all but certain that he was not to remain a newspaperman.

His status as a magazine contributor was more equivocal. Clemens's commitment to the *Galaxy* had been his own idea, not his father-in-law's—had in a sense been intended as an antidote, or a complement, to his newspaper work—and he was determined to meet his deadlines and make a success of it. By about the third day of every month, he had to submit to his publishers his ten-page "Memoranda" for the month following.[8] Although he wrote his family shortly after signing on with the *Galaxy* that "the berth is exceedingly easy" (26 March 1870), he often found himself hard pressed for copy as each succeeding month drew to a close, especially given the demands, upheavals, and shocks generated by the vagaries of Langdon's illness. His first "Memoranda" column (for May 1870) would have been prepared, or perhaps simply gathered together, during a placid, euphoric March and submitted by early April. His second (for June) would have been completed just before he and Olivia were called from Buffalo to help nurse her father in Elmira in early May. That he lacked either the opportunity or the inclination to do *Galaxy*, or any other, work there is suggested by his writing Bliss on 5 May, "Here I only 'loaf.'"

Back in Buffalo by the middle of that month, Clemens undertook his third column (for July) under the tenuous but welcome impression that Langdon was recovering. On 22 May 1870 he wrote him, "For several days the news from you has grown better & better, till at last I believe we hardly seem to feel that you are an invalid any longer." Toward the end of the Clemenses' visit to Elmira earlier in the month Langdon had renewed his generosity to them by presenting Olivia with a check for $1,000.[9] Now Clemens jumped at the chance to exchange roles with his powerful father-in-law by doing him a kindness. "Now we hope to see you up here with Mother, just as soon as you can come," he said. "Everything is lovely, here, & our home is as quiet & peaceful as a monastery, & yet as bright & cheerful as sunshine without & sunshine within can make it. We are burdened & bent with happiness, almost, & we do need to share it with somebody & so save the surplus. Come & partake freely" (22 May 1870). The imagery of surfeit that suffuses the invitation mirrors not only Clemens's sense of luminous good fortune as a newlywed but also the very tangible benefits of Langdon's material generosity.

Clemens's 22 May 1870 letter to his father-in-law makes no mention of his progress on the July "Memoranda," due in early June, but it does acknowledge an anticipated pressure on columns to follow. "We expect to spend a full month in the Adirondacks (August or Sept.)," he says, "& I shall have to do all that amount of Galaxy & Express writing in advance, in order to secure the time. So I shall make myself right busy for a while now—shall write faithfully every day." A week later he wrote Mary Fairbanks that he and Olivia had fixed plans to vacation in the Adirondacks from the first of August to mid-September with their Hartford friends Joseph and Harmony Twichell. "I have to get all literary work done for a month or two ahead," he told her, "so that our proposed holiday will *be* a holiday with no compulsory labor in it" (29 May 1870). He made it clear in the same letter, though, that the advance work had not yet begun and that in fact he had his hands full meeting his present deadline. "We were to have gone [to Elmira] yesterday," he said, "but being dissatisfied with the next Galaxy (July,) I begged a delay of Livy till I could make some changes in the MSS. before mailing them to N.Y." Whatever revising Clemens may have accomplished in postponing the Elmira trip, his column for the July *Galaxy* is chiefly notable for picking up and extending two attacks initiated in its predecessors, one on the pitfalls and annoyances of newspaper editing (in "How I Edited an Agricultural Paper Once" and "An Editorial Office Bore") and one on mawkish, regressive sentimentality (in "The 'Tournament' in A.D. 1870"). Although it lacks focus, the column reflects Clemens's impatience with newspapering and his continuing preoccupation with literary and social criticism.

The Clemenses traveled to Elmira in very late May or early June 1870, but it is unclear to what extent Jervis Langdon's condition lent urgency to their trip. That the visit had been planned and that it was deferable suggest that he was in no grave or immediate danger. However, when Clemens described the trip retrospectively to his sister, Pamela, he described it in terms of dire exigency. "We were snatched away [from Buffalo] suddenly by an urgent call to come to Elmira & help nurse Mr Langdon," he said (12 June 1870). When Langdon decided against taking the entire family to "some Pennsylvania springs" for the sake of his health, Clemens continued, "We simply rested a moment & then hurried back here. I have thus lost valuable time, & must make it up by steady work." Given the extremity of his father-in-law's illness, moreover, he felt that "it is wisest for me to rush my work along & get ready for emergencies."[10] His resolutions notwithstanding, however, he was not ready when the next emergency arose.

On 22 June he and Olivia were notified that Langdon was failing and left immediately for Elmira. "We are summoned here by telegram," he wrote Mary Fairbanks from the family mansion. "It does appear that Mr Langdon's five-month sieze [*sic*] of illness must presently culminate in death. . . . Mr. L. made his will this morning—that is, appointed executors. It is the saddest, saddest time. . . . You understand what trouble we are in, & how the sunshine is gone out. The town is distressed—the solicitude is general" (25 June 1870). Two days later he wrote Elisha Bliss, "Mr. Langdon is very ill. Sometimes we feel sure he is going to get well, but then again hope well nigh passes away." Olivia's brother was called home from his world tour with Professor Ford, and the family waited helplessly for the worst. Clemens alternated with Olivia and Susan in maintaining a round-the-clock bedside vigil. "I can still see myself," he said more than three decades later, "mechanically waving a palm-leaf fan over the drawn white face of the patient. . . . I can recall all the torture of my efforts to keep awake; I can recall the sense of the indolent march of time, and how the hands of the tall clock seemed not to move at all."[11] His watches— from midnight to four in the morning and for three hours at midday—left him drained, anxious, and exhausted.

Under the circumstances, Clemens dealt as best he could with his next *Galaxy* deadline (for the August issue) in early July. When the magazine appeared, it contained just one slight sketch, entitled "A Memory," in the "Memoranda" column, together with the following note of "Personal Explanation" from Mark Twain: "I find the above squib among my MSS., and send it along merely to hold my place and represent me in the August number. Illness has rendered it out of my power to do more than this at present." Clemens's failure to meet his *Galaxy* obligation for August, a failure which resulted from his inability to work in late June and early July, was the most telling manifestation of the problem he faced and would for some time continue to face as a writer: how to function professionally in the midst of personal calamity. In the case of the August "Memoranda" column, he may have sought at some level of consciousness to establish a connection between his private and public selves. "A Memory"—written, or at least submitted, while his "father" by marriage was hovering close to death—turns out to be an anecdotal rendition of Clemens's (or, according to the byline, Mark Twain's) relationship with his own father. This biological father, unlike his Elmira counterpart, is stern, ungenerous, and forbidding—"austere," in the language of the sketch. According to the narrator, "My father and I were always on the most distant terms when I was a boy—sort of armed neutrality, so to speak."[12] Where Jervis Langdon had been a central and abiding presence in the lives of his children, the narrator's father, like Clemens's own, remained aloof and cold. Like John Marshall Clemens, too, this father was a judge, a circumstance the narrator calls upon in picturing him reading "Hiawatha," the one poem he appreciates, "with the same inflectionless judicial frigidity with which he always read his charge to the jury." The central action of "A Memory" involves the narrator's recollection of proposing to write a poem for his father, of his father's derisive response, and of the "daring recklessness" that then took possession of him and led him to offer instead the text of "an imposing 'Warranty Deed'" rewritten in the tom-tom trochaic tetrameter of "Hiawatha." The sketch ends with the father, his features clouded by "a fell darkness," hurling a bootjack at his son. Altogether, the piece amounts to an early depiction of the kind of physical and psychological family violence that was to become generic in the work of Mark Twain. Perhaps it was also Clemens's undeliberate way of summoning, or even of exorcising, the spirit of one father as he faced the prospect of losing another.

But Jervis Langdon was not yet ready to die, and his family once again allowed itself to be cheered by another of his unexpected rallies. On the Fourth of July, 1870, Clemens wrote Bliss, "Mr. Langdon is ever so much better, & we have every reason to believe that he is going to get well, & that speedily." The Adirondack vacation in August was still a possibility, he reckoned, and if Bliss wished to talk business with him in the meantime, the publisher would be a welcome guest either in Elmira or Buffalo. Further demonstration of Clemens's confidence in Langdon's apparent stability was his leaving Elmira for a few days in early July to lobby in Washington, D.C., on behalf of judicial redistricting in Tennessee, a mission he very likely undertook either in the interest of his own family's landholdings in the state or because of Langdon's investments there.[13] He claimed to be pleased with the bill's prospects for passage but was probably even more gratified by the reception he was afforded by the members of Congress he sought out. "I have the advantage of obscure lobbyists," he wrote Olivia, "because I can get any man's ear for a few moments, & also his polite attention & respectful hearing" (6 July 1870). He was back in the public eye, away from home—from both his own home and the Langdons'—for the first time since his lecture tour ended in January, and he was experiencing the effect of the enormous popularity of *The Innocents Abroad*. Senators and representatives, he told Olivia, "tacitly acknowledge an indebtedness to me for wisdom supplied to them by my pen." To cap his triumph, when he "called upon . . . President [Grant] in a quiet way," he was surprised both by his own "calm & dignified self-possession" and by the discovery that "*The General was fearfully embarrassed himself*" (8 July 1870).

His brief Washington expedition offered a striking testimonial to Mark Twain's burgeoning national reputation. Exhilirated and no doubt flattered by the enthusiastic, sometimes fawning, treatment he received at the hands of congressional movers and shakers, Clemens returned to Elmira considerably restored and perhaps a little transfixed by his own celebrity. It was in this frame of mind that he met with Elisha Bliss, who was quick to take him up on his 4 July invitation and visited Elmira in the middle of the month. Clemens had proposed such a meeting earlier, just before Langdon's health had failed, promising his publisher, "When you come we'll talk books & business" (23 April 1870). Now both men were ready to do just that, Bliss in order to secure a successor to *The Innocents Abroad* and Clemens in order to capitalize on the recognition he not only knew he had achieved but had just savored in Washington. The result was a contract, executed on 15 July 1870, for Mark Twain's second book with the American Publishing Company, which promised "to give the book as large a sale as they possibly can do by using all means in their power . . . to make it a great success."[14] Clemens's part of the bargain was only a bit more specific. He agreed with Bliss "to write . . . a book upon such subject as may be agreed upon between them, & to deliver the same . . . as early as 1ˢᵗ of January next if said Company shall desire it."

Perhaps the only unambiguous aspect of the contract referred to Clemens's compensation, which was to amount to 7.5 percent of all sales—at the time, he believed, an extraordinary royalty.[15] When he wrote of the deal later in the day to Orion, he said, "I suppose I am to get the biggest copyright, this time, ever paid on a subscription book in this country." The terms of the contract ratified the good feelings he had brought back from Washington and gave them tangible form. Still basking in satisfaction three days after the signing, he wrote Bliss, who had returned to Hartford, "I am now unquestionably notorious." The Fates were beaming.

All Clemens had to do to secure his happiness was to put in an occasional, perfunctory appearance in the Buffalo *Express*, fulfill his monthly obligation to the *Galaxy*, and write a six-hundred-page book by the end of the year. To him, at midsummer in green and abundant Elmira, it seemed possible. Although he and Olivia had agreed to cancel their Adirondack trip in deference to her father's health, Jervis Langdon appeared to have embarked upon a long, slow, steady period of convalescence, and sunshine once again filled the mansion. Members of the family convinced themselves that his surprising recovery in early July signaled a decided turn for the better in the course of his illness. So Clemens could quietly observe in his 15 July letter to Orion that "Mr. Langdon is very low" and then take heart three days later in writing Bliss, "Mr. Langdon is perceptibly better. The doctor has some hope of his recovery." When he subsequently informed his *Express* partners of Langdon's progress, they duly published "Personal" notices in the paper to keep their readers apprised of the good news. On 26 July they reported, "A dispatch yesterday from our colleague, Mr. Clemens, informs us that Mr. Langdon continues to improve, and that his recovery is now fully expected."[16] Luxuriating in the buoyant mood that accompanied Jervis Langdon's apparent return to health, Clemens produced his September "Memoranda" in time to meet his early August deadline.

Written during a lull between the storms that beset him in 1870, the September "Memoranda" column compactly embodies many of the divergent, sometimes conflicting, impulses that at the time went into making up Mark Twain. His literary-critical interests, for example, dominate "Favors from Correspondents," in which he passes along, with appropriately trenchant commentary, instances of florid writing, gullible reading, and "touching obituaries" that *Galaxy* readers had sent in at his invitation. In a related vein, "The Approaching Epidemic" decries other quasi-literary frauds, the mountebanks and "vagabonds" who, Twain predicts, will flood the lecture circuits in attempts to capitalize on the recent death of Charles Dickens. "A Royal Compliment" is an exercise in Twain's self-spoofing good humor, a piece in which, with perfectly deadpan and perfectly transparent conceit, he expresses his willingness to bow to what he perceives as a groundswell of popular sentiment in his favor and assume the throne of Spain. Not to acknowledge so widespread a consensus, he says, "would be but an ostentation of modesty."

Probably the most successful of the September "Memoranda" sketches and the one to take best advantage of Clemens's late July optimism and relative stability is the column's leadoff piece, "Political Economy." In it Mark Twain is once more the butt of his own joke, or actually of a two-pronged joke. One of the prongs is literary. Twain, who claims to be "seething [with] political economy ideas," is trying to write an essay on the topic. Again the smug innocent, he pictures himself "boiling and surging with prodigious thoughts wombed in words of such majesty that each one of them was in itself a straggling procession of syllables that might be fifteen minutes passing a given point." The glimpses he provides of the essay, of course, reveal it to be a fatuous compilation of abstraction, name dropping, malapropism, and wind: "The great light of commercial jurisprudence, international confraternity, and biological deviation, of all ages, in all civilizations, and all nationalities, from Zoroaster down to Horace Greeley, have . . . wrestled with this great subject."

The second prong upon which Twain impales himself involves the familiar ploy of his being gulled by a stranger from whom he wishes to hide his ignorance. In this case the stranger turns out to be a lightning-rod salesman, and Twain's ignorance, significantly, is of the rudiments of housekeeping. "Political Economy," in fact, is the one published sketch in all his work in which Mark Twain presents himself as or acknowledges that he has ever been a householder in a conventional domestic environment.[17] When his visitor interrupts Twain's fulminations about political economy to observe that his home is in need of lightning rods, Twain's self-consciousness looms up to make him easy prey. "I am new to housekeeping," he confides to the reader, and "have been used to hotels and boarding-houses all my life. Like anybody else of similar experience, I try to appear (to strangers) to be an old housekeeper." The strategy was already a familiar one in Clemens's writing. The innocent compounds his discomfort and so his vulnerability by trying to bluff or bluster his way through an embarrassment—sometimes, to his peril, quite aggressively—and the initiate, or sharper, or con man plays expensively upon his fear of exposure. In "Political Economy" the price Twain pays is $900 for a thicket of lightning rods which call down upon his home no fewer than 764 lightning strikes during their maiden thunderstorm. As he had in a number of earlier pieces, Twain comes off in "Political Economy" as a dupe or schlemiel, but, here as elsewhere, the reader gladly identifies with and likes him because he demonstrates familiar human weaknesses, because he himself tells us of them, and because he does so in contexts that are so obviously and comically overdrawn.

That open, appealing humor is largely missing from the remaining two pieces Clemens wrote in late July for the September *Galaxy*. "John Chinaman in New York" seems essentially an error in his comic judgment, but it is an error that suggests his willingness to vitiate his social criticism for the sake of a joke. Clemens credits the item to a correspondent named "Lang Bemis," but it is pretty clearly his own work and in fact simply reuses a bit of business that he had employed almost a year earlier in "A Day at Niagara" (Buffalo *Express*, 21 August 1869). In "Niagara" he made a fool of himself by failing to recognize that the "Noble Red Men" who peddle their wares around the falls are in reality sons of Ireland got up in blankets and buckskin for the tourist trade. In "John Chinaman," Lang Bemis makes a similar mistake. He comes upon a man, apparently Chinese, who has been hired to sit in front of a New York tea store as a kind of living advertisement. Bemis ruminates at some length and quite seriously about the cruelty of such exploitation—"Is it not a shame that we who prate so much about civilization and humanity are content to degrade a fellow-being to such an office as this?"—before discovering that "John Chinaman," too, is Irish. The gambit is more disquieting here than in "A Day at Niagara" because its effect is to undercut the humane expression of sympathy and outrage that immediately precedes it. Certainly it seems to trivialize the very issue—the disgraceful treatment of the Chinese in this country—that Clemens himself had championed in one of his first "Memoranda" pieces, "Disgraceful Persecution of a Boy" (May 1870). Mark Twain would remain an "unfinished" writer, philosophically undisciplined and more than occasionally inconsistent, throughout his career, but some of his work during this formative period raises the question whether, like Huck Finn, he had a sufficiently sound heart to countervail the deformed conscience society had inculcated in him.

That question is drawn to a point by "The Noble Red Man," a sketch in the September *Galaxy* which takes for its subject the American Indian, a lifelong blind spot in the field of Clemens's moral vision.[18] It bears relation to other instances of his literary-social criticism in that it gets underway as an exercise in deflating sentimental excess or distortion: "In books he is tall and tawny, muscular, straight, and of kingly presence," the sketch begins, marshaling in five paragraphs the various nobilities and excellences customarily attributed to the Noble Red Man by romantic writers. However, Twain asserts, to those who have come to know the Noble Red Man directly, "on the plains and in the mountains . . . , he is little, and scrawny, and black, and dirty; and . . . thoroughly pitiful and contemptible." The rest of the sketch is given over to invective, derogation, and manifest racism. Its intensely personal vituperation carries Twain far beyond the attitude of edgy candor needed to correct romantic misrepresentations. The "Noble Son of the Forest," he claims,

is nothing but a poor, filthy, naked scurvy vagabond, whom to exterminate were a charity to the Creator's worthier insects and reptiles which he oppresses. . . .

He is ignoble—base and treacherous, and hateful in every way. Not even imminent death can startle him into a spasm of virtue. The ruling trait of all savages is a greedy and consuming selfishness, and in our Noble Red Man it is found in its amplest development. His heart is a cesspool of falsehood, of treachery, and of low and devilish instincts. . . . The scum of the earth!

Nor does even this slander exhaust Twain's rancor; he empties a last battery of contempt on those "maids and matrons" who send up "a wail of humanitarian sympathy from the Atlantic seaboard" whenever they learn of some violence done against "the 'poor abused Indian.'"

The September *Galaxy*'s "Noble Red Man" serves as a reminder that the process of getting to be Mark Twain was anything but a series of consistent exercises in that kind of humane egalitarianism that empowered him as "the Lincoln of our literature."[19] It not only bristles with racist virulence but also pits that "manly," vaguely western attitude against an effeminate softness that it identifies with the effete East Coast. It distanced Clemens from his own better impulses, from the eastern establishment whose acceptance he somewhat ambivalently sought, and from the traditions of tolerance, generosity, and racial goodwill that had informed Olivia's upbringing.[20] There is no way of knowing how Jervis Langdon, who had been a conductor on the underground railroad, responded to the piece, or even of ascertaining whether or not Clemens read him the manuscript during one of his bedside watches in late July. He could not have seen "The Noble Red Man" when it appeared in print in mid-August, though, since within a few days of Clemens's sending off his "Memoranda" copy for the September *Galaxy*, Jervis Langdon was dead.

Langdon succumbed on 6 August 1870 to the cancer that had for months suspended him and his family between the torments of hope and despair. Clemens telegraphed his sister, "Father died this afternoon." He could have said "Livy's father," but perhaps appropriating the relationship for himself was a way of expressing the sincerity of his own sense of loss. Clemens was not lucky in the matter of fathers. Having lost his own when he was still a child, he had come to feel for Jervis Langdon the ambiguous mixture of affection, gratitude, deference, resentment, admiration, and awe that often shape a son's regard. Langdon had afforded him acceptance, respect, guidance, and very substantial, sometimes altogether stunning, generosity. In return he had sought not so much to please his father-in-law as to justify these extraordinary and often imposing measures of trust. His eulogy to Langdon, which appeared in the *Express* two days after the Langdon's death and was copied by a number of other papers, began with a testimonial that, although couched in general terms, directly reflected Clemens's experience of him: "Mr. Langdon was a great and noble man, in the

best and truest acceptation of those terms. He stood always ready
to help whoever needed help—wisely with advice, healthfully with
cheer and encouragement, and lavishly with money. He spent
more than one fortune in aiding struggling unfortunates in various
ways, and chiefly to get a business foothold in the world." Given
the lavish help Clemens had received, especially in securing his *Express* partnership, he may well have counted himself among Langdon's struggling unfortunates. His encomium to his father-in-law,
at any rate, describes a man a bit too big and considerably too good
for this world. "All the impulses of Mr. Langdon's heart were good
and generous," Clemens wrote. "He could not comprehend the
base or little. His nature was cast in a majestic mould. . . . He was
a very pure and noble Christian gentleman."[21]

Clemens, who routinely used his "Memoranda" column to ridicule obituary sentimentality and excess, may himself have strayed
beyond the bounds of perfect restraint in eulogizing Jervis Langdon, but his paean to his father-in-law's stature and virtue if anything understated the regard in which Langdon was held by his
family, and particularly by his daughter Olivia. With his death he
was quickly and quite enduringly enshrined as having been the
principal animating force in her life. Six months after his passing,
she wrote her friend Alice Day, "I often feel since Father left us that
he was my back bone, that what energy I had came from him, that
he was the moving spring."[22] Almost fifteen years later, Olivia's
sister looked back on that August in 1870 and observed to her in a
letter that everything changed when "our lives had to be all read-
justed to go on without that great power in them."[23] Writing from
the Elmira mansion a few days after the funeral, Clemens could
measure the impact of Olivia's loss. "This is a house of mourning,
now," he wrote Bliss. "My wife is nearly broken with grief &
watching" (11 August 1870).

The dying and death of Jervis Langdon dominated the early
married life of Samuel and Olivia Clemens. His decline overshad-
owed the other circumstances of their first year together almost
from the beginning, and even at that his passing came as a shock
and, particularly for Olivia, as a devastation. It would be under-
standable if Clemens felt at some level of consciousness relieved by
his father-in-law's death. Langdon had cast a long shadow—across
Elmira, across Buffalo, and across the minds and hearts of his fam-

ily. Clemens had found security within that shadow, but he could hardly avoid the feeling of being measured against it, or the danger of its eclipsing, or at least repressing, his own personality. Langdon's solicitousness toward him no doubt reflected a genuine fatherly affection, but in its way it served to extend Clemens's already lengthy adolescence, even while it half-enabled and half-coerced him to settle down and grow up. Langdon's passing left him fatherless again. It ended a kind of psychological apprenticeship on his part to a man he had permitted to exert enormous influence on the course of his character and his life.

Jervis Langdon was not simply *another* father for Samuel Clemens, in effect replacing the one Clemens had lost as a child, but a *better* father—more successful, more benevolent, and more powerful than the distant and ineffectual John Marshall Clemens. Given Olivia's idealization of her father, it would have been in Clemens's best interest to find a way to accept and even to admire Langdon in any case, but his regard went far beyond the bounds of mere accommodation in both its sincerity and its complexity. For Clemens, Langdon embodied a manly integrity whose qualities his early experience of the world had led him to revere and whose existence his later experience of the world would cause him to doubt. Langdon's material generosity had eased Clemens's translation to the East and helped to enfranchise him as a stable provider. That generosity had emphatically conditioned his choices, and from time to time and at various levels of consciousness Clemens bridled at this kindly coercion. His resistances to Langdon's gentle persuasions, however, were characteristically as mild and as unfocussed as the persuasions themselves.

Langdon's intercessions and benevolences notwithstanding, his most telling influence on Clemens—and so on Mark Twain—grew out of his son-in-law's perception of what he *was* rather than what he *did*. Clemens was drawn to Langdon's mix of power and goodness, to the living proof that a person could achieve success without sacrificing his principles. This achievement on Langdon's part contradicted an impression Clemens may well have gathered from the unspoken testimony of his own family: to live honorably was typically to be frustrated by the very nature of things and often to be exploited by those with fewer scruples. Langdon reaffirmed Clemens's faith in the efficacy of virtue and by doing so served to heighten his indignation at the hypocrisy that characterized what Clemens himself came to call the Gilded Age. Langdon demonstrated that even among wealthy and successful men, venality was a matter of choice and acquiescence rather than necessity. To observe that the moral focus of Mark Twain's criticism sharpened while Clemens was the beneficiary of his father-in-law's patronage is not to imply that Langdon was responsible for that aspect of Clemens's (or Twain's) character, but rather to suggest that Langdon was manifestly important in providing an environment in which Clemens's natural tendency to moralize could and did develop.

In the wake of Langdon's death, Clemens produced a "Memoranda" column for October 1870 that juxtaposed his adolescent and his reformist impulses. The column begins with "The Reception at the President's," a rendition of his July meeting with President Grant in which Mark Twain comes off as an opaque, garrulous western boor who remains provocatively unaware of his own longwindedness and unimportance as he creates a one-man logjam in a White House receiving line. The account bears little apparent resemblance to Clemens's interview with Grant, which had been conducted "in a quiet way" and in private. It is accompanied, in terms of outlook or frame of mind, by "Curious Relic For Sale," Twain's tribute to an almost lethally aromatic pipe he had wielded for a time during the *Quaker City* voyage, and by "Science Vs. Luck," in which a Kentucky jury plays cards all night to ascertain that "the game commonly known as old sledge or seven-up is eminently a game of science and not of chance." These meditations on smoking and gambling, two of the preoccupations Clemens associated with bachelorhood, play up the adolescent-male immaturity Mark Twain sometimes exploited like a talisman, as does his performance as an innocently outrageous outlander afoot in the White House.

They are in that respect substantially at odds with the remaining major feature among the October 1870 "Memoranda," a series of four letters under the general heading "Goldsmith's Friend Abroad Again." Clemens's purpose in the letters—which are supposedly written by Ah Song Hi, originally of Shanghai, to his friend Ching-Foo—is to chronicle the prejudice and abuse the Chinese encounter when they immigrate to the United States. Ah Song Hi's patient, decent, long-suffering hopefulness in what he persists in calling the "Land of the Free and Home of the Brave" is uniformly perverted and betrayed by the Americans he encounters. He is humiliated, beaten, and robbed not simply by men of the mean streets he is forced to inhabit, but by policemen, employers, judges, customs officers, and even by the laws of Congress themselves—that is, by the very system he expected "to welcome all . . . oppressed peoples and offer her abundance." Ah Song Hi's guileless innocence is a foil to Twain's outrage, the outrage of a grown-up witness to American rapacity and cruelty. It was a dynamic that Clemens would develop and refine in his best work, a way of transforming his own persistent immaturity into a vehicle for serious social criticism. Placing himself in the tradition of the genteel Goldsmith, moreover, especially in championing the cause of the unfortunate and the oppressed, emphasized those aspects of his own character that best reflected the noblest qualities he associated with his father-in-law.

Clemens's submission of these October "Memoranda" in late August or early September brought to a close the summer of 1870, a season of distraction, uncertainty, and change. It had begun with the marked decline of Jervis Langdon's health and his consequent degeneration from patriarch to patient. At precisely its midpoint, during a period of relative stability and hopefulness, Clemens had signed a contract to produce his second major book. By the time it ended, his father-in-law was dead, his work was in disarray, and his wife was distraught with grief. The "burden" of happiness he spoke of bearing in late May had been displaced by the real cares of an imperfect world that only *seemed* to play favorites. If Mark Twain were to emerge triumphant from the summer shadows that had overtaken Samuel Clemens and from the indirection and confusion that had characterized his professional life even before those shadows fell, the fall of 1870 would have to be a time of extraordinary coalescence and accomplishment.

Chapter Eight

Writing *Roughing It*

The story of Samuel Clemens's remaining days in Buffalo intertwines with and eventually becomes the story behind the composition of his second big book, *Roughing It*. By his own account, he began work on his sequel to *The Innocents Abroad* in August of 1870 and was still revising and adding to it as late as October of 1871. During those fifteen months he probably produced more than two thousand manuscript pages, of which just three are extant today.[1] Over the course of that time, waves of energetic, sometimes frantic, composition alternated with troughs of torpor, distraction, and despair. There may even have been moments of calm, consistent, workmanlike productivity. But by and large, writing *Roughing It* was a struggle for Clemens: against the odds, which emphasized the unlikelihood of his producing a successful follow-up to a bestseller; against the Fates, which seemed determined to rain an endless stream of catastrophes down upon him; and against the elements of his own temperament, which were inclined from time to time to give way to self-doubt, insecurity, and guilt.

The germ of the book, the impulse to recollect and make literary matter of his western experiences, can be traced back at least as far as the "Around the World" letters Clemens began publishing in the Buffalo *Express* in the fall of 1869. Six of the eight letters he wrote for the series treated Nevada and California.[2] His imagination may have been further stirred by his writing a long congratulatory letter to the New York Society of California Pioneers on 11 October 1869: "If I were to tell some of my experiences, you would recognize Californian blood in me," he wrote the society. "Although

I am not a pioneer, I have had a sufficiently variegated time of it to enable me to talk pioneer like a native, and feel like a Forty-Niner."[3] He seems clearly to have had *some* western project or projects in mind when he wrote to his mother and sister in February or March of 1870 asking that they send him a file of his clippings from the Virginia City, Nevada, *Territorial Enterprise*; the file arrived on 26 March 1870.

Quite some time earlier, however, Clemens was at least toying wth the idea of capitalizing in some way on the popularity of *The Innocents Abroad.* "I mean to write another book during the summer," he wrote Mary Fairbanks on 6 January 1870. "This one has proven such a surprising success that I feel encouraged." Later that month, just before his wedding, he wrote with the same easy assurance to his publisher, Elisha Bliss, "I can get a book ready for you any time you want it." As if to protect himself from the pressure such a promise might generate, though, he added, "but you *can't* want one before this time next year—so I have plenty of time" (22 January 1870). Bliss apparently responded with a combination of enthusiasm and his customary shrewdness to overtures of this kind on Clemens's part, and during the spring the two fenced rather languidly with one another about contracting for a second book. When it seemed likely that the newlyweds might travel to Europe, for instance, either for the sake of their own pleasure or in order to accompany Jervis Langdon on an excursion to restore his health, Clemens wrote, "I have a sort of vague half-notion of spending the summer in England.—I could write a telling book" (11 March 1870).

It was amid these circumstances that he sent for the "coffin" of clippings from the Virginia City *Territorial Enterprise.* Insofar as he and Bliss had any very definite notions at this time about the nature of his second book, those notions pretty clearly centered on his setting off on another round of foreign travels in order to write a sort of "Innocents Abroad II." It seems likely, therefore, that requisitioning the file of *Enterprise* clippings that arrived in late March had more to do with his having agreed earlier that month to edit a regular ten-page column for the *Galaxy* than with his intention to write a book.[4] Every early indication is that the second major work from Mark Twain was, like the first, to chronicle his encounter with the Old World, not the New. While Clemens was securing and assessing those *Enterprise* clippings, in fact, Bliss evidentally put teasing aside and began pressing him in earnest about a European tour. On 1 April 1870 Clemens wrote Olivia's parents, "Bliss is *very* anxious that I go abroad during the summer & get a book written for next spring." Had Jervis Langdon's rapidly failing health not put such a trip out of the question, Clemens would probably have acted on his publisher's urging, since neither of them had come up with a better way of stimulating a follow-up to his best-seller, and set out to write a second *Innocents Abroad*. Only upon acknowledging his inability to do so did he hit, glancingly at first and without much fervor, upon the idea of turning west rather than east—to the past rather than the present, and to the internal world of recollected experience rather than the external world of accident and circumstance—in generating the matter for his second book.

On 29 May 1870 Clemens made his first explicit reference to the idea of writing a western book when he tentatively, perhaps playfully, agreed in a letter to accompany Mary Fairbanks and her family on a trip to California the following spring. "The publishers are getting right impatient to see another book on the stocks," he said, "& I doubt if I could do better than rub up old Pacific memories & put them between covers along with some eloquent pictures." The letter somewhat contradictorily juxtaposes the mention of his publisher's impatience against his expressed intention of waiting almost a full year to undertake the trip that would "rub up" the memories needed to produce the book. But it does indicate a willingness, at least, to draw from those "Pacific memories" in writing his second major work, if only because he doubts that he "could do better." These lukewarm, inconclusive musings about a second book persisted into June, when Clemens expressed the hope to Bliss that his flagging enthusiasm for the project, whatever its nature, would be restored by the late-summer vacation he and Olivia were hoping to take. "I like your idea for a book," he said, apparently in response to a suggestion that has since been lost, "but the *inspiration* don't come. Wait till I get rested up & rejuvenated in the Adirondacks, & then something will develop itself *sure*" (9 June 1870).

Clemens's uncertainty about the subject of his second book, no doubt amplified by the distractions he faced in coping with his

Elisha Bliss, Jr. (Courtesy Mark Twain Memorial, Hartford, Conn.)

father-in-law's decline, became a matter of record when Bliss visited him in Elmira on 15 July and secured his signature on a contract. The agreement obligated him to produce a six hundred-page book for the American Publishing Company "as early as 1ˢᵗ of January next," but was quite unspecific as to what those six hundred pages might treat, stipulating only that Clemens produce for the company "a book upon such subject as may be agreed upon between them."[5] The matter of content was left open, it turned out, because even as he signed the document Clemens was unable to say unequivocally what he would write about. "The subject of it is a secret," he wrote to Orion later that day, "because I may possibly change it. But as it stands, I propose to do up Nevada & Cal., beginning with the trip across the country in the stage." *Roughing It* came contractually and conceptually into existence in this conditional, provisional way. Dealing with an experienced publisher whose impatience and solicitude were carefully orchestrated, flushed with his own success and renown, and momentarily benefiting from a brightening in Jervis Langdon's condition, Clemens found his way into a bargain that stipulated his obligations much more clearly than it did the course he would follow to fulfill them.

In his 15 July letter to Orion he explained that "per contract I must have another 600-page book ready for my publisher Jan. 1," adding, "I only began it today." His subsequent correspondence, however, indicates that Clemens did not start work on *Roughing It* until about six weeks later. In a letter to his mother and sister dated 27 July, he described the contract for the Nevada and California book and said, "I shall begin it about a month from now." The postponement was very likely due to the strain of maintaining Jervis Langdon's sickroom vigil, but it may also reflect Clemens's difficulty in recalling events of a decade earlier. "Do you remember any of the scenes, names, incidents or adventures of the coach trip?" he had asked Orion, "for I remember next to *nothing* about the matter" (15 July 1870). Even had he planned to begin work on the book sooner, those plans would necessarily have been set aside when his father-in-law died on 6 August. Langdon's long decline, which might under other circumstances have helped members of his family prepare for the worst, instead preyed upon their incautious optimism and so relegated them to a deep and troubled mourning. Back in Buffalo by the end of August with Olivia and her mother, Clemens wrote his sister, Pamela, "Livy cannot sleep since her father's death—but I give her a narcotic every night & *make* her" (31 August 1870). His own mourning and ministrations had to be interrupted or cut short in order to allow him to produce copy for his October "Memoranda" column, due in early September. Having excused himself from his *Galaxy* obligations for the preceding month because of Langdon's illness, he found himself in a position where he simply had to resolve to work.

Apparently it was that resolution—intensified, perhaps, by the recognition that his 1 January book deadline was now only four months away—that finally led him to begin *Roughing It*. He was further stimulated when he received the record of the stagecoach trip he had requested from Orion. "I find that your little memorandum book is going to be ever so much use to me," he wrote, "and will enable me to make quite a coherent narrative of the Plains journey instead of slurring it over and jumping 2,000 miles at a stride."[6] The big western book was at last under way. "I am just as busy as I can be," he wrote his sister on 31 August, "am still writing for the Galaxy & also writing a book like the 'Innocents' in size & style. . . . I have got my work ciphered down to *days*, & I haven't a single day to spare between this & the date which, by written contract I am to deliver the MSS. of the book to the publisher." On 2 September 1870 he reported to Mary Fairbanks, "I have written four chapters of my new book during the past few days," and on 4 September he bragged to Bliss, "During the past week have written first four chapters of the book, & I tell you the 'Innocents Abroad' will have to get up early to beat it.—It will be a book that will jump right strait into a continental celebrity the first month it is issued."

Ciphering and enthusiasm, though, were no proof against the misfortunes that plagued the book's early composition. Just as Clemens was writing these initial chapters, he and his wife were paid a visit by Emma Nye, a girlhood friend of Olivia's, who was stricken seriously ill shortly after arriving in Buffalo. With her parents off vacationing in South Carolina, responsibility for their guest's care fell to the Clemenses. On 7 September Clemens wrote Ella Wolcott, an Elmira friend of the Langdons', "Poor little Emma Nye lies in our bed-chamber fighting wordy battles with the phantoms of delirium. Livy & a hired nurse watch her without ceasing,—night & day." On 9 September he told Orion, "I have no time to turn round. A young lady visitor (schoolmate of Livy's) is dying in the house of typhoid fever . . . & the premises are full of nurses & doctors & we are all fagged out." Olivia, who had yet to get over the shock and wearying ordeal of her father's dying, exhausted herself at yet another sickbed, and Clemens watched helplessly as his wife's strength and their patient's life ebbed. The end came as he had foreseen. "Miss Emma Nye lingered a month with typhoid fever," he wrote Mary Fairbanks, "& died here in our own bedroom on the 29th Sept" (13 October 1870).

Almost four decades later Clemens remembered Emma Nye's last days as being "among the blackest, the gloomiest, the most

The Map of Paris as it appeared in the November *Galaxy*. (Courtesy Mark Twain Papers, The Bancroft Library)

wretched of my long life," but he also regarded "the resulting periodical and sudden changes of mood in me, from deep melancholy to half insane tempests and cyclones of humor," as standing out among his life's principal "curiosities."[7] For all its manifest and indisputable wretchedness, September 1870 was a time of quirky, manic productivity for Clemens. Even with his *Express* obligations in abeyance, he was driven by his *Galaxy* and book deadlines to a frenzy of creative energy whose sources were somewhere between desperation and whimsy and whose most notable consequence was his famous "Map of Paris," a parody of the military maps many periodicals were then publishing in connection with their accounts of the Franco-Prussian War. "During one of these spasms of humorous possession," he later recalled, "I sent down to my newspaper office for a huge wooden capital *M* and turned it upsidedown and carved a crude and absurd map of Paris upon it, and published it, along with a sufficiently absurd description of it, with guarded and imaginary compliments of it bearing the signatures of General Grant and other experts."[8] The map appeared in the *Express* on 17 September and 15 October 1870, was reprinted with a bit more elaboration in the November *Galaxy*, and directly became a minor national sensation. Among its admirers was Schuyler Colfax, vice president of the United States, who wrote Clemens on 26 September, "I have had the heartiest possible laugh over it, & so have all my family."[9] The map's patent absurdities—the inclusion, for example, not only of Verdun and Vincennes but also of Omaha, Jersey City, and the Erie Canal—and execrable execution were perfectly set off by Mark Twain's transparent vanity over its supposed brilliance and indisputable uniqueness. The map is a telling manifestation of the internal skirmishing Clemens's impulses were conducting in the wake of Jervis Langdon's death and during the course of Emma Nye's dying. Its botched, infantile look and general silliness aptly reflect his knack for finding imaginative freedom and release from the draining cares of adulthood through childish forms and perspectives. Mourning the loss of one patient, doing his part to nurse another, afraid that his wife was about to break with grief and anxiety, he regressed to a safer—and funnier—place; or rather he was taken there by "spasms of humorous possession" over which he claimed no control and for which, therefore, he could not be held responsible.

A similar release may well have accompanied Clemens's early work on the *Roughing It* manuscript, particularly if that manuscript essentially resembled the book as it was eventually published (a likelihood to be discussed below). For it, too, offers a childish, or puerile, perspective on the world, the outlook of a narrator who opens by allowing that he was "young and ignorant" when he began his western adventures, at least in part because he "never had been away from home."[10] The first of these claims distorts the actual circumstances of Clemens's history and the second wholeheartedly misrepresents them. When he accepted his brother's invitation to head west in the summer of 1861, he was a twenty-five-year-old man who had already seen and lived for a time in such places as St. Louis, New York, Philadelphia, Washington, D.C., and Cincinnati, and who had gained a wide experience of the Mississippi Valley during three years as an apprentice and steamboat pilot. The *Roughing It* narrator, however, is a callow, inexperienced innocent in those opening chapters, a wide-eyed adolescent who anticipates a string of western adventures as breathlessly as Tom Sawyer would, who refers to himself as a "stripling" (*RI*, p. 96), who is on one occasion supposedly mistaken for a child (*RI*, p. 117), and who is carried away from "the States" in a stagecoach that seems to him "an imposing cradle on wheels" (*RI*, p. 47). The regressions in the early going of *Roughing It*, moreover, operate on other levels as well. The trip west seems, at least at the outset, a flight from civilization to conditions more primitive and rudimentary, from relative order to something approaching anarchy, from the rules of decorum and the forms of polite address to the unrestraint of practical usage and the vigor of colloquial language, from the tame to the wild. Aboard their hurtling stagecoach, the narrator and his brother shed their clothes, stow their unabridged dictionary, and revel in a "wild sense of freedom" (*RI*, p. 66); the coach itself undergoes a parallel transformation, eventually devolving to a mud wagon, its horses replaced by mules.

In beginning his book, Clemens was clearly tapping into and in his way extending the myth of the West, but on a much more personal level he was also discovering in the unfettered, childlike joy of "those fine overland mornings" a refuge from the grown-up burdens that weighed upon him in the early fall of 1870. "We bowled away and left 'the States' behind us," he wrote: "It was a superb summer morning, and all the landscape was brilliant with sunshine. There was a freshness and breeziness, too, and an exhilarating sense of emancipation from all sorts of cares and responsibilities, that almost made us feel that the years we had spent in the close, hot city, toiling and slaving, had been wasted and thrown away" (*RI*, p. 47). Like the map of Paris, the opening chapters of his California book offered Clemens the tonic of boyish self-indulgence and release. His early enthusiasm for the project and his ability to stay with it very likely derived from his exploiting it as a means of escape. Vicariously sloughing layers of respectability and obligation, he found in the writing a form of emancipation not only from the close, hot confinement of Buffalo, where his dreams of perfect domestic contentment were fast giving way to a nightmare reality, but also from the specters of age, disease, and mortality that seemed destined to harry him there and from the burdens of gentility and the confinements of newspaper and magazine work that had become his lot.

So it is not altogether surprising that Clemens managed to make some progress on the *Roughing It* manuscript in September 1870, even as Emma Nye was losing her battle with typhoid fever in his home. In the middle of the month he wrote to Hezekiah L. Hosmer, postmaster of Virginia City, informing him that he was "now . . . writing a book" and that "the Overland journey has made six chapters of it thus far & promises to make six or eight more" (15 September 1870). The letter is significant not only because it indicates that Clemens had written chapters 5 and 6 between 4 and 15 September but also because it requests from Hosmer information about Slade, the division agent to whom chapters 10 and 11 of the book in its present form are entirely devoted.[11] The timing of the request suggests that the arrangement and numbering of the early chapters in the manuscript were essentially similar to those of the first edition. That is, Clemens raised an issue at the end of manuscript chapter 6 that he came to treat in book chapter 10. The overland journey, as it turned out, eventually occupied the first twenty chapters of *Roughing It*, not twelve or fourteen as Clemens here speculates.

By 19 September Clemens could report to Bliss that he had "finished 7th or 8th chap of book to-day . . .—am up to page 180— only about 1500 more to write." It had taken him three weeks, under trying circumstances, to produce these 180 manuscript pages; it would be months before he would be able to sustain even this modest pace again. His attention may have been overtaken at this point by the demands of Emma Nye's illness, but it may also, and necessarily, have been diverted by his having to prepare "Memoranda" for the November *Galaxy* in time for his early October deadline. Nothing in that November column approached the antic foolery of the map of Paris, which accompanied it. The "Memoranda" opened with a long encomium to John Henry Riley, a cohort from Clemens's California and Washington days, and included two further letters from Ah Song Hi, "Goldsmith's Friend," depicting the plight of the Chinese in the courts of San Francisco. There were also a five-column "General Reply" to aspiring writers from a seasoned, savvy Mark Twain, and the usual gathering of saccharine verse and other literary overindulgences sent him by correspondents. Each of these pieces reinforced Twain's stature not only as a sage and serious adult but also as a critic in conspiracy with his readers to trim the excesses of unenlightened sentimentality. They were set off by "A Reminiscence of the Back Settlements," in which a vernacular speaker, an undertaker, rhapsodizes about an especially agreeable corpse he has just had the pleasure of interring. "There's some satisfaction in buryin' a man like that," he says. "You feel that what you're doing is appreciated. Lord bless you, so's he got planted before he sp'iled, he was perfectly satisfied." Perhaps Clemens's frustration with the dead and the dying led him to publish this "Reminiscence," which otherwise seems a particularly inappropriate and insensitive performance in light of his circumstances and Olivia's in the early fall of 1870. Perhaps his experiment with a vernacular narrator served as a kind of warm-up or preparation for *Roughing It*. The garrulous, unsentimental undertaker of "A Reminiscence," at any rate, could have held his own with the "sociable heifer" who makes her appearance in chapter 2 of *Roughing It*, and would have been just the man to conduct Buck Fanshaw's funeral in chapter 47.

It would be some time, though, before Clemens could turn his full attention back to the book. Olivia collapsed shortly after Emma Nye's death in late September, exhausted by the month-long sickbed vigil and the strain of her first pregnancy. Mindful that his wife had been something of an invalid for much of her adolescence, Clemens anxiously monitored her slow recovery. She was still too weak on 12 October to attend the wedding of her brother, Charles, to Ida Clark in Elmira. On 13 October Clemens wrote Bliss that he had recently been able to return to the manuscript. "I am driveling along tolerably fairly on the book," he said, "getting off from 12 to 20 pages (MS.) a day." But the demands of his literary obligations, augmented by his worries at home, were growing burdensome. "The reason I haven't written before," he admitted the same day in a letter to Mary Fairbanks, "is because I am in such a terrible whirl with Galaxy & book work that I am so jubilant whenever each day's task is done that I have to dart right off & play—nothing can stop me. I never want to see a pen again till the task-hour strikes next day."

An important change had taken place, not in the big western book, but in Clemens's attitude toward it, and toward himself. It had become *work*, and he the harried worker. No longer a lark or an escape, it was an incessant daily obligation—an obligation, moreover, bearing a deadline he could not hope to meet. And he was no longer the world-class raconteur, the darling of senators and congressmen, tossing off another six hundred-page best-seller in a few carefree months, but a drudge and perhaps even a fraud, straining to produce by tedious effort and under grim circumstances the kind of thing he wished to believe he could turn out in a fit of happy inspiration. As the fall of 1870 deepened, so did Clemens's experience of the slow, anxious, frustrating toil that was so much at odds with the widely held and assiduously perpetrated image of the offhand, drolly spontaneous Mark Twain. His *Galaxy* "Memoranda," which he originally undertook as an outlet for "fine-spun stuff" and an antidote to the grind of newspaper work, had grown arduous as well. Five days after telling Mary Fairbanks of the terrible whirl he was in, Clemens warned *Galaxy* co-editor Francis P. Church, "Sometimes I get ready to give you notice that I'll quit at the end of my year because the Galaxy work crowds book work so much" (18 October 1870).

It was in this frame of mind that Clemens ground out his "Memoranda" for the December 1870 *Galaxy*. The main feature of the column and its leadoff piece, "An Entertaining Article," is a densely humorless review of *The Innocents Abroad* which Clemens attributed at the time to an English critic but later revealed he had written himself. The point of the exercise, by this time a familiar point to Mark Twain's *Galaxy* readers, is to hold up to ridicule those people too opaque or too much in earnest to get a joke or to penetrate even the most transparent irony. It was in keeping, then, with Twain's ongoing endeavor to challenge and educate his public in the matter of appreciating strategies and subtleties important to the humorist. It is accompanied by several other pieces that in one way or another also touch upon a writer's role or prerogatives or frustrations: "Running for Governor," for example, points up the press's willingness to resort to slander in its biased coverage of political campaigns. "The 'Present' Nuisance" attacks the practice common among tradesmen of giving newspaper editors merchandise in return for free advertising in the form of favorable "notices." In it Twain quite disingenuously says, "I am not an editor of a newspaper, and shall always try to do right and be good, so that God will not make me one." Finally, among these writer's laments, "Dogberry in Washington" lodges a complaint against the Buffalo postmaster who misinterprets an inscrutable postal regulation in such a way as to prohibit an author's sending his manuscripts through the mail at a reduced rate. Twain resolves

Langdon Clemens.
(Courtesy Mark Twain Memorial, Hartford, Conn.)

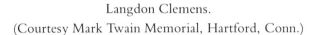

to take no action against this "misguided officer," but, perhaps with the vigilante justice of *Roughing It* fresh in his mind, says, "If he were in California, he would fare far differently—very far differently—for there the wicked are not restrained by the gentle charities that prevail in Buffalo."

Soon, however, the *Galaxy*, the *Express*, and even the book would seem only petty distractions. On 7 November 1870 Olivia gave birth to the Clemenses' first child, Langdon, prematurely. For a time her health and the baby's life were in such jeopardy that Clemens could think of little more than his anxiety for the two of them. As he did, it registered with him that his dainty palace in Buffalo, despite its particular graces and the "gentle charities" that operated in that city, had become a source of torment rather than satisfaction. On 11 November 1870 he vented some of his worry and desperation in a letter to Orion:

I am looking for heavy bills to come in during the next few weeks—a four or five hundred-dollar doctor's bill, a sixty-dollar nurse bill, a hundred & seventy-dollar sleigh-bill, a two-hundred dollar life-insurance bill, a three-hundred dollar carpenter's bill, & a dozen or two of twenty-five dollar debts, & we owe the servants seven hundred dollars which they can call for at any time—*& I am sitting still with idle hands*—for Livy is very sick & I do not believe the baby will live five days.

It had been just four months since Clemens, flush with a sense of his own power, had signed what he thought was a fat contract with Elisha Bliss to produce a fat new work designed to capitalize on his swelling popularity. All things had seemed possible, including the restoration of his father-in-law to health and the writing of "a book like the 'Innocents' in size & style" by the turn of the new year. Now, his life a turmoil and his work in disarray, his responsibilities seemed about to overwhelm him. As the late fall drew on he temperamentally careened between poles of giddiness and despair, and the *Roughing It* manuscript slipped into twilight.

In letters he wrote during the summer of 1870, Clemens often observed that his deadline for completing the California book was 1 January 1871. He makes no mention of that deadline, however, after 15 September, a circumstance that suggests his willingness to forget or ignore it once the work of composition began. The *Roughing It* contract is somewhat equivocal on the matter, stipulating that Clemens was to submit the completed manuscript to his publishers "as soon as practicable, but as early as 1st January next if they . . . shall desire it."[12] Perhaps in the hope that the American Publishing Company might suppress any such desire, Clemens kept Bliss well informed of his domestic tribulations throughout the fall, treating him more like a confidant than their mutual wariness would otherwise have made likely. He also managed in November to secure a spot for Orion on Bliss's staff as editor of a house organ called the *American Publisher*. Bliss was pleased to secure Orion as a kind of hostage to his brother's loyalty and to develop an opportunity to exploit his name. Clemens once remarked that Bliss's purpose in hiring Orion was to keep him—that is, Clemens himself—from "whoring after strange gods."[13] For his part, Clemens may have liked the idea of placing an insider in

Orion Clemens. (Courtesy Mark Twain Papers, The Bancroft Library)

Bliss's firm to look after his interests and to plead his case when, for example, he sought to extend a deadline.

By the end of 1870 Clemens had moved all members of his immediate family to the East—his mother, his sister, and his sister's children to Fredonia, New York, in April, and his brother and sister-in-law to Hartford in November. As he did so, ironically, he was becoming increasingly unsettled in Buffalo. The baby survived his first five days, but he did not grow strong. Olivia's hold on health was tenuous. The *Express*, which had long since ceased to exert any real attraction for Clemens, had come to claim little hold even on his attention or loyalty. On 26 November 1870 he wrote to Charles Henry Webb, "I never write a line for my paper, I do not see the office oftener than once a week, & do not stay there an hour at any time." His January 1871 "Memoranda" showed to what extent his work for the *Galaxy* had likewise grown labored and uninspired. Its leading piece showcased a crude Twain engraving of King William III of Prussia, executed after the fashion of the map of Paris and amounting to no more than a knockoff or plagiarism of that earlier success. The sketches that followed it largely substantiate his later observation that few things are drearier than "to be a monthly humorist in a cheerless time."[14] If Clemens's hands were no longer idle as winter set in, neither had they taken a purposeful hold on a single enterprise. Rather than working to meet the chief obligation before him, he chose in the last months of 1870 to spawn a bewildering array of *new* projects which served, whether intentionally or not, to distract him, and sometimes even Bliss, from his failure to make headway in *Roughing It*.

The most spectacular of these schemes was his proposal, made in November, to write a book about prospecting for diamonds in South Africa, where strikes and claims were making news that sounded an ever-resonant chord in Clemens. The idea was to send a surrogate—a less taciturn, more dependable version of Professor Ford—to the diamond fields to gather facts and impressions, which Mark Twain would then convert to a thick, profitable book. "*That book will have a perfectly beautiful sale*," he wrote Bliss, asking for a 10 percent royalty and claiming that he had already found "the best man in America" to send to Capetown. His enthusiasm for the project stopped just short of frenzy: "Say yes or no quick, Bliss, for this thing is brim-full of fame & fortune for both author [and] publisher. Expedition's the word! I don't want any timidity or hesitancy now" (28 November 1870). His "best man" was John Henry Riley, the same Riley to whom he had devoted four columns of praise in his November "Memoranda." In a long, importunate letter of 2 December, Clemens tried to pry Riley loose from his commitments in Washington. "This thing is the pet scheme of my life," he wrote. "I *urge* upon you, 'Expedition's the word!' Clear out *now*, & let us publish the FIRST book & take the richest cream. . . . But *hurry*, now. There is no single moment of time to lose. If you could start *now*, it would be splendid." Clemens knew his man, having said of him in the November *Galaxy*, "He will put himself to any amount of trouble to oblige a body." Riley gave way to this assault and, with Bliss not only concurring but issuing him an advance of $1,500, set sail on 7 January 1871.

The diamond-book enterprise epitomizes the feverish scheming that overtook Clemens during the winter of 1870–71. Frustrated by illness, misfortune, and perhaps by the vagaries of his own unruly talent, he seems to have sought reassurance that he was both a popular writer and a promising entrepreneur by conjuring up and committing himself to a series of literary speculations, all of them taking precedence at least for a time over the *Roughing It* manuscript. Unable or unwilling to attend to the work before him, he went on a spree of contract signings that may have bolstered his ego at the expense of his common sense and whatever remained of his peace of mind. The diamond-book idea was only the sparkling tip of that speculative iceberg. Moving on another front during this troubled winter, he agreed with Isaac Sheldon, publisher of the *Galaxy*, to produce a pamphlet which eventually appeared as *Mark Twain's (Burlesque) Autobiography and First Romance*. When it was all Bliss could do to contain his consternation over this seeming defection, Clemens contracted with *him* in mid-December to compile *another* book of short pieces for almost immediate publication. "To-day I arranged enough sketches to make 134 pages of the book," he wrote Bliss on 22 December 1870. "I shall go right on till I have finished selecting, & then write a new sketch or so." By 3 January 1871 he was pressing Bliss hard on this latest undertaking: "Name the Sketch book '*Mark Twain's Sketches*' & go on canvassing like mad. Because if you don't hurry it will tread on the heels of the *big* book next August." The "big book," of course, was *Roughing It*; this letter indicates that Clemens still hoped somehow to complete the *Roughing It* manuscript in time to allow for its August 1871 publication.

All together, then, by the turn of the new year Clemens had pledged himself to produce a substantial volume of sketches for Bliss (to appear in the late winter or early spring), a pamphlet for Sheldon (to appear in March), a six hundred-page western book for Bliss (to appear in August), and another six hundred-page work, also for Bliss, on the African diamond fields (to appear, as Clemens wrote Riley, on "Feb. 1, 1872, & sweep the world like a besom of destruction" [2 December 1870]). All the while he had to prepare his monthly "Memoranda" columns and make some show at fulfilling his editorial obligations to the *Express*. In Clemens's mind, Mark Twain had somehow become an enterprise of vast proportions, a literary fabricating plant modeled on the prevailing industrial strategies of bulk processing and mass production. Whatever else these schemes may have accomplished, they seem to have supplanted in Clemens's imagination the notion of the writer-as-inspired-artist with that of the writer as manager or processor. While there is considerably less magic or mystery in the latter conception than in the former, there is also less isolation and pressure. What these new projects had in common, whether pasteups of new sketches and old or retellings of someone else's diamond-field escapades, was that they diverted their would-be author from the awful obligation of having miraculously to *invent* the California book. Their sheer number, though, destined them to stymie rather than soothe the frantic conjurer.

Something had to give. By the end of a few months, almost everything had. Sheldon got and printed his pamphlet by mid-March 1871, and the *Galaxy* publishers continued to receive "Memoranda" until Clemens had fulfilled his contract in April, but all else slid to confusion. Bliss convinced Clemens that to put a book of sketches on the market would be to jeopardize sales of the still popular *Innocents Abroad*. Clemens deferred to this reasoning and to Bliss's subsequent postponements as well, with the consequence that *Mark Twain's Sketches, New and Old* remained unpublished until 1875. The diamond book proved to be not only a failure, but a failure bearing the cast of tragedy. Riley performed dutifully, often under difficult circumstances. "Your letters have been just as satisfactory as letters could be," Clemens wrote him on 3 March 1871. But by the time Riley returned from his long odyssey, Clemens was preoccupied with other projects, and the diamond book, together with Riley himself, was left to languish. When Riley died of cancer of the mouth in September of 1872, unbidden and unvisited by Clemens, the book died with him.[15]

Roughing It proved vulnerable to both the pipe dreams and the vnightmares of early 1871. In a frenzy of enthusiasm for the book, perhaps after several weeks of having neglected it, Clemens wrote Bliss on 27 January, "Tell you what I'll do, if you say so. Will write night & day & send you 200 pages of MS. every week (of the big book on California, Nevada & the Plains) & finish it all up the 15th of April if you can without fail *issue* the book on the 15th of May. . . . I have to go to Washington next Tuesday & stay a week, but will send you 150 MS pages before going, if you say so." This is a big promise, even for a man given to making big promises, as Clemens indisputably was, particularly at this moment in his life. No evidence suggests that he had yet experienced a two hundred-page week in working on the *Roughing It* manuscript. The record established by his correspondence, in fact, implies that he may not have written a *total* of two hundred manuscript pages since he began the book five months earlier in late August. Whether or not he could have delivered on such a promise, however, was destined to become an irrelevant question. Within a few days of Clemens's writing this letter, his grand schemes came crashing down around him as his wife again collapsed, seriously ill. The diagnosis was typhoid fever.

Clemens's February 1871 "Memoranda," which he would have submitted to his publishers just before this latest calamity, included a piece entitled "The Dangers of Lying in Bed," whose humor depended on the argument that since many more accidents occurred in the home than on the road, people had a much greater need for accident insurance when they were at rest than when they were in motion. "THE PERIL LAY NOT IN TRAVELLING," its astonished author exclaims, "BUT IN STAYING AT HOME." He continues, "my advice to all people is, Don't stay at home any more than you can help; but when you have *got* to stay at home a while, buy a package of those insurance tickets and sit up nights. You cannot be too cautious." Although it is hardly likely that he meant this as a veiled commentary on his own home life in Buffalo, it was an observation that came abundantly to be borne out by his subsequent experience. For as long as they lived in Buffalo, at least, home was not a safe place for Samuel and Olivia Clemens. During their courtship Clemens took particular pleasure in promulgating a vision of domestic life that stressed shelter, security, repose, and contentment. The "great world" might do its worst, he had written Olivia, "we will let it lighten & thunder, & blow its gusty wrath about our windows & our doors, but never cross our sacred threshold" (12 January 1869). Two years later he stood in the ruins of that dream. Married life offered no special protection against the world's tumultuous thunder, and in fact brought its own burdens of care and vulnerability. The heft of those burdens might eventually strengthen and deepen Mark Twain, but at the time, in early 1871, it all but crushed him. For months Clemens had needed a chance to relax and find his bearings in Buffalo, both personally and professionally, after a spring and summer of uncertainty, distraction, and loss. Instead the fall brought further and even more dire calamities. When Olivia fell ill with typhoid in the dead of winter, just as their first married year was ending, he found himself at his wit's end. There would be no writing a big book now while the nightmare continued; there would be no writing at all.

Chapter Nine

Lighting Out

Olivia Clemens's battle with typhoid, the disease she and her husband had watched claim the life of Emma Nye just a few months earlier, was both serious and protracted. "Sometimes I have hope for my wife," Clemens wrote Elisha Bliss on 15 February 1871, "so I have at this moment—but most of the time it seems to me impossible that she can get well. I cannot go into particulars—the subject is too dreadful." The Buffalo house again filled with nurses and even, he wrote his brother, for a time with "a non-resident physician . . . hired at fifty dollars a day" (22 February 1871). Under the circumstances, his creative life was abruptly suspended, and Mark Twain, the embodiment and the chief manifestation of that life, went into eclipse.

Olivia was stricken with typhoid early in February, very shortly after Clemens had sent off his contribution for the March *Galaxy*. By the eighth of the month her condition was so grave that he dispatched a telegram to Francis P. Church, one of the magazine's editors, asking that the March "Memoranda" column not be published. He could not bear the thought of appearing before the public in his role as humorist at the very moment his wife was dying. It was a fear he had expressed and acted upon in a similar way twice before, during Jervis Langdon's illness the previous summer and when he thought baby Langdon might not survive his first few days in early November. Church's first response to this latest crisis was to advise Clemens that his telegram had arrived too late. "The Galaxy had already gone to press days before," he wrote, "and it was impossible to please you by leaving out the department" (9 February 1871).[1] He was, however, able to act on Clemens's request to suppress *Mark Twain's (Burlesque) Autobiography and First Romance*, the pamphlet that *Galaxy* publisher Isaac E. Sheldon had produced and was at just that time shipping to his agents. "I will tell Sheldon to stop the book," he said. Later that afternoon Church went even further: "I have found after consultation with Sheldon that by delaying & reversing things generally I can leave out Memoranda & gratify your wish & my desire to please you" (9 February 1871).[2] Such gratification, he was careful to point out, did not come without a cost: "It is making a great trouble in the printing office, but as it *can* be done, it *shall* be done." The next day he wrote again to make the same point, saying, "It will delay the Galaxy several days, but I keenly appreciate your feeling & honor you for it."[3] He was joined by Sheldon himself, who in a letter of his own let it register with Clemens that he had "spent all the afternoon in arranging to leave your department out of the March no & I assure you it has been no light task" (10 February 1871).[4] As for the pamphlet, Sheldon said, it might be briefly delayed, but "our orders are very large & our promises & contracts are such that it will be possible to hold it but a few days." So Clemens did manage to suppress his March "Memoranda"—the magazine carrying instead a notice that "the sudden and alarming illness of his wife deprives us this month of his usual contribution"—but he did so only by subjecting himself to a certain indebtedness to his publishers.[5]

Church and Sheldon had good reason for wishing to incur such a debt. Even before the dramatic events of early February, Clemens had made it clear to them that he would drop out of the *Galaxy*, an unhappy development for the magazine, when his contract year ended with the April issue. Together with the unpublished March "Memoranda," he had included his "Farewell" to *Galaxy* readers, leaving it up to Church whether to print it in the March or April issue. Church had chosen to put off its appearance until April even before Clemens asked that he suppress the March column, possibly in the hope that Clemens might reconsider his decision to resign as a contributing editor. There can be little doubt that he was an important *Galaxy* attraction. Since his contract year began, the magazine displayed across the top of its cover, "MARK TWAIN, the Great Humorist, writes for THE GALAXY every Month." By playing upon his senses of guilt and gratitude, Church and Sheldon may have sought to cajole or obligate Clemens into extending rather than terminating his commitment with them. But he was not to be moved, perhaps especially because their subtleties were all but lost in the welter of more immediate and pressing demands he faced at home. His hopes and grand designs for the spring of 1871 were among the earliest casualties of sickness and chagrin. "We have had doctors & watchers & nurses in the house *all* the time for 8 months," he complained to his diamond-field alter ego, John Henry Riley, "& I am disgusted" (3 March 1871). In the throes of yet another sickbed watch, this one more personally harrowing than its predecessors, he admitted to Orion, "I am nearly worn out" (4 March 1871).

It was in this spirit that Clemens came to the end of his con-tractual commitment to the *Galaxy* and terminated his editorial as-sociation with the magazine. "I have now written for THE GALAXY a year," he explained in his April "Valedictory,"

> For the last eight months, with hardly an interval, I have had for my fel-lows and comrades, night and day, doctors and watchers of the sick! Dur-ing these eight months death has taken two members of my home circle and malignantly threatened two others. All this I have experienced, yet all the time been under contract to furnish "humorous" matter once a month for this magazine. . . . Please to put yourself in my place and con-template the grisly grotesqueness of the situation. I think that some of the "humor" I have written during this period could have been injected into a funeral sermon without disturbing the solemnity of the occasion.

The "Valedictory" is ostensibly a statement from Mark Twain, but the circumstances it describes are those of Samuel Clemens, insofar as it serves any purpose to try to distinguish between the two. Clemens, after all, was the one with the "home circle" and its ac-companying domestic burdens; Twain, with his fictive brothers, uncles, and grandmothers, was the untethered one who invented or annihilated a family for himself as the need arose, like Huck Finn. In the "Valedictory" Clemens steps out from behind the Mark Twain mask and confides in his readers not only his reasons for bringing the "Memoranda" column to a close but also his anx-iety that his performance may not have measured up to their ex-pectations and his excuses for falling short. It is an apology that openly acknowledges, even exploits, the interrelationship between Clemens's life and work; it also betrays a characteristic self-doubt about his worthiness or sufficiency as a writer. Perhaps most tellingly, it demonstrates that the mask itself was in many ways almost transparent, that the line between Clemens and Twain was a blurred one, and that both Clemens and his readers were familiar with the nature of that not-quite-double identity.

Taking his public into his confidence, though, would not in itself remedy the plight he found himself in during those last dark months with the *Galaxy*. The very identity of Mark Twain as anything but a flash-in-the-pan celebrity who could on occasion write divertingly for magazines—a "mere humorist," to use a phrase he even then disdained—depended on his ability to do sustained work on a project as substantial and challenging as the California book that had sometime earlier been lost in that darkness.

Before leaving his *Galaxy* audience altogether, Clemens sounded a few notes that seem to have been intended to bolster its confidence, and perhaps his own, in certain bits of what might be called the Mark Twain myth. In bringing his "Valedictory" to an end he said, "At last I am free of the doctors and watchers, and am so exalted in spirits that I will cut this final MEMORANDA very short and go off and enjoy the new state of things. I will put it to pleasant and diligent use in writing a book. I would not print any MEMORANDA at all this month, but the following short sketch has dropped from my pen of its own accord and without any compulsion from me, and so it may as well go in." Resilience and a persistent durability in the face of bad fortune, two Twain hallmarks, have finally carried him to a "new state of things" where the gods will have the chance to regain their accustomed smiles. Writing a book will require diligence, but it will also be "pleasant." In fact, writing is hardly work at all; words, sketches, and eventually entire books drop of their own accord and without compulsion, like the specimen piece accompanying the "Valedictory," which recounts Twain's taking over the production of his uncle's newspaper at the age of thirteen. Sickness and the deaths of loved ones might for a time distract a gifted writer from the effortless magic he practices, but the magic abides, awaiting only the magician's ease to reassert itself. The question is not one of talent, ingenuity, or invention, but simply of opportunity. This vision of writing as magic, a vision absolving the writer of blame, credit, or responsibility for his work, was then and thereafter among the most beguiling and powerful myths in Clemens's repertoire. Such were his temperament and ability, in fact, that at times he was very nearly able to make it a reality. Rarely in his early career had he a greater need to believe in that myth than during the late winter of 1871, when his confidence in his still somewhat dubious gifts gave way to the latest and most serious of his distractions.

The onset of Olivia Clemens's illness in early February widened the already yawning chasm between her husband's intentions regarding the *Roughing It* manuscript and what he was actually able to accomplish. It brought to a standstill work that had at best been limping along by fits and starts since the preceding August. On 4 March 1871 he put the matter plainly to Orion: "I am still nursing Livy night & day & *cannot* write anything." Two weeks later he confided to Bliss, "In three whole months I have hardly written a page of MS" (17 March 1871). Overextended, uncertain of his endowment, and beset by misfortunes even before his wife's sickness, he may well have felt that his protracted unproductivity had placed both his California book and his career in jeopardy. The record of his *Roughing It* output to this point shows that he had good reason to worry.

Clemens's mid-March acknowledgment that he had "hardly written a page" in three months provides a useful point of departure for speculation about the size and nature of the *Roughing It* manuscript he *had* produced before this long interruption. His correspondence, much of it cited in the previous chapter, indicates that the first four chapters of the book were written betwen 28 August and 4 September, 1870, that chapters 5 and 6 were added before 15 September, that chapter 7 and perhaps chapter 8 were completed by 19 September, and that at that point Clemens was "up to page 180" in the manuscript with "only about 1500 to go" (SLC to Elisha Bliss, 19 September 1870). Although he told Bliss in mid-October that he was "driveling along tolerably fairly on the book—getting off from 12 to 20 pages (MS.) a day"—considerable later evidence suggests that he could not have sustained this pace for very long and that he may have produced very little more than those initial 180 manuscript pages by March of 1871. This conjecture is substantially at odds with assumptions customarily made by the book's critics and commentators, many of whom imagine that Clemens driveled along fairly productively during the late fall and winter of 1870–71.[6] As a gloss on the book's composition it is important not simply because it offers a corrective, or at least an alternative, to the prevailing view, but also because it necessarily implies that the burst of creative energy that carried the book to its conclusion was even more formidable than has been supposed.

How much more than those first 180 pages did Clemens write between mid-September 1870 and mid-March 1871? Aside from Clemens himself and perhaps Olivia, the only person likely to have known was Mary Fairbanks, who visited them in Buffalo not long after Langdon's birth in early November 1870. Just before the baby arrived, Clemens had urged her to "Come along . . . & prune my manuscript" (5 November 1870). After she left he wrote Bliss, "Mrs. Fairbanks (my best critic) likes my new book WELL, as far as I have got" (28 November 1870). Inadvertently or otherwise, though, he neglected to say in the letter just how far he had gotten, and apparently no record of Mary Fairbanks's impressions of her visit or of the manuscript have survived. Some light is shed on the matter, however, by Clemens's later correspondence. Just before Olivia fell ill with typhoid, he had written to Bliss, peremptorily offering to go ahead full-tilt with the California book, pledging him "200 pages of MS. every week" and proposing to send along "150 MS pages [before] next Tuesday [31 January]" to show his good faith (27 January 1871). The offer itself proves little, especially since Olivia's imminent collapse prevented his acting upon it, but it may suggest that Clemens had few more than those 150 pages completed at the time. The letter was intended to wring from Bliss a guarantee "without fail [to] *issue* the book on the 15th of May"; it would seem to have been in Clemens's best interest, given this intention, to provide as impressive an initial installment of text as he could, particularly if he were looking to drive a bargain with so shrewd a Yankee businessman as he took Bliss to be. Whatever the case, the record implies that the 150 manuscript pages Clemens offered Bliss on 27 January 1871 were probably those he had written before 19 September 1870.

The 27 January letter is revealing in at least one other way. In it Clemens promises to send Bliss "200 pages of MS. every week . . . & finish it all up the 15th of April"—that is, to write two hundred pages a week for about ten weeks, producing a total of about two thousand manuscript pages. At the time he should certainly have known how much manuscript was required to make the kind of six-hundred-page book called for in the *Roughing It* contract; he had produced just such a book, *The Innocents Abroad*, not long before. In the 19 September letter, where he reported to Bliss having finished one hundred and eighty pages of manuscript, he added, "only about 1500 to write." The clear implication is that he imagined he needed a total of about one thousand seven hundred manuscript pages. But the scheme he proposed to Bliss in late January, with its implicit pledge of about two thousand additional pages (or, say, one thousand five hundred pages, if he meant to allow himself two to three weeks for revision), indicates that he could hardly have been much further along at that time than he was in September. These inferences suggest, although of course they cannot prove, that Clemens produced very little manuscript after his initial spurt in the fall of 1870. As it happened, Olivia's falling ill in early February effectively consigned this latest battery of promises to limbo, and in the end he sent Bliss no manuscript at all.

By the time he could return to *Roughing It*, the long winter of 1870–71 drawing to a close and his wife's precarious health returning, Clemens understandably felt that changes were in order. In the early spring he began making some. "I have come at last to loathe Buffalo so bitterly," he wrote Riley, "that yesterday I advertised our dwelling house for sale" (3 March 1871). His share in the *Express* was also to go on the block, bringing his connection with the city entirely to a close and at last substantiating rumors about his intending to leave that had begun to circulate virtually from the moment the newlywed Clemenses had taken up housekeeping there. He and Olivia would spend the summer in Elmira, he told Riley, and eventually "build a house in Hartford just like this one." From the beginning there had been nothing wrong with the house, their wedding house, and certainly it had been the gift of the right people, Olivia's parents. It had simply stood in the wrong city. Jervis Langdon's influence had brought them to that city, and their leaving it was to some extent a measure of their unhappiness there and also of Clemens's readiness to step out of his father-in-law's shadow.

Regarding his work Clemens was emphatic: "I quit the Galaxy

with the current number," he informed Riley in his 3 March letter, "& shall write no more for any periodical. . . . Shall simply write books." The next day he reiterated these plans in a letter to Orion, plainly expecting his brother to represent both his intentions and his frame of mind to Bliss: "We shall go to Elmira ten days hence . . . & stay there till I have finished the California book—say three months. But I can't begin work right away when I get there—*must* have a week's rest, for I have been through 30 days' terrific siege. That makes it after the middle of March before I can go fairly to work—& then I'll have to hump myself & not lose a moment." It may be worth noting that the interval he says he needs to finish the *Roughing It* manuscript, even if he humps himself and doesn't lose a moment, is about the same as, or even a bit longer than, that he specified at the end of January. Again the implication, given his expressed intention to work at his best pace (allegedly, two hundred pages per week), is that very little of the manuscript lay behind him.

How little? At least a partial answer to that question emerges from the record of Clemens's comments and behavior as he tried to return to composing the book. While the 4 March letter to his brother dramatizes his tribulations and emphasizes his determination to get back to work, it also, if a bit more subtly, reveals the frustration, guilt, anger, and defensiveness of a man who feels put upon not only by the Fates but also by his publisher. In his oblique but unrelenting way, and often through Orion, increasingly his hostage and go-between, Bliss had begun again to press his most salable author for copy; he wanted to see *some* manuscript from the California book, and he needed something under Mark Twain's by-line to draw attention to the *American Publisher*, the advertising venture he had hired Orion to edit. Convincing himself that he was being poorly used, particularly by a publisher, was never a matter of great difficulty for Clemens, and the 4 March letter consequently has about it the edge of a complaint. "You & Bliss put yourselves in my place," he wrote Orion, "& you will see that my hands are full & *more* than full. When I told Bliss in N.Y. that I would write something for the Publisher *I* could not know that I was just about to lose FIFTY DAYS. Do you see the difference it makes?"

Then, having worked himself into something of a dudgeon, he

made another of his promises, this one with a proviso: "Just as soon as ever I can, I will send some of the book MS., but right in the first chapter I have got to alter the whole style of one of my characters & re-write him clear through to where I am now. It is no fool of a job I can tell you, but the book will be greatly bettered by it.—Hold on a few days—four or five,—& I will see if I can get a few chapters fixed & send to Bliss." The implication here is that despite his claim of having lost fifty days' work, Clemens had at the very least been thinking about the manuscript and had determined the necessity of a sweeping revision. It may be prudent to wonder when, during the hectic winter of 1870–71, he found the opportunity for this penetrating and uncharacteristic editorial reflection, especially since he claims in the same letter that he is "still nursing Livy night & day & *cannot* write anything," but critics have tended to accept his declaration here as unskeptically as Orion evidently did and to set about the business of identifying the altered character, offering in the process conjectures regarding the terms of and reasons for his alteration. Their ingenuity notwithstanding, the fact is that only a single figure, the narrator, is present "all the way through" the early chapters of *Roughing It*. And while it is possible to imagine Clemens describing him as "one of my characters" and speaking of altering his "style," that language seems curiously and atypically imprecise as a means of indicating a change in the narrator—that is, essentially, a change in voice.[7]

Given the context of frustration in which the 4 March letter was written and bearing particularly in mind the feelings of indignation and inadequacy that tormented Clemens at the time, a skeptic might be forgiven for raising a further possibility: the character in need of alteration was itself a piece of fiction, a creature Clemens conjured—with some justification, he probably felt—to keep Orion and Bliss at bay while he made his way back to the long-neglected manuscript. He may well have needed to buy time to "get a few chapters fixed," but under the circumstances that "fixing" might have involved Clemens's assessing and reacquainting himself with work he had done months earlier rather than his revising a character no one has yet convincingly identified. Exhausted and beleaguered, perhaps he stretched the truth in dealing with Orion, who was after all dunning him at the very worst time on Bliss's behalf. Perhaps there was no "altered character," only a driven and uncertain writer whose ability to do sustained, coherent work was very much in doubt.

Clemens's excuses and protestations did not mollify Bliss, who largely ignored both in applying his own peculiar brand of pressure, a tactic compounded of about equal parts hurt, disappointment, and dismay. "I was in hopes Orion found something from you on my return," he wrote Clemens on 7 March 1871, "but poor Orion says he has nothing from you relating to matters."[8] The reference to "poor Orion" would remind Clemens of Bliss's doing him the favor of hiring his brother in the first place and perhaps even imply that Clemens was keeping Orion—and conceivably Bliss as well—"poor" by producing no manuscript. "Now then," Bliss chided, "if you have got as far as to give us something I think it would be well to get at it very soon." Then too, there was the matter of the *American Publisher*, the enterprise upon which Orion's welfare most directly depended. Bliss's appeal on behalf of the *Publisher* was couched in even more plainly personal terms: "We trust you will not disappoint us this month."

Orion again wrote the next day, doing his part in a campaign that Bliss was clearly directing. In his 4 March letter Clemens had indicated his intention to move eventually to Hartford and had asked about taxes and furniture storage there. From Hartford Orion responded, plaintively, "We will hunt up any information you want, and do anything else you want done, if you will only write"—that is, if Clemens would only produce manuscript for the American Publishing Company.[9] Of Bliss and his hopes of making a go of the *Publisher* Orion wrote, "He is in earnest. He is decidedly worked up about it. He says, put yourself in our place. . . . Squarely, we *must* have something from you, or we run the risk of going to the dickens."

From his outpost in Buffalo Clemens capitulated. "Tell Bliss 'all right,'" he wrote Orion; "I will try to give him a chapter from the *new* book every month or nearly every month, for the Publisher" (9 March 1871). Seen against the backdrop of his other pledges, predictions, and promises, this may not seem a major concession, but it did acknowledge Clemens's sense of obligation to Bliss—particularly in light of his having declared the intention less than a week earlier to "write no more for any periodical"— and it did signal his commitment to return to the *Roughing It* manuscript. Of the book he told Orion in the same letter, "I have got several chapters (168 pages MS.) revised & ready for printers & artists, but for the sake of security shall get somebody to copy it & then send the original to [Bliss]."

At least two observations might be made about this 9 March progress report on the book, one regarding the scope of the manuscript and the other concerning its status as "revised and ready." Of the latter point: on 4 March Clemens claimed to have discovered a character "right in the first chapter" in need of alteration "all the way through." For him to say on 9 March that 168 manuscript pages were "revised & ready for printers" implies that he somehow managed at least a considerable portion of that comprehensive revision—"no fool of a job," as he put it—in just five days, all the while "nursing Livy night & day." To the extent that this accomplishment seems improbable, even for a writer as susceptible to fits of creativity as Mark Twain, it reinforces speculation that the "altered character" was a ploy or a "stretcher." Of the former point, the scope or size of the manuscript, it might simply be remarked that Clemens had spoken of having produced 180 pages as early as 19 September 1870 and had proposed, on 27 January 1871, to send Bliss 150 pages. That he speaks of having just 168 pages "ready" on 9 March 1871 promotes the suspicion—although, again, it cannot confirm it—that Clemens added little or nothing to the *Roughing It* manuscript during the fall and winter of 1870–71.

That suspicion is further reinforced by Clemens's writing to Orion the next day, 10 March, asking, as he had before, for help in recalling details of the overland journey: "Please sit down right away & torture your memory & write down in minute detail every fact & exploit in the desperado Slade's life. . . . I want to make up a telling chapter from it for the book." The desperado Slade would appear toward the end of chapter 9 in *Roughing It*, and his history would occupy all of chapters 10 and 11. In trying to rekindle his memories of Slade, Clemens had written to Hezekiah Hosmer, postmaster of Virginia City, for Slade recollections and anecdotes, but he had done so on 15 September 1870, almost six months before making this request of Orion.[10] An available inference, and one that gains force in the context of other contemporaneous evidence, is that during the six months in question Clemens had managed to get only marginally beyond the six chapters he mentioned having written in the Hosmer letter. Whatever the case, Orion responded promptly to the request on 11 March 1871, and Clemens eventually made substantial use of that response in treating Slade.[11]

At the time of these exchanges Clemens was putting in his last days in Buffalo, the city he had come to loathe so bitterly that he took heavy losses in liquidating his assets there, watching over his still-ailing wife, and, apparently, muttering through clenched teeth as he considered the incandescent success of Bret Harte, his chief rival among "western" writers.[12] "Do you know who is the most celebrated man in America to-day?" he asked Riley in his 3 March 1871 letter, "the man whose name is on every single tongue from one end of the continent to the other? It is Bret Harte. . . . His journey east to Boston was a perfect torchlight procession of eclat & homage." Watching that brilliant progress from the domestic and professional shadows that had come to engulf him in Buffalo, Clemens was quick to spot accomplices to his misfortune. While his complaints against Bliss and Orion, in this case, fall short of the paranoiac vituperations that characterize his later career, they nevertheless bear the stamp of those dark ravings. "Now why do you & Bliss go on urging me to make promises?" he asked Orion in a letter of 11 March 1871 concerning the pledge he had made to them only two days earlier to be a monthly contributor to the *American Publisher*. "I have suffered damnation itself in the trammels of periodical writing and I will *not* appear once a month nor once in *three* months, in the Publisher nor any other periodical."

Clemens had just completed his year-long obligation to provide monthly "Memoranda" for the *Galaxy* when he sent this letter off. His writing regularly for a magazine had not, as he had hoped and expected, provided him the chance to enhance his reputation by going before the public in a more relaxed and reflective way than his newspaper work allowed. Mulling Harte's success, rather, he managed to convince himself that he had compromised his own popularity by appearing too often, and trivially, in print.[13] Under these circumstances it was easy to discover villainy in Bliss and Orion's nagging him for copy and thereby to deflect or ignore the real issue, his own unproductivity on the *Roughing It* manuscript. "There isn't money enough between hell & Hartford to hire me to write once a month for *any* periodical," he wrote Orion. "The more I turn it over in my mind how your & Bliss's letters of yesterday are making the Publisher a paper which the people are to understand is Mark Twain's paper & to sink or swim on his reputation, the more outrageous I get." When it came to cultivating a hurt or an imagined abuse, even so early in his career, Clemens *could* be outrageous: "I lay awake all last night," he told Orion, "aggravating myself with this prospect of seeing my hated nom de plume (for I do loathe the very sight of it,) in print *again* every month. . . . As for being the high chief contributor & main card of the Publisher, I won't hear of it for a single moment. I'd rather break my pen & stop writing just where I am." Given how little writing he apparently had done since the preceding fall and the sense of oppression he clearly felt at the prospect of resuming his work, the temptation to find a justification for breaking his pen must have been considerable.

Clemens uncharacteristically brooded over the 11 March letter for two days before mailing it—to allow his mind "to cool," he said. He seems to have spent the time nurturing his indignation. "The more I think of it the more I feel wronged," he added on 13 March, indulging himself in a series of insinuations to the effect that Bliss had regularly taken advantage of him and proposing a disclaimer to appear in the *Publisher* saying that Mark Twain would "doubtless appear less frequently than any other contributor." Taken as a whole, the letter is a convincing demonstration of Clemens's capacities for self-dramatization and scapegoating. Beneath the outrage and outrageousness, however, runs the poignant appeal of a very public man who wants to regain his privacy, who wants, in fact, to disappear. "I must & will keep shady & quiet till Bret Harte simmers down a little," he wrote Orion, "& then I mean to go up head again & *stay* there. . . . I will 'top' Bret Harte again or bust. But I can't do it by dangling eternally in the public view."

Clemens's concern for how he fared in the public view was genuine and at times obsessive. Recent critics and readers, viewing the beginnings of his career from a distance of more than a hundred years, can easily fail to recognize that in the early 1870s Mark Twain was not yet the national institution with which they are so familiar. He was regarded at the time, rather, as one of a number of Pacific Slope writers—perhaps the best of the lot, perhaps not

quite so good as Bret Harte—who had begun to find a wider audience. No one, including Clemens himself, knew whether he had
in him a sequel to *The Innocents Abroad*, and no one understood
more pointedly than he how accidentally that first book had come
into being. Now, with the spring thaws of 1871, his domestic circumstances were changing for the better, changing in such a way
as to make it possible for him to return full-time to the task of writing that sequel. On 14 March he wrote Mary Fairbanks that "Livy
was decidedly & distinctly out of danger & . . . had become wonderfully better & hungrier & chattier & cheerfuller." Olivia's improvement coincided with Clemens's escaping Buffalo, ridding
himself of the *Express*, and cutting his ties with the *Galaxy*. As his
worries and obligations fell away, however, so did the ground
upon which he based his excuses for not writing. For the first time
in months he was "free" to confront the expectations of his public
over his writing desk and to face directly the question his audience,
his publisher, and he himself were asking: Could he write a second
book? "The Great Public's is the only opinion worth having," he
wrote Orion on 15 March; the time had come when he could no
longer put off working to regain his place in that public's
imagination.

Clemens was emerging from the oppressions of misfortune, illness, and obligation to take on the burden of self-discipline necessary to sustain him in writing *Roughing It*. "I am & have been for
weeks so buried under beetling Alps of trouble," he told Orion,
"that yours look like little passing discomforts to me" (15 March
1871). During his last, despairing days in Buffalo his anxieties
about the work that lay ahead rose up to meet those that seemed at
last to lie behind. He wrote his brother, in the same letter, "I am
simply half-crazy—that is the truth. And I wish I was the other
half."

Two days later he again resorted to the lexicon of madness, this
time in writing to Bliss. The letter begins, "Out of this chaos of
my household . . . ," ends with Clemens proposing to "butt my
frantic brains out & try to get some peace," and closes, "Yours, in
perfect distraction." The body of the letter is a maelstrom of indignation, confession, apology, outrage, petulance, and resolution.
Bliss had written a characteristically chastening and manipulative
note on 15 March, deftly assuming the role of the wounded in-

nocent. "I cannot conceive what we have done to draw your fire so strongly," he said, referring to the explosion of anger and in-nuendo Clemens had aimed at Orion two days earlier in refusing to be obligated to the *American Publisher*.[14] Sensing, perhaps, that Bliss had taken the high ground from him, Clemens exercised his own talent for self-justifying lamentation:

You do not know what it is to be in a state of absolute frenzy—despera-tion. I had rather die twice over than repeat the last six months of my life. . . . Do you know that for *seven weeks* I have not had my natural rest but have been a night-&-day sick-nurse to my wife?—& am still—& shall continue to be for two or three weeks longer—yet must turn in now & write a damned *humorous* article for the Publisher, because I have *promised* it—promised it when I thought that the vials of hellfire bottled up for my benefit *must* be about emptied.—By the living God I don't believe they ever *will* be emptied.

This was Clemens's last transmission from Buffalo. The next day he and his family left the city for a protracted stay in Elmira before settling in Hartford. No rendition is likely to match his own in dra-matizing the "frenzy" to which the catastrophes of the Buffalo res-idence drove him. Then and later he tended to think of the time he and Olivia spent there as a torture. "Our year and a half in Buffalo . . . saturated us with horrors and distress," he declared in his "Au-tobiographical Dictation," claiming that they finally made the break for Elmira and beyond "when we could endure imprison-ment no longer."[15] Elsewhere in that dictation he described the days immediately preceding Emma Nye's death in the late summer of 1870 as being "among the blackest, the gloomiest, the most wretched of my long life."[16] His last weeks in Buffalo must surely have vied for that distinction. Perhaps what mitigated his recollec-tion of them was that in retrospect he recognized that Emma Nye's death was among the early disasters of 1870–71, in its way herald-ing those that were to follow. These dark last days in Buffalo, con-versely, led to a brightening.

When Clemens complained to Bliss on 17 March 1871 that "in three whole months I have hardly written a page of MS," he in-advertently corroborated his 4 March lament to Orion that he had lost fifty days' work; in fact, it considerably extends the period dur-ing which he admits having made no progress on *Roughing It*.

Taken literally, it implies that his last bout of sustained work on the manuscript took place in mid-December 1870. Other evidence, such as his correspondence with Hezekiah Hosmer and with Orion about the Slade chapters and his intimations to Orion and to Bliss about the number of pages he had completed, however, suggests that even this admission fails to give a true measure of his inattention to the book, which seems more likely to have extended over five or six months rather than three. Whatever the case, as he left Buffalo the full weight of the obligations he had undertaken during the preceding year came pressing down upon him. "If I *dared* fly in the face of Providence & make one more promise," he wrote Bliss, "I would say that if I ever get out of this infernal damnable chaos I am whirling in at home, I will go to work & amply & fully & freely fulfill some of the promises I have been making to you— but I don't dare! Bliss—I don't dare!" He was, though, at long last able to deliver on one of those promises. The 160 pages of *Roughing It* manuscript that he had mentioned in his 10 March letter to Orion were back from the copyist. In sending these initial chapters to Bliss, Clemens said he found "nothing . . . that can be transferred to the Publisher"; however, he added, "When I get to Elmira I will look over the *next* chapters & send something—or, failing that, will write something—my own obituary I hope it will be."

This last Buffalo letter hit most of the notes that Clemens would sound with increasing stridency and bitterness at the far end of his career. But unlike those later protestations it allowed for the possibility of release and renewal. The damnable chaos was still external and circumstantial, not woven into the fabric of personality, of experience. So Clemens could say to Bliss, "Now do you see?— I want *rest*. I want to get clear away from all hamperings, all harassments. I am going to shut myself up in a farm-house alone, on top of an Elmira hill, & *write*—on my book. I will see no company, & worry about nothing. I will never make another promise again of any kind, that *can* be avoided, so help me God." The Clemenses left Buffalo for Elmira the next day, Olivia's frail health requiring her to make the trip on a mattress. In the former city they had passed the first year of their marriage, harried by calamities that deepened and persisted through its long winter. In the latter they were to spend most of the next twenty summers. It was 18 March 1871; spring had arrived.

Chapter Ten

Coming of Age in Elmira

Elmira must have seemed more than ever a haven to the fugitive Clemenses as they made their way there in the spring of 1871, driven by the devastations they had suffered in Buffalo into a retreat that offered them a chance at recuperation. Owing to the various calamities and confinements that beset them in Buffalo, neither had been in Elmira since the preceding August, when Jervis Langdon had died. For Olivia especially this homecoming of sorts, however welcome, was tinged with misgiving. Two months earlier she had written of Elmira to her friend Alice Day, "I dread very much my first visit at home—I know that I shall realize more than I possibly can away from there that Father has left us never to return any more."[1] Olivia intuited that her father's death would necessarily change the nature of "home" and alter the status of those he left behind. She may or may not have foreseen that in the absence of her father her husband would become the dominant figure in the domestic circle they were rejoining.[2]

Moving to Elmira essentially returned or restored Olivia to her family's keeping and lifted the burden of her care from Clemens's shoulders, enabling him, as he had hoped and pledged, to shut himself up in a farmhouse and write on his book. The farmhouse itself, once a stonecutter's cottage, was the main feature of a tract the family called Quarry Farm, a place that was to be from that time on a principal influence on the character and development of Mark Twain. The Langdons had bought the property, situated at the top of East Hill, overlooking Elmira and the Chemung Valley, as an upland rural retreat in 1869. At his death Jervis Langdon left

Quarry Farm. (Courtesy Elmira College)

the farm to his elder daughter, Susan, Olivia's adopted sister, and to Susan's husband, Theodore Crane. When the Clemenses arrived in Elmira in March 1871, most family activity, especially given Olivia's invalid condition, was still centered on the commodious Langdon home on Elmira's Main Street. With Olivia comfortably in the hands of relatives and servants, Clemens was able almost daily to make the two-and-a-half-mile climb to the Quarry Farm hilltop and there to work on fulfilling his manifold obligations.

After he had been in Elmira just two days, in fact, he began living up to the promises he had made to Elisha Bliss by sending him a long-awaited submission for the *American Publisher*. "Here is my contribution," Clemens wrote, "(I take it from the book,) & by all odds it is the finest piece of writing I ever did" (20 March 1871). He enclosed what was to become chapter 8 of *Roughing It*, the pony-express episode, taken, he said, "from along about the 160th to 170th page of the MS." Since he had mailed Bliss the first 160 pages just before leaving Buffalo, it seems fair to assume that the pony-express chapter immediately followed them. That those 160 pages comprise the first seven chapters of the book as it was eventually printed is suggested by Clemens's disinclination, made clear in subsequent correspondence, to make substantial revisions in the manuscript before publication.

How much more of *Roughing It* had Clemens written by the time he left Buffalo? When, for that matter, did he write the pony-express episode? The record of his correspondence sheds little light on either question. In fact, the note which accompanied his submission of the pony-express material to Bliss on 20 March was followed by two weeks of silence, a virtual news blackout from Quarry Farm. While he may have completed the pony-express chapter considerably earlier—when he was "driveling along tolerably fairly," say, in October of 1870—he seems hardly to have got much further than that in the ensuing months, as seen in his 10 March 1871 appeal to Orion for information about the desperado Slade that would eventually help to shape chapters 9–11.[3] It is even conceivable that he dashed off the pony-express episode between the time he arrived in Elmira and the time he sent it off to Bliss two days later. Perhaps the likeliest conjecture, however, is that he deliberately held back the pony-express chapter when he mailed the first block of manuscript from Buffalo, thereby allowing himself the chance not only to placate Bliss with a submission for the *Publisher* two days later but also to give the impression that the submission was drawn from a substantial portion of additional manuscript. Bliss, equal to his part in any cat-and-mouse drama, responded rather coolly to Clemens's enthusiasm for the episode by using less than half of it in the *Publisher*.

To ask why Bliss might want to dampen the spirits of the most popular author in his stable is to glimpse a complex relationship between two very clever and very suspicious men at just the time it was assuming its full complement of quirky convolutions. What particularly provoked Bliss at the time, apart from Clemens's glacial progress on the *Roughing It* manuscript, his reluctance to contribute to the *American Publisher*, and his charge that the American Publishing Company was "crowding" him, was the appearance in March 1871 of *Mark Twain's (Burlesque) Autobiography and First Ro-*

mance, published by Isaac Sheldon. Bliss had to handle Clemens's defection from the company gingerly, but he clearly felt wronged by what he regarded as Clemens's disloyalty, especially since the *Roughing It* contract specifically forbade that Clemens "write or furnish manuscript for any other book unless for said company" while *Roughing It* was in preparation.[4] To make a bad matter worse, the *(Burlesque) Autobiography* was little more than a quick and careless attempt to capitalize on Mark Twain's popularity. Its insubstantiality and its consequent failure to find a wide audience threatened to diminish Twain's reputation, a reputation upon which Bliss, like Clemens, was banking. Bliss was determined not to allow Clemens again to jeopardize the company's best interests by straying into schemes involving other publishers, and he was quick to spot and discourage feelings of overconfidence or independence. The strategy he evolved, perhaps without quite intending to, was to try to keep Clemens sufficiently at ease regarding his talent and popularity to enable him to function as a writer but always to leave him slightly off balance, chronically in need of reassurance and support.

However much or little of this strategy Clemens may have discerned, he had begun by the time he negotiated the *Roughing It* contract to regard Bliss as the archetypal Gilded Age entrepreneur and to treat him with befitting measures of admiration and caution. "Bliss is the very liveliest kind of a Yankee business man," he warned Orion when his brother wrote about plans for a new invention. "Don't reveal anything to him about your main, big machine, but at the proper time if there is any money or success in it you can just rely on him every time to *get it out of it*" (after 2 November 1870). Clemens's lifelong, ambivalent fascination with successful men of business, the carnivores of the marketplace, as he came to see them, may not have begun with his relationship with Elisha Bliss—that distinction may well have belonged to Jervis Langdon—but it must have been furthered by that relationship. From time to time the wariness that became habitual between the two men could harden to distrust, a sentiment they rarely expressed overtly. Clemens brought the matter into the open when he wrote Bliss, concerning his own intention to live up to the *Roughing It* contract, "You see you can't get it out of your head that I am a sort of rascal, but I ain't. I can stick to you just as long as you can stick to me, & give you odds" (2 August 1870). It was language that either man could have applied to the other. Just a year earlier, in fact, Bliss had responded to an insinuating letter from Clemens, "hereafter, if you want to say such things to me again, just come out plain & call me a d——d cheat & scoundrel—which will really it seems to me cover the whole ground & be a great deal more brief."[5]

Suspecting that he was dealing with a rascal, or that he was re-garded as one, occasionally brought out the rascal in Clemens. Misrepresenting his progress on the *Roughing It* manuscript may have been one manifestation of this penchant; publishing the *(Bur-lesque) Autobiography* was pretty surely another; sending John Henry Riley off to be his eyes and ears in Africa has, for all his enthusiasm for the project, the look of a third. It might still come as something of a shock, though, to discover that shortly after es-tablishing himself in Elmira, Clemens apparently corresponded with Isaac Sheldon about the possibility of Sheldon's publishing a *novel* he had in mind. On 4 April 1871 Sheldon responded, "As regards the story, I like the idea & it would sell well if it were a good story & had a quiet vein of humor. . . . I do not see why you could not write such a story."[6] Two days later Clemens wrote back, "I am glad you agree with me. I begin to think I can get up quite a respectable novel, & mean to fool away some of my odd hours in the attempt, anyway." Although the proposed novel never came into being, Clemens's flirtation with Sheldon about it indicates that Bliss had hardly cured his wanderlust. Not only did the negotia-tions with Sheldon take place directly in the wake of the contro-versy surrounding his publication of the *(Burlesque) Autobiography*; they also occurred while Clemens was under exclusive contract with Bliss for *three* books, the first of which was already three months overdue and, by anybody's reckoning, very largely unwritten.

Perhaps the most remarkable thing about Clemens's exchange with Sheldon is that a man who could write convincingly of butt-ing his frantic brains out on 17 March could toy with the notion of fooling away some of his odd hours in writing a novel on 6 April. To observe by way of explanation that Clemens's was a "mercurial temperament" is in this case to try to stretch a commonplace be-yond its reasonable limits. The real answer to the puzzle presented by his dramatic change in attitude probably lay in Quarry Farm itself, and in the realization of Clemens's wish to find solitude, refreshment, and peace there. His perch on East Hill allowed him an outlook that was literally above the cares of the city below; it set him apart, in place and time, from the kinds of obligations, responsibilities, and interruptions that had made his life in Buffalo unendurable. The logistics of his circumstances in Elmira that spring helped establish the rhythms he would follow during his most productive periods for the rest of his life. After breakfast in town he would set off for his hilltop, working there without a break until just before dinnertime, often sharing a portion of the day's work with his family in the evening. It was for him the right combination of isolation and belonging, of solitude and nurture. A certain sense of separation, not just from the cares of domestic life, but from domestic life altogether, seems to have been an important condition of freeing Clemens to function as Mark Twain.

When, after the two-week hiatus, progress reports on the *Roughing It* manuscript began flowing out of Elmira, they were distinguished by a change in tone. Lamentation, justification, and apology gave way to buoyant enthusiasm. From the very first report Clemens turned the tables and began pushing Bliss about the book's production schedule. On 4 April 1871 he wrote to Orion, "Is Bliss doing anything with the MS I sent? Is he thinking of beginning on it shortly?" At this point the manuscript Clemens had sent Bliss amounted, apparently, to the first eight chapters of the book—about 180 pages, by his own count. By "beginning on it" Clemens probably meant beginning the process of selecting and commissioning illustrations as well as setting the book in type, particularly with an eye toward the production of the prospectuses that Bliss's canvassers would use in their sales pitches. It seems a bold question considering how little of that book Clemens had placed in Bliss's hands.

Behind Clemens's brashness, though, was the surge of creativity he seems to have experienced during those two initial weeks at Quarry Farm. For the first time in months—perhaps since the preceding September—he had managed to do sustained and sustaining work on the manuscript; the book which had seemed dead or doomed had come alive. In the 4 April letter he told Orion, "In moving from Buffalo here I have lost certain notes & documents—

among them what you wrote for me about the difficulties of opening up the Territorial government in Nevada & getting the machinery to running. And now, just at the moment that I want it, it
is gone. . . . Have you time to scribble something again, to aid my
memory[?] Little characteristic items like Whittlesey's refusing to
allow for the knife, &c are the most illuminating things." The request helps to locate Clemens in the manuscript and to chart his
progress. "The struggles of a new-born Territorial government to
get a start in this world," including the knife incident, are part of
chapter 25 of *Roughing It*. That he claims to be ready to work on
this material "just at the moment" indicates that by 4 April 1871
he was closely approaching that section of the book.

By 20 March Clemens had sent Bliss the book's first eight chapters; by 4 April he was preparing for what would be chapter 25.
Just how many of the intervening seventeen chapters were written
during those first two weeks in Elmira, no one can say with certainty. Had he been able to match the facility he demonstrated in
producing later portions of the book, he could quite conceivably
have written all seventeen during that period. Critics have been reluctant to make a claim of this kind, preferring, generally, to credit
Clemens with having made some substantial contribution to
Roughing It during the fall and winter of 1870–71. Given, on the
one hand, his travails, dodges, and apologies while in Buffalo and,
on the other, his ebullience and aggressiveness after two weeks of
writing in Elmira, it seems reasonable to speculate that the first,
invigorating explosion of work at Quarry Farm may well have
been considerably more energetic and productive than has typically
been acknowledged.

Chapters 9–25 are among the most vivid and strategic in *Roughing It*, fixing the book's tone and developing the tensions that lend
it complexity and resonance. They begin with the Slade episode
(chapters 9–11 of the first edition), which Clemens could *not* have
written before mid-March 1871, given his 10 March letter to
Orion, and end with the attempt to establish a fledgling legislature
in the Nevada Territory. In their undeliberate way, that is to say,
they move from a depiction of desperado lawlessness to the feeble
beginnings of communal lawmaking. Although he is anything but
philosophically consistent, here and elsewhere, Clemens is considerably drawn to the wildness of the West, epitomized in the Over-

land Stage Company's Rocky Ridge division, a "very paradise of outlaws," a place where "violence was the rule [and] force . . . the only recognized authority" (*RI*, p. 93). Like the West generally, it is a man's land, dominated for a time by the intrepid Slade, "a man of peerless bravery" (*RI*, p. 104). The West in these chapters might be described not only as uncivilized, for better and for worse, but also as either antedomestic or antidomestic. A brutal reduction of conventional domesticity prevails here, as for instance in the overland stage stations, where the rocking chairs and sofas of eastern sitting rooms are represented by a scattering of three-legged stools and greasy pine-board benches and where table service consists of a few pieces of battered tinware. It is a place not yet "ready" for women, a kind of never-never land with guns and gold and Goshoot Indians. White shirts and manners are not simply optional here but scorned as the earmarks of the "emigrant," that pitiful eastern arrival whose complacency over "the cut of his New York coat" and genteel grammar necessarily fails him in the presence of "that proudest and blessedest creature that exists on all the earth, a 'FORTY-NINER'" (*RI*, pp. 138–39). The eastern emigrant is an adult—but certainly not a *man*—in a world of "boys" whose perfect happiness it is to be wholly unfettered by his restraints and to celebrate that freedom in their dress. "I had grown well accustomed to wearing a damaged slouch hat, blue woolen shirt, and pants crammed into boot-tops," the narrator says, "and gloried in the absence of coat, vest and braces. I felt rowdyish and 'bully'" (*RI*, p. 162).

Married life is presented in these pages chiefly through the distorting lens provided by the narrator's burlesque accounts of Mormon polygamy. His rowdyish and bully freedom is strikingly juxtaposed to the nightmare confinement of Brigham Young, whose legions of wives and children make him a prisoner of his commitments and responsibilities. "Bless my soul," Young moans to him, "you don't know anything about married life. It is a perfect dog's life, sir—a perfect dog's life" (*RI*, p. 125). The life of choice, by contrast, is one of adolescent male camaraderie and irresponsibility, the kind of life epitomized in the idyll the narrator experiences at Lake Tahoe with his friend Johnny K——. Reflecting on that time at the beginning of chapter 23 he says, "If there is any life that is happier than the life we led on our timber ranch for the next two or three weeks, it must be a sort of life which I have not read of in books or experienced in person. We did not see a human being but ourselves during the time, or hear any sounds but those that were made by the wind and the waves, the sighing of the pines, and now and then the far-off thunder of an avalanche" (*RI*, p. 167). The same carelessness that both typifies this way of life and makes it possible, however, eventually brings it to an end when the narrator's neglected campfire rages to consume the Tahoe timber tract he and Johnny had claimed, leaving them "homeless wanderers again, without any property" (*RI*, p. 170).

In their celebration of this wayward, rootless, heedless life, these early chapters of the California book stand in contrast to the "imprisonment" Clemens claimed to have suffered in Buffalo. In their boy's dream of the West as a man's land uncluttered by any but the most rudimentary rules and largely free of social constraint, they offer an early rendition of an idealized territory into which, throughout his career, he would attempt to light out. In their rejection or reduction of domestic conventions, and particularly in their sometimes slighting, sometimes idolatrous, treatment of women, they suggest an adolescent impulse to flee rather than confront the realities of home and hearth. In their proclaiming the superiority of the happiness they describe to any he has known since, they imply that the satisfactions of adulthood, including those of marriage, even of marriage to an angel, are only second best. If, as seems likely, many of these chapters were written from his roost at Quarry Farm, they may well reflect the disburdening and exhilaration he experienced there, above and apart from a world of grownup cares—of obligation, decorum, family ties and roots—which, like his narrator, he rejoiced to leave behind.

One of the three extant manuscript pages Clemens wrote for the book peculiarly corroborates the notion that at some level of consciousness these early chapters tacitly reject adult cares and attachments. The page, a fragment of about one hundred words, was originally a part of what became chapter 12 of *Roughing It*, an account of the narrator's arrival at the Great Divide and his fascination at discovering two streams there, one destined for the Gulf of California and the other for the Gulf of Mexico. In the book, he contemplates the journey of the eastbound stream, a journey reversing the course of his own, and imagines it finally managing to "pass the Gulf and enter into its rest upon the bosom of the tropic sea, never to look upon its snow-peaks again or regret them." "I freighted a leaf with a mental message for the friends at home," he says, "and dropped it in the stream. But I put no stamp on it and it was held for postage somewhere" (*RI*, p. 109).

The manuscript page in question offers an earlier version of this episode, a version Clemens apparently chose to discard:

[The eastbound stream would eventually] pass the Gulf and enter into its rest upon the bosom of the tropic sea, never to look westward again.

The incident had such a gentle air of romance about it that I was subdued into a vein of thoughtfulness; & as I sat dreaming of the wanderings of my leaf across the continent, & the vague possibility that many weeks to come *she* might take it out of the water as it drifted by the old city, & by the unerring instinct of love know instantly the tender freight it bore, the tears came into my eyes. However, when I reflected that I had forgotten to put a postage stamp on it. . . .[7]

Clemens may have rejected the fragment for a number of reasons, including its somewhat incongruous rendition of the narrator as a treacly sentimentalist or its implication of a love interest in his life antedating Olivia Langdon, but in more general terms he may have excised it because he recognized how out of character it would have been for Mark Twain to be romantically involved with a woman, even if that involvement amounted to no more than puppy love. The taboo here is not so much against sex or affection or even sentimentality as against the most fundamental of those attachments that compromise an adolescent's fleeting freedom. At his best or most characteristic, Mark Twain came to be poised at the fringes of that scant free territory, either behind his own mask or behind those of such alter egos as Huck Finn, Tom Sawyer, Hank Morgan, and Young Satan. Much of the release Clemens experienced in the course of writing *Roughing It* derived from its carrying him back through time to the borders of that territory, partly because it prodded him to recall or create a younger self, partly because of the adolescent character of the West itself as he imagined it, and partly because his daily climb up East Hill enabled him to suspend the demands of his own adulthood and keep them at a safe distance.[8]

Clemens began making these ascents of the hill and assaults on his manuscript soon after arriving in Elmira in mid-March. On 8

April he could report to his brother that he was "to the 570th page & booming along," an indication that by then, if not before, he had hit an exhilarating writing stride. Two days later he added, "Am to 610th page, now." Encouraged by the pace he had established, he again urged Orion to work to set the machinery of publication in motion: "Tell Bliss to go ahead & set up the MSS & put the engravers to work." This time he made it quite clear that it was the production of the text itself, and not simply the prospectus, that he had in mind: "Tell Bliss to go ahead setting up the book just as it is." Directing his publisher to print the manuscript "just as it is" was a pointed indication of how little revising Clemens planned to do and contributes to validating the supposition that the relationship between manuscript and book chapters is very nearly direct. In the same letter he told Orion that "what I am writing now is so much better than the opening chapters . . . that I do *wish* I could spare time to revamp the opening chapters, & even write some of them over again." As his tone here suggests, it was a wish he had no intention of acting on; the subsequent publication history of *Roughing It* reinforces the likelihood that little such revamping took place.

In an 18 April letter to Orion, for example, Clemens expressed his dissatisfaction with "the Bull story" in chapter 7, but said, "I cannot alter it—too much trouble." The attitude he betrayed here and elsewhere toward the prospect of wholesale revision reflected both his impatience with editorial responsibilities and his reluctance to interrupt the momentum his work had gathered in Elmira. Once again in his life, a reality had lived up to his expectations: he had found the contentment and release he had associated with the Cranes' hilltop farmhouse. "I am up here at the farm," he crowed to Orion, "a mile & a half up a mountain, where I write every day" (8 April 1871). In mid-April he was joined on his treks to Quarry Farm by Joe Goodman, former publisher and co-owner of the Virginia City *Territorial Enterprise*, who proposed to "come up every day for 2 months & write a novel." Goodman was a flesh-and-blood totem of Clemens's Nevada days and so abetted both his recollection of and his regression to that earlier time, all the while reinforcing the status of Quarry Farm as an imaginative outpost, a kind of literary boys' club. Clemens assured his brother, "He is going to read my MSS critically" (18 April 1871).[9]

Invigorated and in many senses rejuvenated, Clemens hardly had a month to boom along on the *Roughing It* manuscript before Bliss himself, in one of his most perverse performances, effectively ran him aground. Perhaps, again, Bliss saw in Clemens's new friskiness a too-ready, too-demanding independence. Perhaps he resented Clemens's urging him to spring to work at producing the book after allowing both manuscript and publisher to languish for months. Perhaps he nurtured a grudge over Clemens's disloyalty in allowing Isaac Sheldon to publish the *(Burlesque) Autobiography*. Whatever the case, Bliss wrote a letter on 22 April 1871 that sharply succeeded, whatever its intention, in curbing Clemens's boisterous spirits.

Clemens may have innocently fired the first volley in this skirmish by observing to Bliss that with the publication of *The Innocents Abroad* Mark Twain had become a well-known and very salable commodity. As early as 2 August 1870 he made this observation in suggesting that the American Publishing Company could afford to offer him a higher royalty, "there being no *risk*, now, in publishing me, which there *was*, before." Just prior to Olivia's bout with typhoid, when he was proposing to write two hundred pages of *Roughing It* manuscript a week in order to rush the book to press, Clemens told Bliss, "My popularity is booming, now, & we ought to take the very biggest advantage of it" (27 January 1871). Bliss turned this argument around in his 22 April letter, maintaining that Mark Twain's popularity had diminished so precipitously that his publisher and agents would have to work hard and shrewdly to secure a profitable audience for his next book:

Standing where I do, with so many agents all over, coming in contact with the masses, I can feel the pulse of the community, as well as any other person's. I do not think there is as much of a desire to see another book from you as there was 3 months ago. Then anything offered would sell— people would subscribe to anything of yours without . . . looking at it much. Now they will inspect a Prospectus closer & buy more on the strength of *it*—, than they would have done a few months ago.[10]

A few months before, of course, Clemens had not yet published the anemic *(Burlesque) Autobiography*. But Bliss was doing more in this letter than simply skewering Clemens for his defection. He was observing that the decision to publish with Sheldon, something that Clemens had obviously done without Bliss's guidance or supervision, had been a serious professional misstep. The implication was that Clemens lacked the acumen to direct the course of his own career and that he needed a shrewd Yankee businessman to provide that direction. The letter also stressed Clemens's dependence on the American Publishing Company, in the wake of the failure of the *(Burlesque) Autobiography*, to mount a restorative advertising campaign on behalf of his next book. Without "a *splendid Prospectus* . . . to reawaken the appetite," Bliss suggested, a skeptical, fickle, and recently disappointed public might have little reason to give Mark Twain another chance. Bliss represented himself as being perfectly eager to conduct such a campaign, but the cost to Clemens would be to acknowledge that he needed the company at least as much as the company needed him.

Together with Bliss's decision to use only half of the pony-express episode—according to Clemens, "the finest piece of writing I ever did"—in the *American Publisher*, the 22 April letter amounted to a skillful and altogether deflating dressing down. It was a bitter dose of put-you-in-your-place discouragement, but Clemens seems to have swallowed the entire measure. More sensitive than ever about the negative reviews that the *(Burlesque) Autobiography* had drawn, he complained to Mary Fairbanks on 26 April, "I am pegging away at my book, but will have no success. The papers have found at last the courage to pull me down off my pedestal & cast slurs at me—& that is simply a popular author's death rattle. Though he write an *inspired* book after that, it would not save him."[11] One index of Bliss's power over Clemens at the time is the extent to which Clemens implicitly acceded here to the view of authorship and reputation that Bliss proposed in his 22 April letter: a popular writer, whatever his gifts, enjoys a standing with his public that he never quite deserves, a standing that depends more upon perception than performance and that therefore locates his fate in his image rather than his talent.

Clemens protested—to Orion, not Bliss—on 30 April 1871. "You both wrote me discouraging letters," he said. "Yours stopped my pen for two days—Bliss's stopped it for three." And he added a warning, in the high-handed tone he sometimes took with his brother: "Hereafter my wife will read my Hartford letters & if they are of the same nature, keep them out of my hands." Still, his work was proceeding, if not at the same pace he had managed a few weeks earlier. "Don't be in a great hurry getting out specimen chapters for canvassers," he told Orion, "for I want the chapter I am writing *now* in it—& it is away up to page 750 of the MS." Again Orion found himself caught in the middle of the undeclared hostilities carried on by his brother and his employer. In his 22 April letter Bliss had pressed Clemens, with characteristic indirection, for more of the *Roughing It* manuscript. Part of his reason, in fact, for stressing the strategic importance of "a *splendid Prospectus*" was to drive home the point that he needed more material from Clemens from which to fashion one: "The first part of a book alone," he warned, "is not sufficient to make a proper prospectus of." Clemens was now advising Orion not to be in a great hurry in preparing a prospectus, putting a bright face on the implicit acknowledgment that he still had a long way to go on *Roughing It*. Emphasizing the progress he *had* made, Clemens added, "I sent Bliss MSS yesterday, about 100 pages of MS."

By 3 May 1871 Clemens could tell Bliss, "My book is half done. I mailed you the 12th, 13th, 14th & 15th chapters yesterday, & before that I had sent you the previous 11 chapters." This report helps to clarify how much manuscript Bliss had so far received and when he received it. Clemens sent the first seven chapters of the book, something in the neighborhood of 160 manuscript pages, just before leaving Buffalo in mid-March. He submitted the pony-express episode, chapter 8, on 20 March. The next installment, "about 100 pages of MS," went out on 29 April and apparently consisted of chapters 9, 10, and 11. Chapters 12–15 followed on 2 May. Those fifteen chapters would probably have comprised fewer than four hundred manuscript pages, which is to say that by 3 May Clemens had sent Bliss a bit less than half of the manuscript he had written— given that he was "away up to page 750" on 30 April and "half done" with the book three days later. Being "half done" implies that he may have completed as many as 840 pages, if his early estimate that the book would require about 1,680 pages is taken literally.[12] Whatever the case, Clemens seems to have had a good deal more manuscript on hand than he had sent to Bliss. As that manuscript accumulated, so did his enthusiasm for the project. "This book will be pretty readable, after all," he told Bliss; "& if it is well & profusely illustrated it will crowd the 'Innocents'" (3 May 1871).

The reference to illustration was a transparent reminder that Bliss had better live up to his part of the publishing bargain.

The floodgates had opened. Not even his skirmishing with Bliss could check the flow of creative energy Clemens generated in the late spring of 1871. After months of doubt and frustration, he had entered into one of those remarkable states of grace when, as he later put it, books seemed to write themselves. "I am writing with a red-hot interest," he told Bliss on 15 May. "Nothing grieves me now—nothing troubles me, bothers me or gets my attention—I don't think of anything but the book, & don't have an hour's unhappiness about anything & don't care two cents whether school keeps or not." Quarry Farm provided just the right environment for this outlook, and at his perch there he was experiencing the most productive period of his career to that date. "I have 1200 pages of MS already written," he reported, "& am now writing 200 a week—more than that, in fact." He spoke, as he came characteristically to do at such times, like a man possessed: "I can't bear to lose a single moment of the inspiration. So I will stay here & peg away as long as it lasts."

Those twelve hundred pages, Clemens wrote Bliss in the same letter, were enough "to make (allowing for engravings) about 400 pages of the book"; he felt that he was "consequently . . . two-thirds done." This judgment ought to figure strategically in any assessment of the composition of *Roughing It*, since it indicates that Clemens believed the ratio of manuscript to book pages was about three-to-one, a ratio that is generally reflected in other instances of his writing. It also reemphasizes his determination that *Roughing It* would be a six-hundred-page book, one that would require approximately eighteen hundred pages of manuscript. These estimates are essentially identical to those he held from the outset of the undertaking and therefore provide a consistent baseline of Clemens's own devising against which subsequent critical conjectures might be measured. Further, Clemens's report that he was now writing two hundred pages a week shows that under the right circumstances he actually *could* live up to the terms of the proposal he had made to Bliss in late January, 1871, when he had offered to "write night & day & send . . . 200 pages of MS. every week."

So enthusiastic was Clemens about his progress, in fact, that he even toyed in the 15 May letter with the prospect of full-scale revision. "My present idea," he told Bliss, "is to write as much more as I have already written, & then cull from the mass the very best chapters & discard the rest. I am not half as well satisfied with the first part of the book as I am with what I am writing now. . . . If I keep up my present lick three weeks more I shall be able & willing to scratch out half of the chapters of the Overland narrative—& shall do it." Whatever this intention implies about Clemens's critical insight into his own work—he never discarded large portions of the overland narrative, which is surely one of the liveliest and most satisfying parts of the book—it indicates that *Roughing It* was not being typeset at the time and that he was no longer pressing Bliss on that front. He did, however, renew his charge to Bliss to provide top-notch illustrations: "It will be a starchy book, & should be full of snappy pictures." And he added in a postscript a freshening rejoinder in the debate over the status of his reputation: "My stock is looking up. I am getting the bulliest offers for books & almanacs, am flooded with lecture invitations." It was, again, a good time to be Mark Twain.

There would be lapses and moments of distraction over the course of its completion, but Clemens was not again to founder and grow desperate while he was writing *Roughing It*. For his part, Bliss was able to restrain himself from trying to curb Clemens's mid-May exuberance, despite the author's references to other publishers. He simply responded, "I think you are in the mood to do good work, at which I *heartily rejoice*—Glad to know you are so pressed with overtures for works."[13] In reality it seems that Clemens may have been making more overtures than he was receiving, as, after all, he made most of the distractions that came between him and the book. On 10 June, for instance, he wrote to James Redpath, his lecture agent, claiming to have written a lecture "just for amusement" the day before and proposing a four-month tour to begin in the fall. On 21 June he offered Bliss three articles, which he had apparently just written, for inclusion in the *Publisher*. On 27 June he told Orion of having written two *additional* lectures and promised, "Tomorrow I go back on the book again."[14]

The "red-hot interest" he reported taking in *Roughing It* on 15 May had sufficiently cooled by 9 June to allow him to meander off into these other projects. With more than two-thirds of the manuscript written, he diverted his quicksilver enthusiasm elsewhere at just the moment he needed it to make one last push. By the time he turned his attention back to the manuscript, it had again assumed the shape of hard, deliberate work. He wrote Mary Fairbanks that "the book has been dragging along just 12 months, now, & I am *so* sick & tired of it. If I were to chance another break or another move before I finish it I fear I never *should* get it done" (27 June 1871). Clearly, the manuscript had stopped writing itself.

It may be more to the point to say that like many of the good and great books that were to follow it, it had written its way out of ease and innocence, back into the very kinds of hardship, travail, and responsibility it began by escaping. Clemens's imagination, for all its whimsy and iconoclasm, was chastened by the ambient Calvinism of his day and upbringing. Allowed to function freely, it would by virtue of its own gravity carry him and his creations to the fatalities of a fallen world. Play would give way to work, innocence to experience, and freedom to an inevitable tethering. The big California book was no better able to escape these fatalities than its successors would be or, for that matter, than Clemens himself had been. The release that he had found in the early stages of writing *Roughing It* naturally diminished as his own imagination insisted that the world's sober realities be permitted to overtake and reclaim his narrator.[15]

Consider, for example, the course of the narrator's fortunes in the gold and silver fields. In chapter 28 he describes his first frenzy of silver prospecting along the Humboldt River, recalling in particular his fervid, wide-eyed naïveté. "I confess, without shame," he says, "that I expected to find masses of silver lying all about the ground." Imagining his younger self scrambling among the Humboldt hills, jealously hoarding bits of bright stone, he acknowledges that "of all the experiences of my life, this secret search among the hidden treasures of silverland was the nearest to unmarred ecstasy" (*RI*, p. 194). When his nuggets are revealed to be "rubbish," however, he is made to confront the real work of silver mining, work that teaches him "how hard and long and dismal a task it is to burrow down into the bowels of the earth" (*RI*, p. 233). When his burrowing comes to nothing he is forced to earn a living even more dismally as a laborer in a quartz mill. "It is a pity," the narrator reflects, "that Adam could not have gone straight out of Eden into a quartz mill, in order to understand the full force of his doom to 'earn his bread by the sweat of his brow'" (*RI*, p. 234). The implication here is that the narrator's exile from his own Eden, the Eden of the American West, is even more severe than was Adam's. In fact, though, the West is revealed to be no Eden at all but a very real and not altogether romantic place whose precious ores are well and even grudgingly hidden, whose picturesque deserts are trackless expanses of cutting alkali dust and whose Noble Red Men are the despised and despicable Goshoots. The narrator's fall into experience, a fall precipitated by an innocence of Clemens's own enthusiastic contriving, necessarily darkens the California book and lends resonance and poignancy to the narrator's early, precarious freedom. But retelling the Fall was never an easy matter for Clemens, whether in this book or those that were to follow, and his imagination characteristically balked at the necessity of having finally to conform to his somber moral vision.

Perhaps it was at this time, with the manuscript once more threatening to lapse in late June 1871, that Clemens turned, or resorted, to the Sandwich Island material. Whether he had originally planned to do so or not, the temptation to lean at this point on a crutch of previously published letters—to return, in other words, to the method that had seen *The Innocents Abroad* satisfactorily to its conclusion—must have been considerable. Above all, given his expressed weariness with the book, his obligation to and interest in turning to other projects, and his recent boasting to Bliss, he simply could not afford to allow *Roughing It* again to stagnate. Later in his career he could permit himself the luxury of pigeon-holing a manuscript when his imagination ran dry or refused to follow the course of its own momentum; in the summer of 1871, his tenuous self-esteem and the rising tide of his commitments made it a luxury too dangerous to indulge.

Just where he was in *Roughing It* at this time is a question that requires some extrapolation to answer. On 29 June 1871, having pledged to "go back to the book again" two days earlier, he reported to Orion, "Wrote 2 chapters of the book to-day—shall write chapter 53 to-morrow." On 2 July he told his brother that he was "just finishing Chapter 56." These references locate Clemens in the manuscript, but they leave unclear the relationship between the numbering of manuscript chapters and that of chapters in the first edition. That is, they fail to establish whether or not manuscript chapter 56 corresponds to book chapter 56. The matter is of some interest inasmuch as the Sandwich Islands narrative begins in chapter 62 of the first edition. If chapter numbers in the manuscript corresponded to those in the book, that is to say, it would follow that when Clemens returned to work on *Roughing It* in late June he wrote several California chapters—at least ten, in fact—before turning to the Sandwich Islands material.

There is some evidence to indicate, however, that those chapter numbers do not correspond, evidence that suggests that Clemens may have taken up the Sandwich Islands very soon after returning to work on the manuscript. He made it clear, for instance, that he added and inserted chapters to the book after it ostensibly was done. On 10 August 1871, as he was working over the "completed" text, he told Olivia, "I wrote a splendid chapter to-day, for the middle of the book." That he made such insertions implies that the manuscript chapter numbers he mentioned in late June and early July were very likely to have been lower than the numbers of corresponding chapters in the first edition. Further, he reported to Mary Fairbanks on 29 June that a lecture he had just written, "Reminiscences of some Un-Commonplace Characters I have Chanced to Meet," included the stories of "Dick Baker, California Miner, & his wonderful cat" and "Blucher's curious adventure with a beggar." These two episodes make up parts of chapters 61 and 59, respectively, in *Roughing It*—at the very end of the California sequence and immediately before the Sandwich Islands narrative begins. Were Clemens working this material into a lecture and the book manuscript at about the same time, as seems probable, he would have written these chapters before, or perhaps just after, returning seriously to the manuscript on 29 June. The evidence would indicate, in any case, that he soon came to depend on the Sandwich Islands material to give substance and direction to what remained of writing *Roughing It*.

When he wrote Orion on 2 July that he was "just finishing Chapter 56," Clemens added, "Have already nearly MS enough, but am still writing—intend to cut & cull liberally." His plan for the book had apparently remained essentially the same as the one he outlined to Bliss on 15 May: to produce an overabundance of

manuscript "& then cull from the mass the very best chapters &
discard the rest." The Sandwich Islands material was supposed not
simply to complete the book, then, but to fill it out sufficiently to
allow Clemens to make excisions—to "cut & slash & lick & trim
& revamp it," as he said in the 10 August letter to Olivia. He found,
however, upon arriving in Hartford with what he thought was too
much manuscript, that he had underestimated the requirements of
a six-hundred-page book. He wrote Olivia, "It takes 1800 pages of
MS to make this book?—& that is just what I have got—or rather,
I have got 1,830. *I thought that just a little over 1500 pages would
be enough* & that I could leave off all the Overland trip—& what
a pity I can't" (10 August 1871). Actually, what seems to have happened is that Clemens relaxed and lowered his own estimates of
what was required of him as *Roughing It* again grew hard to write.
On 15 May he had imagined—accurately, as it turned out—that the
book would require eighteen hundred pages of manuscript. Sometime before 10 August, and probably by 2 July, he had convinced
himself that fifteen hundred pages would do and that whatever he
wrote after that point—after what he was then calling chapter 56—
would allow him to trim away a proportional part of the earlier
manuscript. Hawaiian material, in effect, would displace the overland chapters. Discovering that his 1,830 pages were just enough
to meet his commitment to Bliss, Clemens was prevented from
omitting or substantially shortening the story of the overland journey, or any other section of *Roughing It*, for that matter. The lick-
ing and revamping he did in Hartford was consequently restricted,
in all likelihood, to editorial fine-tuning rather than to sweeping
revision. He may have added a few chapters, as his 10 August letter
to Olivia indicates, but it is improbable that he changed the book's
basic shape or pace.

That shape, and particularly that pace—the bright, breathless
sprint of the overland section; the anecdotal meander of the Nevada and California episodes; and the final, desultory procession of
Hawaiian chapters—reflected the three important periods of the
book's composition: the initial spurt in late summer 1870; the long-
delayed resurrection of the manuscript at Quarry Farm in March
1871; and the last, long haul through the Sandwich Islands material
in midsummer of that year. The book that Clemens had proposed
and contracted to write in about five months had in fact taken him

more than a year to complete. During that year, as the vials of hell-fire emptied upon him, he experienced in new and sobering ways the burdens of responsibility he would have to bear as a professional writer, and, remarkably, he found his way back to the gifts of imagination and craft that enabled him from time to time to transcend those burdens.

Afterword

Getting To Be Mark Twain

Over the course of the year he spent writing *Roughing It*, Clemens established most of the important circumstances that would direct his career over the next two decades. He would be a writer of books, not a journalist and not, primarily, a platform performer. In those books he would continue to lay claim to his own experience, sometimes panning for anecdotes, sometimes mining for something more essential. He would carry on a battle of wills and wits with Elisha Bliss that neither man would decisively win. He would write best in a condition that might be described as genial privacy, a condition that allowed him to work apart from the daily cares and turmoil of a household without sacrificing the nurture and support of a domestic circle; he would write best in Elmira.

And finally, as the summer of 1871 drew to a close and *Roughing It* was being set in proof, he moved to Hartford. The book whose composition began in Buffalo, the city Clemens could not love, took him eventually to the city that was to be his principal home for the next twenty years. He had first set foot in Hartford in January 1868 to negotiate the publication of *The Innocents Abroad* with Bliss's American Publishing Company and returned there in August of that year to submit the finished manuscript. At the time he had written, "Of all the beautiful towns it has been my fortune to see this is the chief."[1] Exactly three years later, in August 1871, he was again in the city with a manuscript to deliver, that of the long-awaited California book. It was during this visit that he finally acted on the impulses that had attracted him to Hartford from the outset, arranging to rent the home of John and Isabella Hooker, longtime friends of the Langdon family, in Nook Farm, a genteel enclave of writers and well-to-do people at the edge of the city.

It was a move Clemens could not have made, and in fact was not welcome to make, in the summer of 1869, when he and Olivia had been casting about for a nesting site. Some of the Hartfordians who were now to become his neighbors were then not at all prepared to welcome Mark Twain to their society. *The Innocents Abroad* had changed that, by virtue of its enormous popularity, certainly, but also, perhaps, because it revealed its author to be something other than a vulgar comedian. Clemens's persistent regard for Hartford, despite the snub, was no doubt reinforced by his affection for Joe Twichell, his ties to Bliss, and his appreciation of Olivia's friendships there, but from the outset what had chiefly drawn him to the city was his sense of its upright and elevating character. It was a land of steady habits, he said, a place where morality and huckleberries flourished. Given Clemens's passing resemblance to the man who would not want to belong to a club that would have him for a member, the snub may only have whetted his appetite to find acceptance there.

In one of the paeans to Hartford he wrote during his first visits to the city, Clemens spoke of its moral and moralizing atmosphere with such enthusiasm as to conclude, "We may expect the lion and the lamb to lie down together shortly in Connecticut." That the millennium might soon come to pass in Hartford should hardly be surprising, he says, but "to me, a sinner, the prospect is anything but inviting."[2] At the time it suited his purposes and his persona to place himself beyond the pale of Hartford respectability, thereby anticipating and perhaps even preparing the way for the rejection he suffered there a year later. By August of 1871, however, Hartford was glad to have him, and he was still glad to have Hartford, its wholesome, pervasive rectitude undiminished among the fixtures of his imagination. The sinner had not become a saint, but he had undergone some fundamental changes and clarifications over the course of the three years that separated his delivery of the second book manuscript from his delivery of the first.

By the time he and Olivia took up residence in Hartford at the beginning of October 1871, Clemens was within two months of his thirty-sixth birthday. His son, Langdon, was almost a year old, and Olivia was expecting their second child. He had managed,

against considerable odds and in the face of all but relentless ad-
versity, to draft a follow-up to *The Innocents Abroad*, a follow-up
which proved not to be a sequel but a kind of precursor of the first,
at least in terms of the chronology of his life. He had begun a pattern, that is to say, of reaching back further into his past with each
succeeding book, a pattern he continued, with occasional interruptions, through the heart of his career. He was about to become
a lecturer again and would in fact have a chance to settle into his
new home for only about two weeks before setting out for Beth-
lehem, Pennsylvania, where his 1871–72 tour began on 16 October. He was on the road, in New England and the Midwest, until
the tour closed on 6 February 1872.

Although his lecture persona might seem to his audiences to
have changed little since his previous tour two years earlier, Clemens's sense of Mark Twain had, like his sense of vocation, sharpened over the course of that time. Most fundamentally, Twain had
ceased for the most part to be an innocent himself and had become
instead a commentator on innocence, frequently the innocence of
his earlier life. Writing *Roughing It*, in particular, had helped him
establish his perspective in time; the book revealed him to be not
simply a retrospective teller but a seasoned, reflective adult, an initiate able to recall his former naïveté vividly and with contagious
enthusiasm even though he could no longer participate in it. This
perspective aligned writer and persona more closely than ever before. The contemporaneous Mark Twain was older and more
knowing than, say, the Mark Twain who had assumed an editorship at the Buffalo *Express* two years earlier. He was no longer
available to such catastrophes as being thrown over Niagara Falls
by Irish Indians or shot full of holes by outraged newspaper readers, although he might recall such incidents from his earlier life. In
this regard he came nearer than he ever had to serving as a mask
for Clemens himself. He had ceased to function primarily as a
comic actor and become instead an impresario or raconteur capable
of fashioning a younger self to fill that role and the related roles of
butt, victim, novice, tenderfoot, and fledgling. This shift or evolution in point of view afforded Mark Twain a certain maturity
without curtailing his access to the essentially adolescent springs
of his imagination and "adventures." It enabled him to take his
place, as Clemens had, in a world of grown-ups. Eventually it

would enable him to create other selves, other innocents, and to trace their uneasy accommodations to that world.

In 1877 Clemens learned, or came to believe, that his old nemesis Captain Charles C. Duncan of the *Quaker City* had slandered him in a lecture treating their 1867 "pleasure voyage." He responded, as Mark Twain, in a public letter to the editor of the New York *World*,

Where is the use in bothering about what a man's character was ten years ago, anyway? Perhaps the captain values his character of ten years ago? I never have heard of any reason why he should; but still he may possibly value it. No matter. I do not value my character of ten years ago. I can go out any time and buy a better one for half it cost me. In truth, my character was simply in course of construction then. I hadn't anything up but the scaffolding, so to speak. But I have finished the edifice now and taken down that worm-eaten scaffolding. I have finished my moral edifice, and frescoed it and furnished it, and I am obliged to admit that it is one of the neatest and sweetest things of the kind that I have ever encountered. I greatly value it, and I would feel like resenting any damage done to it. But that old scaffolding is no longer of any use to me; and inasmuch as the "captain" seems able to use it to advantage, I hereby make him a present of it. It is a little shaky, of course, but if he will patch it here and there he will find that it is still superior to anything of the kind he can scare up upon his own premises. (14 February 1877)[3]

Not far beneath the humor of these observations, empowering their counterattack on Duncan, is Clemens's ready acknowledgment that when he stepped off the *Quaker City* a decade earlier, the terms of Mark Twain's identity, like those of his own, were radically uncertain. But if the scaffolding needed to frame his character was barely in place then, in 1867, its work was largely accomplished by the time the Clemenses moved to Hartford in 1871.

Like Gatsby, Clemens had come a long way in arriving at the enclave of respectability and status he sought, his land of steady habits. Over the four years that had passed since the *Quaker City* returned him from the Old World to the New, he had sifted or blundered among the many courses he might have followed to discover the future that was to hold him. During those years he found the stable personal identity that would make a stable literary identity possible; he settled the sources of Mark Twain. Now he was ready to build on those sources, to bring to life over the next two decades voices that refracted that complex and dynamic identity. His search for a home had brought him at last to Hartford, but in the process of arriving there he had begun his approach to another, even more fertile Promised Land. Having been carried east during the course of writing *Roughing It*, the most western of his books, Clemens was, in the fall of 1871, poised to discover that his richest imaginative resources lay at neither extremity, East or West, but in what he was to call "the body of the nation," the Mississippi Valley. On 27 November of that year, as he was out lecturing for James Redpath and reading proof for Elisha Bliss, he mused to Olivia, "When I come to write the Mississippi book, *then* look out!" Writing *Roughing It* had brought him to the brink of finding his real and lasting fortune, a fortune buried in the very riverbanks he had earlier left in boarding an overland stagecoach in search of more promising Territory.

Notes

Preface

1. Quotations from Clemens's letters bearing dates before 1867 are drawn from *Mark Twain's Letters*, Volume 1: *1853–1866*, ed. Edgar Marquess Branch, Michael B. Frank, and Kenneth M. Sanderson (Berkeley, Los Angeles, and London: University of California Press, 1988). Those from letters dated 1867–68 are drawn from *Mark Twain's Letters*, Volume 2: *1867–1868*, ed. Harriet Elinor Smith and Richard Bucci (Berkeley, Los Angeles, and London: University of California Press, 1990). Those from letters dated 1869 and later are drawn from printer's copy of later volumes in the series, prepared by the Mark Twain Project in the Bancroft Library for publication by the University of California Press. Dates of letters cited appear in the text. All previously unpublished material by Mark Twain is © 1991 by Edward J. Willi and Manufacturers Hanover Trust Company as trustees of the Mark Twain Foundation, which reserves all reproduction or dramatization rights in every medium. Previously published letters by Mark Twain quoted from *Collected Letters* have been correctly established from the authoritative documents for the first time and are © 1991 by the Regents of the University of California. All quotations from Mark Twain are published here with the permission of the University of California Press and Robert H. Hirst, general editor of the Mark Twain Project.

Chapter 1

1. An early version of this chapter appeared as "How Mark Twain Survived Sam Clemens' Reformation," in *American Literature* 55 (October

1983): 299–315, and was reprinted in *On Mark Twain: The Best from American Literature*, ed. Louis J. Budd and Edwin H. Cady (Durham, N.C.: Duke University Press, 1987), pp. 259–75.

2. Dixon Wecter makes a similar observation about Clemens's susceptibility to Mary Fairbanks's ministrations and generalizes that "he enjoyed a touch of feminine domination all his life—believing . . . that woman with her finer sensibilities was the true arbiter of taste, manners, and morals." *Mark Twain to Mrs. Fairbanks* (San Marino, Calif.: Huntington Library, 1949), p. xxiii.

3. A year after their first meeting, Clemens explained to Olivia how he had resisted falling immediately in love with her: "I did have such a struggle, the first day I saw you at the St Nicholas [Hotel], to keep from loving you with *all* my heart! But you seemed to my bewildered vision, a visiting *Spirit* from the upper air—a something to *worship*, reverently & at a distance—& *not* a creature of common human clay, to be profaned by the *love* of such as I" (6 January 1869).

4. See Leon T. Dickinson, "Mark Twain's Revisions in Writing *The Innocents Abroad*," *American Literature* 19 (1947): 139–57. For a later consideration of these changes see Robert H. Hirst, "The Making of *The Innocents Abroad*: 1867–1872," Ph.D. diss., University of California, Berkeley, 1975, pp. 112–67. Robert Regan has shown that Clemens's revisions did nothing to mitigate his indictment of the more sanctimonious of his fellow *Quaker City* passengers, the so-called pilgrims. In fact, Regan observes, "In the process of revising and expanding his travel letters to produce *The Innocents Abroad*, Mark Twain roughly doubled the number of attacks on the pilgrims and trebled their aggregate length." "The Reprobate Elect in *The Innocents Abroad*," *American Literature* 54 (May 1982): 257.

5. The letters quoted here are from Clemens to Charles Henry Webb (26 November 1870) and to Thomas Bailey Aldrich (27 January 1871), respectively. Writing of Harte's editorial suggestions in the letter to Webb, Clemens said, "I followed orders strictly." Hirst maintains that in doing so Clemens cut more than one thousand pages from the manuscript. For his account of Harte's role in the book's revision, see "The Making of *The Innocents Abroad*," pp. 156–66.

6. Holograph letter in MTP.

7. Max Eastman defends the Langdons and their Elmira community from such charges in "Mark Twain's Elmira," *Harper's Monthly Magazine* 176 (1938): 629. Henry Nash Smith makes a related, more general, comment about the roots of Clemens's impulse to reform in *Mark Twain: The Development of a Writer* (Cambridge, Mass.: Harvard University Press, 1962), p. 3.

8. A few months later Olivia wrote Mary Fairbanks that she "felt proud and humble" to receive an encouraging letter from her, "proud that you should feel that I might *help* Mr. Clemens—Humble when I remembered how much I must strive to do, as a Christian woman, in order to accomplish what you believe me capable of accomplishing." Letter dated 15 January 1869; holograph in MTM.

9. Clipping in MTP.

10. Quoted in Smith and Bucci, ed., *Mark Twain's Letters*, Volume 2, p. 286n.

11. Cleveland *Herald*, 18 November 1868, p. 8; clipping in MTP.

12. "Personal Habits of the Siamese Twins," *Packard's Monthly*, n.s. 1 (1869): 249.

13. This claim is substantiated by a letter from Mrs. Langdon to Mrs. Fairbanks dated 25 November 1869. There Mrs. Langdon wrote, "It is just a twelve-month since Mr Clemens first talked with me of his love for Livia, now he seems so incorporated into our whole being that I seem hardly to remember when it was not so. . . . We are all increasingly attached to Mr. Clemens, every time he leaves us loving him better than when he came" (quoted in Wecter, *Mark Twain to Mrs. Fairbanks*, p. 112n).

14. Letter dated 13 November 1869; holograph in MTP.

Chapter 2

1. See, e.g., Justin Kaplan, *Mr. Clemens and Mark Twain: A Biography* (New York: Simon and Schuster, 1966), pp. 113–14.

2. *Alta California*, 3 March 1868; reprinted in " 'American Travel Letters Series Two,' Ninth in Series in 'Alta California,' " *Twainian* 7 (September–October 1948): 3–4.

3. Clemens claimed in a letter to Olivia that from the beginning of their slight acquaintance he instinctively regarded Bowles as "a born & bred *cur*," only to have that impression borne out when he learned later from Twichell "that last June both Hawley & Warner were full of the idea of having me on the Courant, but ran to consult Bowles . . . , & he advised them not to do it" (24 November 1869).

4. Holograph letter in MTP.

5. Perhaps to protect her feelings and to mask his own, Clemens dwelt in his letter to Mary Fairbanks not on her husband's financial manipulations but on his stipulation that Clemens join the *Herald* as its political editor. "The more I thought of trying to transform myself into a political editor," he said, "the more incongruous & the more hazardous the thing looked. I always did hate politics, & the prospect of becoming its servant at last . . . was anything but attractive. It just offered *another* apprentice-

ship—another one, to be tacked on to the tail end of a foolish life *made up* of apprenticeships" (14 August 1869).

6. Albert Bigelow Paine sketches the terms of that transaction: "The Buffalo *Express* was at this time in the hands of three men—Col. George F. Selkirk, J. N. Larned, and Thomas A. Kennett. Colonel Selkirk was business manager, Larned was political editor. With the purchase of Kennett's share Clemens became a sort of general and contributing editor, with a more or less 'roving commission'—his hours and duties not very clearly defined." *Mark Twain: A Biography* (New York: Harper, 1912), 1:386–87.

7. Nor was this attitude entirely one-sided. On 1 December 1868 Olivia's mother wrote to Mary Fairbanks of the "utter surprise & almost astonishment with which Mr Langdon & myself listened to Mr Clemens declaration" of love, confessing that "at first our parental hearts said no.—to the bare thought of such a stranger, mining in our hearts for the possession of one of the few jewels we have." Holograph letter in University of Virginia Library; photocopy in MTP.

8. Buffalo *Express*, 16 August 1869; clipping in MTP.

Chapter 3

1. Since this chapter begins a discussion of Clemens's work at the Buffalo *Express*, it might be well to acknowledge here the one book-length attempt to treat that work, Henry Duskis's *Forgotten Writings of Mark Twain* (New York: Philosophical Library, 1963). In his ambition to gather all of "Mark Twain's" *Express* articles, Duskis mistakenly attributes to Clemens a great deal of writing that Clemens clearly had no hand in producing, with the result that Duskis's conclusions about both the man and the material are often seriously flawed. Toward the end of the book, Duskis says, "Let the reader decide for himself—or herself—whether the writings herein contained are the works of Mark [Twain]" (p. 351). A number of knowledgeable readers have since shown good reason for deciding that many of them are not.

2. Albert Bigelow Paine, *Mark Twain: A Biography* (New York: Harper, 1912), 1:398. Justin Kaplan echoes Paine's assessment, observing that Clemens "was at the start, ambitious for his paper, energetic, willing to work late hours." *Mr. Clemens and Mark Twain: A Biography* (New York: Simon and Schuster, 1966), p. 109.

3. Paine remarks of Clemens at about this time, "It is curious to reflect that Mark Twain still did not regard himself as a literary man. He had no literary plans for the future; he scarcely looked forward to the publication of another book. . . . He still regarded himself merely as a lecturer and journalist, temporarily popular, but with no warrant to a permanent seat

in the world's literary congress. He thought his success something of an accident. The fact that he was prepared to settle down as an editorial contributor to a newspaper in what was then only a big village is the best evidence of a modest estimate of his talents." *Mark Twain: A Biography,* 1:385, 398.

4. Buffalo *Commercial Advertiser*, 19 August 1869; Buffalo *Express*, 20 August 1869. On 16 August 1869 the *Commercial Advertiser* had politely welcomed "the widely-known 'Mark Twain' . . . to the editorial circle in Buffalo," describing him as "a gentleman of decided ability and of long experience in the newspaper business." These excerpts from the *Commercial Advertiser* and *Express*, and all future excerpts from the *Express*, are from clippings in the Mark Twain Papers.

5. I am grateful to editors at the Mark Twain Project for making this information available to me, chiefly in the form of a note to a letter from SLC to OL dated 19 August 1869. See also Martin B. Fried, "Mark Twain in Buffalo," *Niagara Frontier* 5 (1958): 92.

6. Consider, e.g., Dixon Wecter: "Never patient under routine, Clemens seems early to have grown bored with his editorial duties in Buffalo." *The Love Letters of Mark Twain* (New York: Harper, 1949), p. 112.

7. Wecter, p. 106.

8. Harriet Beecher Stowe had brought the matter of Byron's incestuous relationship with his half-sister Augusta to national attention in this country in an *Atlantic Monthly* article published in the summer of 1869. Clemens treated the matter, sometimes obliquely, in a number of early *Express* pieces, among them "More Byron Scandal" (7 September 1869), "The Last Words of Great Men" (11 September 1869), and "The 'Wild Man' Interviewed" (18 September 1869). His account of the "Private Habits" of Henry Ward Beecher (25 September 1869), mentioned later, is at least indirectly related to the controversy. Henry Ward Beecher was the brother not only of Harriet Beecher Stowe but also of Thomas K. Beecher, the Langdons' Congregationalist minister in Elmira.

9. J. N. Larned, "Mark Twain," Buffalo *Express*, 26 April 1910; clipping in MTP.

10. Earl D. Berry, "Mark Twain as a Newspaper Man," *Illustrated Buffalo Express*, 11 November 1917; clipping in MTP.

Chapter 4

1. "'American Travel Letters Series Two,' Thirteenth in Series in 'Alta California,'" *Twainian* 8 (May–June 1949): 3.

2. Petroleum Nasby, Buffalo *Express*, 9 October 1869. This and all future excerpts from the *Express* are from clippings in MTP.

3. William Dean Howells, *My Mark Twain: Reminiscences and Criticisms*

(New York and London: Harper, 1910), p. 112; first published in *Atlantic Monthly*, December 1869.

4. See chap. 3.

5. Buffalo *Express*, 16 October 1869.

6. Holograph letter in MTP.

7. Letter dated 27 December 1869; holograph in MTP. The misspellings are Slee's.

8. Document in MTP.

9. Justin Kaplan, *Mr. Clemens and Mark Twain: A Biography* (New York: Simon and Schuster, 1966), p. 113. As further evidence of the character of this indenture, Kaplan offers the following anecdote: "Not long after the marriage Jervis Langdon offered [Clemens] ten thousand dollars and a trip to Europe if, having already given up spirits, he would now give up drinking ale and smoking. Clemens rejected the bribe—'I can't sell myself,' he told Langdon—but he did cut down his smoking drastically, to Sunday afternoons. . . . 'If I had sold myself,' he said to James T. Fields in 1876, after telling him about Langdon's offer, 'I couldn't have written my book, or I couldn't have gone to sleep'" (p. 118).

10. The anecdote is passed along by Samuel Charles Webster, Annie Moffett's son, in *Mark Twain, Business Man* (Boston: Little, Brown, 1946), p. 113. Its accuracy is impossible to verify. It would seem remarkable for Jervis Langdon to betray such a fear to a virtual stranger like young Annie Moffett, who was one of only two members of Clemens's family to attend the wedding, her mother, Pamela Moffett, being the other. It might seem equally remarkable, on the other hand, for Annie Moffett simply to invent the episode in later depicting the wedding to her son.

11. The familiar story of Langdon's accepting Clemens as his daughter's fiancé, even in the face of the skepticism expressed by people Clemens himself had named as references, is told, for instance, by Albert Bigelow Paine in *Mark Twain: A Biography* (New York: Harper, 1912), 1:376–78, and by Kaplan in *Mr. Clemens and Mark Twain*, pp. 88–92. According to Clemens's own account, "The friends that I referred to in California said with one accord that I got drunk oftener than was necessary and that I was wild and Godless, idle, lecherous and a discontented and unsettled rover & they would not recommend any girl of high character & social position to marry me—but as I had already said all that about myself beforehand there was nothing shocking or surprising about it to the family" (SLC to Charles Warren Stoddard, 25 August 1869).

12. Albert Bigelow Paine, ed., *Mark Twain's Autobiography* (New York and London: Harper, 1924), 1:257.

Chapter 5

1. Cleveland *Daily Herald*, 8 February 1870. Excerpts from the *Daily Herald* and from other contemporaneous newspapers, including the Buffalo *Express*, are from clippings or photocopies in MTP.

2. Buffalo *Express*, 16 August 1869.

3. New York *Tribune*, 15 January 1870.

4. Elmira *Saturday Evening Review*, 5 February 1870.

5. Earl D. Berry, himself later a city editor of the *Express*, recalled that when the news broke that Mark Twain was to join the paper, "Bright visions of an immediate expansion of circulation were indulged in and every person on The Express staff confidently expected that the old locally restricted publication would be lifted into a nationwide prominence. 'Petroleum V. Nasby' (D. R. Locke) had done just that thing for the Toledo Blade. . . . Why should not the famous Mark Twain build up The Buffalo Express?" However, according to Berry, in the final analysis "the circulation and business prosperity of the paper did not respond, in the manner expected, to Mark Twain's work. The Buffalo Express did not achieve a nation-wide fame because of his connection with it." "Mark Twain as a Newspaper Man," *Illustrated Buffalo Express*, 11 November 1917, p. 40.

6. Holograph letter in MTM.

7. Letter dated 6 February 1870; holograph in MTM.

8. Letter dated 26 February 1870; holograph in MTP.

9. Letter dated 20 February 1870; holograph in MTM.

10. Letter dated 9 November 1869; holograph in MTP.

11. Holograph manuscript in MTP; to be published in *The Works of Mark Twain: Early Tales & Sketches*, Volume 4: *1869–1870* (Berkeley and Los Angeles: University of California Press, forthcoming), item 279.

12. Holograph manuscript in MTP; to be published in *The Works of Mark Twain: Early Tales & Sketches*, Volume 4: *1869–1870* (Berkeley and Los Angeles: University of California Press, forthcoming), item 280.

13. The three stories are "Experience of the McWilliamses with the Membranous Coup" (1875), "Mrs. McWilliams and the Lightning" (1880), and "The McWilliamses and the Burglar Alarm" (1882).

Chapter 6

1. Letter dated 22–24 March 1870; quoted in Dixon Wecter, ed., *Mark Twain to Mrs. Fairbanks* (San Marino, Calif.: Huntington Library, 1949), p. 129.

2. Letter dated 17 March 1870; holograph in the Katherine S. Day Col-

lection, Stowe-Day Library, Hartford, Connecticut. In the same letter Olivia goes on to give Alice Day an account of the discomforts of making calls in an unfamiliar city: "There is something very comical," she says, "about driving to a street and number and when the servant opens the door find that you have been only intent on the street and number and have no possible idea of the ladies name, so you hand your card in silence, and while your card is being taken to the lady of the house you look at your list to prepare yourself to address her by name when she enters."

3. Clipping in MTP.

4. Holograph manuscript in MTP; to be published in *The Works of Mark Twain: Early Tales & Sketches*, Volume 4: *1869–1870* (Berkeley and Los Angeles: University of California Press, forthcoming), item 283. That Clemens drafted "A Wail" on 7 or 8 March 1870 is indicated by its having been immediately precipitated by a letter he received from writer and stage performer Steven Massett dated 6 March 1870 (holograph in MTP). Massett wrote from Bloomer's Hotel in Buffalo to "thank" Mark Twain sarcastically for a slighting mention of him in the *Express* for 5 March. Clemens incorporated Massett's letter toward the end of "A Wail," clearly intending that the entire piece be set for publication in the newspaper. Perhaps he suppressed "A Wail" not only because it betrayed negative attitudes on his part toward the *Express* but also because it eventually dwindled into yet another slap at Massett. "The idea," it concludes, "of a great overgrown thing like me attacking that lamb!"

5. See chap. 3.

6. Holograph manuscript in MTP; to be published in *The Works of Mark Twain: Early Tales & Sketches*, Volume 4: *1869–1870*, item 282. That "A Protest" was written at about the same time as "A Wail" is primarily suggested by their dealing in such closely related ways with the same subject matter and is reinforced by the observation that both were drafted in the same purple ink on identically embossed paper.

7. Bruce R. McElderry, Jr., ed., *Contributions to the "Galaxy," 1868–1871, by Mark Twain* (Gainesville, Fla.: Scholars' Facsimiles and Reprints, 1961), p. 37. All excerpts from the *Galaxy* are from this text.

8. The sketch appeared as "The Christmas Fireside" on 23 December 1865 in the San Francisco *Californian*, then edited by Bret Harte. The title Clemens assigns the piece here is actually a paraphrase of the original's subtitle, "The Story of the Bad Boy That Bore a Charmed Life." "The Christmas Fireside" is reprinted in *The Works of Mark Twain: Early Tales & Sketches*, Volume 2: *1864–65*, ed. Edgar Marquess Branch and Robert H. Hirst (Berkeley, Los Angeles, and London: University of California Press, 1981), item 148, pp. 405–10.

9. The timing of Clemens's "Memoranda" deadlines is made evident

in his correspondence. On 26 April 1870, for example, *Galaxy* editor Francis P. Church requested copy for his June column "soon," stipulating, "I ought to have all in by May 3ᵈ." Observing a similar schedule, Clemens wrote Mary Fairbanks on 29 May 1870, "We were to have gone [to Elmira] yesterday, but being dissatisfied with the next Galaxy (July,) I begged a delay of Livy till I could make some changes in the MSS. before mailing them to N.Y." Clearly, "Memoranda" manuscript for any given month had to be in Church's hands by the very first days of the month preceding.

10. The notice, entitled "Mark Twain on Agriculture," appeared in the Buffalo *Express* for 12 April 1870 and was no doubt widely copied.

11. "Petrified Man" evidently appeared for the first time in the Virginia City *Territorial Enterprise* for 4 October 1862; it is reprinted in *The Works of Mark Twain: Early Tales & Sketches*, Volume 1: *1851–1864*, ed. Edgar Marquess Branch and Robert H. Hirst (Berkeley, Los Angeles, and London: University of California Press, 1979), item 28, pp. 155–59. "A Bloody Massacre near Carson" was first published in the *Territorial Enterprise* for 28 October 1863; it is reprinted in *Early Tales & Sketches*, Volume 1, item 66, pp. 320–26.

12. Clemens's impatience with this practice dated back at least as far as 1854, when, at eighteen, he had worked as a compositor for the Philadelphia *Ledger*. Writing to the Muscatine, Iowa, *Journal*, then edited by his brother, Orion, he said, "The people here seem very fond of tacking a bit of poetry(?) to the notices of the death of friends." By way of example he included in his letter "a few lines of most villainous doggerel, and worse measure, which may be found in the 'death' column" (3 February 1854).

13. The suspicion is borne out by *Express* veteran Earl D. Berry, who witnessed Clemens's first encounter with a gathering of "enlightened politicians" encamped in the newspaper's offices on the day of his arrival. "The new editor frowned them down," Berry recalls, "and made no bones of letting them know that the nature of his work made it desirable that he be alone. Mark Twain and the politicians never affiliated." "Mark Twain as a Newspaper Man," *Illustrated Buffalo Express*, 11 November 1917, p. 40.

14. See chap. 3.

15. The phrase is a chapter title from Henry Nash Smith, *Mark Twain: The Development of a Writer* (Cambridge, Mass.: Harvard University Press, 1962), pp. 52–70.

16. David Gray, Buffalo *Courier*, 19 March 1870; clipping in MTP. When Clemens later recalled his time in Buffalo as one of stark and forbidding isolation, he allowed that "there was one exception—a single ex-

ception. David Gray—poet, and editor of the principal newspaper,— was our intimate friend. . . . David had a young wife and a young baby. The Grays and the Clemenses visited back and forth frequently, and this was all the solace the Clemenses had in their captivity." "Autobiographical Dictation" for 16 February 1906; original in MTP.

17. Holograph letter in MTP.

18. More than three decades later, Clemens remembered Gray with the same fondness, a fondness that was made poignant by his own lingering bitterness about newspapering in Buffalo. David Gray, he said, "was a poet, but was doomed to grind out his living in a most uncongenial occupation—the editing of a daily political newspaper. He was a singing bird in a menagerie of monkeys, macaws, and hyenas. His life was wasted." "Autobiographical Dictation" for 22 February 1906; original in MTP.

Chapter 7

1. Letter dated 17 June 1872; holograph in MTP.

2. Dixon Wecter cites Langdon's illness as the reason for Abel and Mary Fairbanks's postponing a visit to Elmira that had been planned for November 1868. *Mark Twain to Mrs. Fairbanks* (San Marino, Calif.: Huntington Library, 1949), p. 48n. The diagnosis is specified in a letter from Susan Crane to Anna Dickinson dated 14 June 1870; holograph in the Anna Dickinson papers, Library of Congress, photocopy in MTP.

3. Letter dated 2 April 1870; holograph in MTP.

4. Susan Crane to Anna Dickinson, 14 June 1870.

5. This new arrangement is indicated in a letter from Clemens to Mary Fairbanks dated 25 June 1870.

6. Letter dated 25 April 1870; holograph in the Langdon Collection, MTM.

7. Susan Crane to Anna Dickinson, 14 June 1870.

8. See chap. 6, n 9.

9. Clemens's note of thanks to Langdon for the $1,000 gift is an interesting exercise in the politics of gratitude. He wrote, "We did enjoy the check father, just exactly as much as if we had found the money buried in a pot in the backyard, because a present from you never frets, or humiliates or loads one with the sense of having contracted a debt & given an invisible note for it secured by a lien on the recipient's pride & peace of mind" (13 May 1870).

10. The contrast between the apparently unremarkable circumstances of this brief Elmira visit and the breathless account of it Clemens gave

his sister probably has less to do with the demands of Olivia's family than it does with those of his own. In April 1870, he helped arrange to move his mother, sister, niece, and nephew from St. Louis to Fredonia, New York, a village about forty-five miles from Buffalo. Once they were established there, he variously encountered and constructed a number of reasons for not visiting and did not make the trip until October.

11. "Autobiographical Dictation" for 15 February 1906; original in MTP. Albert Bigelow Paine quotes further portions of the dictation dealing with Clemens's recollections of Langdon's decline in *Mark Twain: A Biography* (New York and London: Harper, 1912), 1:415–16.

12. In his "Autobiographical Dictation," Clemens says that his father, John Marshall Clemens, "was exceedingly dignified in his carriage and speech, and in . . . manner he was austere" (29 December 1906; original in MTP). Paine provides a similar characterization in *Mark Twain: A Biography*, 1:14. While John Marshall Clemens and the fictive father in "A Memory" share much the same temperament, Clemens typically bends the facts of his own biography in the sketch. The narrator speaks of a half-brother named Orrin Johnson; Clemens's full brother was named Orion. Moreover, as Bruce R. McElderry, Jr., points out, "Hiawatha," the fictive father's favorite poem, was published in 1855, eight years after John Marshall Clemens's death. *Contributions to the "Galaxy," 1868–1871, by Mark Twain* (Gainesville, Fla.: Scholars' Facsimiles and Reprints, 1961), p. 146.

13. The second of these speculations about Clemens's reasons for involving himself in the passage of Senate Bill 1025 was brought to my attention by a note accompanying his letter to Olivia dated 6 July 1870 in *Mark Twain's Letters*, Volume 3, forthcoming.

14. Signed holograph contract in MTP.

15. Clemens's view of the terms of the *Roughing It* contract, and of Elisha Bliss, eventually darkened. His later appraisal of both is included in his "Autobiographical Dictation" for 23 May 1906, published in *Mark Twain in Eruption*, ed. Bernard DeVoto (New York and London: Harper, 1922), pp. 151–55. Interestingly, Clemens claimed to have discussed the terms of the contract in theory with Jervis Langdon early in the day on 15 July and then because of Bliss's misrepresentations to have settled for what turned out to be far less than what he and his father-in-law had agreed was fair. See *Mark Twain's Autobiography*, ed. Albert Bigelow Paine (New York and London: Harper, 1924), 2:126–28.

16. Clipping in MTP.

17. This is the kind of generalization that invites qualification or outright refutation, but grounds for either are hard to discover, except per-

haps in the later, blatantly autobiographical writing. There are later pieces—the McWilliams stories, for instance—in which more-or-less fictive characters dramatize aspects of Clemens's (or, conjecturally, of Twain's) domestic circumstances, but none in which either Clemens or Twain identifies himself as a householder or a husband or a father. This does not apply, of course, to the two unpublished fragments he attempted on housekeeping (see chap. 5). Some might consider "A Mysterious Visit" (Buffalo *Express*, 18 March 1870) an exception to this generalization since it begins, "The first notice that was taken of me when I 'settled down,' recently . . . ," but the sketch makes no further reference to the narrator's domesticity.

18. See, in particular, James C. McNutt, "Mark Twain and the American Indian: Earthly Realism and Heavenly Idealism," *American Indian Quarterly* 4 (August 1978): 223–42.

19. The phrase is from William Dean Howells, *My Mark Twain: Reminiscences and Criticisms* (New York and London: Harper, 1910), p. 101.

20. On the matter of the abolitionist and humanitarian elements in Olivia Clemens's training, see Max Eastman, "Mark Twain's Elmira," *Harper's Monthly*, 176 (May 1938): 620–32.

21. Clipping in MTP.

22. Letter dated 25 January 1871; holograph in the Katharine S. Day Collection, Stowe-Day Library, Hartford, Connecticut. The Clemenses' own daughter Susy put the matter succinctly in writing a biography of her father based on stories she had been told as a girl: "About six months after papa and mamma were married grandpa died; it was a terrible blow on mamma, and papa told Aunt Sue he thought Livy would never smile again, she was so broken hearted." Quoted in *Mark Twain's Autobiography*, 2:113.

23. Letter dated 16 April 1885; quoted in *Mark Twain's Autobiography*, 2:129.

Chapter 8

1. Holograph MS in MTP. The three pages were apparently rejected; they were not transcribed as part of the published book. One of them is discussed in chap. 10.

2. The letters appeared in the *Express* between 27 September 1869 and 22 January 1870. Several months earlier, in late May 1869, he had written to his agent, James Redpath, to propose a lecture for the 1869–70 season entitled "Curiosities of California." "There is *scope* to the subject," he urged, "for the country is a curiosity." Among the topics he promised to

treat were "the fluctuations of fortunes in the mines, where men grow rich in a day & poor in another; . . . Lake Tahoe, whose wonders are little known & less appreciated here; . . . [and] the *never-mentioned* strange Dead Sea of California." Despite these intentions, Clemens lectured on the Sandwich Islands, not the American West, during the 1869–70 season.

3. The letter was published in the New York *Tribune* for 14 October 1869 and appeared in the Buffalo *Express* five days later.

4. Clemens did in fact draw upon his western newspaper exploits in his early "Memoranda" pieces, for example in "The Petrified Man," "My Famous 'Bloody Massacre,' " and "The Facts in the Great Land Slide Case," all of which had to have been prepared by very early May in order to appear in the June 1870 *Galaxy*.

5. Signed holograph contract in MTP; a transcription of the contract appeared in *Mark Twain Quarterly* 6 (Summer/Fall 1944): 5.

6. The letter is dated only "Buf., 1870," but was pretty certainly written in July or August of that year because Clemens had asked for the memorandum book on 15 July. Orion's memoranda were a sufficiently valuable and timely aid to his memory to prompt Clemens to promise his brother $1,000 from the new book's royalties in return for his help. Although the memorandum book itself has been lost, a portion of it is preserved—was perhaps transcribed—in a letter Orion wrote his wife, Mollie, on 8 September 1861. The text of the letter is reproduced as "Supplement D" in *Roughing It*, ed. Franklin R. Rogers (Berkeley, Los Angeles, and London: University of California Press, 1972), pp. 546–50.

7. "Autobiographical Dictation" for 15 February 1906; original in MTP.

8. "Autobiographical Dictation" for 15 February 1906; typescript in MTP. Other renditions of the map's creation offer interesting variations. Clemens's 1906 version implies that executing the woodcut was a kind of involuntary and irrational response to the torment he was undergoing at the time, a "half insane tempest . . . of humorous possession" that caused him to send for the block, which he then apparently carved at home. In 1910 his *Express* co-editor, Josephus N. Larned, recalled the incident differently: "I doubt if he ever enjoyed anything more than the jacknife engraving that he did on a piece of board for a military Map of the Siege of Paris, which was printed in The Express from his original 'plate,' with accompanying explanations and comments. Half his day of whittling and the laughter that went with it are something that I find pleasant to remember" (Buffalo *Express*, 26 April 1910; quoted in Albert Bigelow Paine, *Mark Twain: A Biography* [New York and London: Harper, 1912], 1: 399). Larned pretty clearly places Clemens in the *Express* offices during

the map's creation and makes the occasion seem more like a lark than an instance of tempestuous possession.

A more contemporaneous account of the event casts it in another light still. In 1871 fellow humorist Donn Piatt shared with a reporter the description Clemens had given him of the day the map came into being. "Only think," Piatt recalled him saying, "with a dear friend [Jervis Langdon, apparently, given that Emma Nye was still alive at the time] lying dead before me, and my wife half distracted over the loss, I had to get off my articles so as not to disappoint my publishers; and when I sat down with a board and pen-knife to engrave that map of Paris, I did so with a heavy heart and in a house of lamentation" ("Funny in Spite of Himself," *Every Saturday* 2, no. 71 [6 May 1871]: 415).

9. Holograph letter in MTP. The letter also contains Colfax's tribute to Jervis Langdon. "I heard of the death of your excellent father in law with deepest sorrow," he wrote. "He will long be missed by all."

10. Mark Twain, *Roughing It*, ed. Franklin R. Rogers, p. 43. Future references to this edition, abbreviated *RI*, will appear parenthetically in the text.

11. On 4 September Clemens had written Bliss, "During the past week have written first four chapters of the book."

12. See chap. 7.

13. SLC to Orion Clemens, 5 November 1870. Clemens initiated the matter of Bliss's hiring Orion by putting it to his publisher as a point-blank favor: "Say, for instance—I have a brother about 45—an old & able writer & editor," he wrote. "Have *you* got a place for him?" (31 October 1870). Bliss responded on exactly those terms: "You see we have no real place for him just now, but would like for *your sake* to *create a position* for him if possible—would this do?" (2 November 1870; holograph letter in MTP). Clemens did not hesitate to burden Orion with a sense of obligation, pointing out that Bliss's whole purpose in undertaking the arrangement was to win his—Clemens's—gratitude and loyalty. "But all right," he grumbled to his brother, "I am willing" (5 November 1870).

14. The line is from Mark Twain's "Valedictory" in the *Galaxy* "Memoranda" for April 1871. Of the engraving Clemens himself later admitted to Webb, "Yes *sir*—King William was a mistake & a big one, for it was repeating a joke" (14 January 1871).

15. For a discussion of the diamond-book agreement and its collapse, see *Mark Twain's Notebooks and Journals*, Volume 2: *1877–1883*, ed. Frederick Anderson, Lin Salamo, and Bernard L. Stein (Berkeley, Los Angeles, and London: University of California Press, 1975), p. 291 n 4. The story is also told in Justin Kaplan, *Mr. Clemens and Mark Twain* (New York: Simon and Schuster, 1966), pp. 124–28.

Chapter 9

1. Holograph letter in MTP.
2. Holograph letter in MTP.
3. Holograph letter in MTP.
4. Holograph letter in MTP.
5. The "Memoranda" column Clemens wrote for the March issue of the *Galaxy* has been entirely or substantially lost, even though it was at one time actually set in print. On 2 March 1871 Church suggested that some material from the column might be salvaged for later publication in the magazine. "But I will have the plates of those pages destroyed," he said, "so that they need never arise to bother you if you dont want them." It is possible that the one piece signed by Mark Twain that later appeared in the *Galaxy*—"About Barbers," in the August 1871 issue—was part of the March submission.

6. In the two most recent editions of *Roughing It*, for example, Franklin R. Rogers and Hamlin Hill at least tacitly imply that Clemens made such progress on the manuscript. See Rogers, introduction to *Roughing It* (Berkeley, Los Angeles, and London: University of California Press, 1972), pp. 7–8; and Hill, introduction to *Roughing It* (New York: Penguin Books, 1981), pp. 13–14. In other places, too, both Rogers and Hill argue plausibly, but not necessarily convincingly, that Clemens worked substantially on the *Roughing It* manuscript during the winter of 1870–71. Rogers believes that nearly all of the overland section—through chapter 19 of the first edition—was written before March 1871 (*The Pattern for Mark Twain's "Roughing It": Letters from Nevada by Samuel and Orion Clemens, 1861–62* [Berkeley and Los Angeles: University of California Press, 1961], pp. 16–21). Hill maintains that during this time Clemens was recasting his Sandwich Islands letters for inclusion in *Roughing It* (*Mark Twain and Elisha Bliss* [Columbia: University of Missouri Press, 1964], pp. 47–50).

7. Rogers observes that "most scholars . . . have believed that the character [to be changed] was the narrator," and is himself inclined to agree, both in his introduction to *Roughing It* (p. 10) and in *The Pattern for Mark Twain's "Roughing It"* (pp. 16–17). Henry Nash Smith made this argument early and placed it in a thoughtful critical context ("Mark Twain as an Interpreter of the Far West: The Structure of *Roughing It*," in *The Frontier in Perspective*, ed. Walker D. Wyman and Clifton B. Kroeber [Madison: University of Wisconsin Press, 1957], p. 210). Justin Kaplan simply asserts, without discussion or substantiation, that "the character [Clemens] rewrote was that of the narrator himself" (*Mr. Clemens and Mark Twain* [New York: Simon and Schuster, 1966], p. 135). DeLancey

Ferguson was perhaps responsible for stimulating these conjectures as rebuttals to an assertion he made decades ago that the altered character was the narrator's brother, the Secretary (*Mark Twain: Man and Legend* [Indianapolis: Bobbs-Merrill, 1943], p. 157).

    8. Holograph letter in MTM.

    9. Typescript of letter in MTP.

    10. See chap. 8.

    11. The text of Orion's 11 March 1871 letter is published in *Roughing It*, ed. Franklin R. Rogers, pp. 542–45. Hill discusses Clemens's adaptation of this material in *Mark Twain and Elisha Bliss*, pp. 45–47.

    12. Of the dainty palace on Delaware Avenue Clemens wrote John Henry Riley, "The man that comes forward & pays us what it cost a year of ago, ($25,000,) can take it." As for his share of the *Express*, "The man that will pay me $10,000 less than I gave can take *that*" (3 March 1871). A week later he wrote his brother, "We won't take less than $25,000 for the house, . . . & so it may take us 6 months to a year to sell it" (10 March 1871). After six months of advertising the house on the front page of the *Express*, he sold it to Mrs. J. Condit Smith on 23 September 1871 for $19,000 (title search owned by J. W. Bayliss [document in MTP]; the selling price is given in Martin B. Fried, "Mark Twain in Buffalo," *Niagara Frontier* 5 [1958]: 109). On 1 March 1871 Clemens sold his shares in the Express Printing Company to George H. Selkirk for $15,000. He had paid $25,000 for the shares the preceding August (articles of agreement in MTM).

    13. Ironically, the fame Bret Harte was at the time enjoying rested very largely on his poem "The Heathen Chinee," which had appeared in the September 1870 *Overland Monthly* and was subsequently copied by many papers. Hardly more than a jingle, "The Heathen Chinee" seems in retrospect to epitomize the kind of journalistic ephemerality Clemens here disparages.

    14. "Have you ever seen anything from us that has placed you in any difficult position, or thrust you prominently forward?" Bliss went on. "*We have in no way intimated* that you were *sponsor* or *father* to the paper or that you had any connection with it, except as above *in common with other authors and contributors*." Quoted in *Mark Twain's Letters to His Publishers, 1867–1894*, ed. Hamlin Hill (Berkeley and Los Angeles: University of California Press, 1967), p. 60n. In *Mark Twain and Elisha Bliss* Hill refers to this as "another of those remarkable letters that succeeded in keeping Twain in line for an entire decade" (p. 51).

    15. "Autobiographical Dictation" for 16 February 1906; original in MTP.

    16. "Autobiographical Dictation" for 15 February 1906; original in MTP.

Chapter 10

1. Letter dated 25 January 1871; holograph in Katharine S. Day Collection, Stowe-Day Library, Hartford, Connecticut.

2. For a useful gathering of materials relating to the Elmira community and Clemens's association with it, see *Mark Twain in Elmira*, ed. Robert D. Jerome and Herbert A. Wisbey, Jr. (Elmira, N.Y.: Mark Twain Society, 1977).

3. See chap. 9.

4. See chap. 8.

5. Letter dated 4 August 1869; holograph in MTP.

6. Holograph letter in MTP.

7. Holograph manuscript (DV79) in MTP.

8. Within a few years, when they had made it their summer home, the Cranes were inspired by the freedom and informality of Quarry Farm to christen it "Go-as-you-please Hall," in a way perpetuating those aspects of the place Clemens had earlier mined. In 1874, after the Crane and Clemens families had taken over the house at the farm as a summer retreat, Susan Crane surprised her brother-in-law by having an octagonal study built for him on a nearby crest of land, thus recapitulating the circumstances that had drawn him to the farm in the first place by allowing him an amiable escape from domestic cares and distractions.

9. The only surviving record of Goodman's criticism, apparently, is Paine's. He credits Goodman with reviving Clemens's confidence by reviewing the manuscript of *Roughing It* and pronouncing it "a great book!" *Mark Twain: A Biography*, 1:435–36.

10. Holograph letter in MTP.

11. The full publication history of *Mark Twain's (Burlesque) Autobiography* is given in *The Works of Mark Twain: Early Tales & Sketches*, Volume 1, *1851–1864*, ed. Edgar Marquess Branch and Robert H. Hirst (Berkeley, Los Angeles, and London: University of California Press, 1979), pp. 561–71. Branch and Hirst observe that "reviews were relatively scarce, invariably brief, and, with few exceptions, negative in tone," citing a number of contemporary instances. The Chicago *Tribune*, e.g., judged that "the work is not up to Twain's average of humor, and suggests, perhaps, that the well has been pumped too long." *Godey's Lady's Book and Magazine* imagined that "the necessity of making a book must have borne very heavily upon him to compel him to send before the public such a collection of weak jokes and mild witticisms as this." Boston's *Literary World* maintained that the author's name aroused the "suspicion that the work is one of humor; but the book itself affords not the feeblest fibre of corroboration" (pp. 568–69).

12. See chap. 9.

13. Letter dated 17 May 1871; holograph in MTP.

14. Paine mentions other self-inflicted distractions from the same period, including Clemens's plan to co-write a book with Goodman, his beginning a western play, and his inventing and patenting an adjustable vest strap. *Mark Twain: A Biography*, 1:440.

15. These observations tie into and benefit from fuller discussions of the initiation motif in *Roughing It* and of Clemens's presentation of the West in the book. See, in particular, Henry Nash Smith, *Mark Twain: The Development of a Writer* (Cambridge, Mass.: Harvard University Press, 1962), pp. 52–70, and "Mark Twain as an Interpreter of the Far West: The Structure of *Roughing It*," in *The Frontier in Perspective*, ed. Walker D. Wyman and Clifton B. Kroeber (Madison: University of Wisconsin Press, 1957), pp. 210–25. Smith argues that the book's narrator is initiated into a system of western vernacular values which ultimately prove unsatisfying. Hamlin Hill agrees essentially with Smith and extends his judgments to include Clemens's personal circumstances and his implied critique of the American Dream. "*Roughing It*," he says, "is Mark Twain's renunciation of his footloose bachelorhood [and] his rejection of that myth of the frontier West that obsessed the American imagination in the nineteenth century." Introduction to *Roughing It* (New York: Penguin Books, 1981), p. 19. Hill also acknowledges William M. Gibson's assertion that a primary theme of the book is "that luck is for the lucky, who are few, and that work and a vocation are for the many, of whom Mark Twain counted himself one." *The Art of Mark Twain* (New York: Oxford University Press, 1976), p. 35. William C. Spengemann cites the narrator's eventual disillusionment with the West as an instance of Twain's exploiting the tension between "adventure" and "domesticity." *The Adventurous Muse: The Poetics of American Fiction, 1789–1900* (New Haven and London: Yale University Press, 1977), p. 217. James M. Cox dissents, in a way, maintaining that the narrator is never truly initiated but rather is made to experience the same western disillusionment over and over. *Mark Twain: The Fate of Humor* (Princeton: Princeton University Press, 1966), p. 98.

Afterword

1. *Alta California* for 6 September 1868; reprinted in "'American Travel Letters Series Two,' Tenth in Series in 'Alta California,'" *Twainian* 7 (November–December 1948): 6.

2. "American Travel Letters Series Two," p. 7.

3. The letter appeared in the New York *World* on 18 February 1877.

Bibliography

Anderson, Frederick, Lin Salamo, and Bernard L. Stein, eds. *Mark Twain's Notebooks & Journals*, Volume 2: *1877–1883*. Berkeley, Los Angeles, and London: University of California Press, 1975.

Berry, Earl D. "Mark Twain as a Newspaper Man." *Illustrated Buffalo Express*, 11 November 1917.

Branch, Edgar Marquess, Michael B. Frank, and Kenneth M. Sanderson, eds. *Mark Twain's Letters*, Volume 1: *1853–1866*. Berkeley, Los Angeles, and London: University of California Press, 1988.

Branch, Edgar Marquess, and Robert H. Hirst, eds. *The Works of Mark Twain: Early Tales & Sketches*, Volume 1: *1851–1864*. Berkeley, Los Angeles, and London: University of California Press, 1979.

———. *The Works of Mark Twain: Early Tales & Sketches*, Volume 2: *1864–1865*. Berkeley, Los Angeles, and London: University of California Press, 1981.

Cox, James M. *Mark Twain: The Fate of Humor*. Princeton: Princeton University Press, 1966.

DeVoto, Bernard, ed. *Mark Twain in Eruption*. New York and London: Harper, 1922.

Dickinson, Leon T. "Mark Twain's Revisions in Writing *The Innocents Aborad*." *American Literature* 19 (1947): 139–57.

Duskis, Henry. *The Forgotten Writings of Mark Twain*. New York: Philosophical Library, 1963.

Eastman, Max. "Mark Twain's Elmira." *Harper's Monthly* 176 (May 1938): 620–32.

[Fairbanks, Mary Mason]. "The Wedding of 'Mark Twain.'" Cleveland *Daily Herald*, 8 February 1870, p. 2.

Ferguson, DeLancey. *Mark Twain: Man and Legend*. Indianapolis: Bobbs-Merrill, 1943.

F[ord], D[arius] R. "Around the World: Letter No. Nine." Buffalo *Express*, 12 February 1870.

———. "Around the World: Letter No. Ten." Buffalo *Express*, 5 March 1870.

Fried, Martin B. "Mark Twain in Buffalo." *Niagara Frontier* 5 (1958): 89–110.

Gibson, William M. *The Art of Mark Twain*. New York: Oxford University Press, 1976.

Hill, Hamlin. *Mark Twain and Elisha Bliss*. Columbia: University of Missouri Press, 1964.

———, ed. *Mark Twain's Letters to His Publishers, 1867–1894*. Berkeley and Los Angeles: University of California Press, 1967.

Hirst, Robert H. "The Making of *The Innocents Abroad*: 1867–1872." Ph.D. diss., University of California, Berkeley, 1975.

Howells, William Dean. *My Mark Twain: Reminiscences and Criticisms*. New York and London: Harper, 1910.

Jerome, Robert D., and Herbert A. Wisbey, Jr., eds. *Mark Twain in Elmira*. Elmira, N.Y.: Mark Twain Society, 1977.

Kaplan, Justin. *Mr. Clemens and Mark Twain: A Biography*. New York: Simon and Schuster, 1966.

Larned, Josephus N. "Mark Twain." Buffalo *Express*, 26 April 1910.

"Mark Twain on Agriculture." Buffalo *Express*, 12 April 1870.

"Mark Twain's First Visit to Niagara Falls." Buffalo *Commercial Advertiser*, 19 August 1869, p. 2; reprinted in Buffalo *Express*, 20 August 1869, p. 1.

McElderry, Bruce R., Jr., ed. *Contributions to the "Galaxy," 1868–1871, by Mark Twain*. Gainesville, Fla.: Scholars' Facsimiles and Reprints, 1961.

McNutt, James C. "Mark Twain and the American Indian: Earthly Realism and Heavenly Idealism." *American Indian Quarterly* 4 (August 1978): 223–42.

Paine, Albert Bigelow. *Mark Twain: A Biography*, Vol. 1. New York: Harper, 1912.

———, ed. *Mark Twain's Autobiography*. 2 vols. New York and London: Harper, 1924.

Piatt, Donn. "Funny in Spite of Himself." *Every Saturday* 2, no. 71 (6 May 1871): 415.

"Press Greetings." Buffalo *Express*, 9 October 1869.

Regan, Robert. "The Reprobate Elect in *The Innocents Abroad*." *American Literature* 54 (May 1982): 240–57.

Rogers, Franklin R. *The Pattern for Mark Twain's "Roughing It": Letters from Nevada by Samuel and Orion Clemens, 1861–62*. Berkeley and Los Angeles: University of California Press, 1961.

Smith, Harriet Elinor, and Richard Bucci, eds. *Mark Twain's Letters*, Volume 2: *1867–1868*. Berkeley, Los Angeles, and London: University of California Press, 1990.

Smith, Henry Nash. "Mark Twain as an Interpreter of the Far West: The Structure of *Roughing It*." In *The Frontier in Perspective*, ed. Walker D. Wyman and Clifton B. Kroeber. Madison: University of Wisconsin Press, 1957, pp. 210–25.

———. *Mark Twain: The Development of a Writer*. Cambridge, Mass.: Harvard University Press, 1962.

Spengemann, William C. *The Adventurous Muse: The Poetics of American Fiction, 1789–1900*. New Haven and London: Yale University Press, 1977.

Steinbrink, Jeffrey. "How Mark Twain Survived Sam Clemens' Reformation." *American Literature* 55 (October 1983): 299–315; reprinted in *On Mark Twain: The Best from American Literature*, ed. Louis J. Budd and Edwin H. Cady. Durham, N.C.: Duke University Press, 1987, pp. 259–75.

Twain, Mark. "About Smells." *Galaxy*, May 1870, pp. 721–22.

———. " 'American Travel Letters Series Two,' Ninth in Series in 'Alta California' "; reprinted in *Twainian* 7 (September–October 1948): 3–4. Originally published 3 March 1868.

———. " 'American Travel Letters Series Two,' Tenth in Series in 'Alta California' "; reprinted in *Twainian* 7 (November–December 1948): 5–7. Originally published 6 September 1868.

———. " 'American Travel Letters Series Two,' Thirteenth in Series in 'Alta California' "; reprinted in *Twainian* 8 (May–June 1949): 3–6. Originally published 25 July 1869.

———. "The Approaching Epidemic." *Galaxy*, September 1870, pp. 430–31.

———. "Around the World: Letter No. One." Buffalo *Express*, 16 October 1869.

———. "Around the World: Letter No. Three." Buffalo *Express*, 13 November 1869.

———. "Around the World: Letter No. Four." Buffalo *Express*, 11 December 1869.

———. "Around the World: Letter No. Five." Buffalo *Express*, 18 December 1869.

———. "Around the World: Letter No. Six." Buffalo *Express*, 8 January 1870.

———. "Around the World: Letter No. Seven." Buffalo *Express*, 22 January 1870.

———. "Around the World: Letter No. Eight." Buffalo *Express*, 29 January 1870.

———. "The Blondes." Buffalo *Express*, 28 February 1870.

―――. "A Couple of Sad Experiences." *Galaxy*, June 1870, p. 858.

―――. "Curious Dream: Containing a Moral." Buffalo *Express*, 30 April and 7 May 1870.

―――. "Curious Relic for Sale." *Galaxy*, October 1870, pp. 571–74.

―――. "The Danger of Lying in Bed." *Galaxy*, February 1871, pp. 317–18.

―――. "A Day at Niagara." Buffalo *Express*, 21 August 1869.

―――. "Disgraceful Persecution of a Boy." *Galaxy*, May 1870, pp. 722–24.

―――. "Dogberry in Washington." *Galaxy*, December 1870, pp. 881–83.

―――. "The Editorial Office Bore." *Galaxy*, July 1870, pp. 140–41.

―――. "English Festivities." Buffalo *Express*, 28 August 1869.

―――. "An Entertaining Article." *Galaxy*, December 1870, pp. 876–78.

―――. "The Facts in the Case of George Fisher, Deceased." *Galaxy*, January 1871, pp. 152–55.

―――. "The Facts in the Case of the Great Beef Contract." *Galaxy*, May 1870, pp. 718–21.

―――. "The Facts in the Great Land Slide Case." Buffalo *Express*, 2 April 1870.

―――. "Fortifications of Paris." Buffalo *Express*, 17 September 1870.

―――. "Goldsmith's Friend Abroad Again." *Galaxy*, October 1870, pp. 569–71.

―――. "Goldsmith's Friend Abroad Again (Continued)." *Galaxy*, November 1870, pp. 727–31.

―――. "Goldsmith's Friend Abroad Again (Continued)." *Galaxy*, January 1871, pp. 156–58.

―――. "Hogwash." *Galaxy*, June 1870, pp. 862–63.

―――. ["Housekeeping No. 1"]. Holograph manuscript in MTP; to be published in *The Works of Mark Twain: Early Tales & Sketches*, Volume 4: *1869–1870*. Berkeley and Los Angeles: University of California Press, forthcoming, item 279.

―――. ["Housekeeping No. 2"]. Holograph manuscript in MTP; to be published in *The Works of Mark Twain: Early Tales & Sketches*, Volume 4: *1869–1870*. Berkeley and Los Angeles: University of California Press, forthcoming, item 280.

―――. "How I Edited an Agricultural Paper Once." *Galaxy*, July 1870, pp. 133–35.

―――. *The Innocents Abroad*. Hartford: American Publishing Company, 1869.

―――. "Introductory." *Galaxy*, May 1870, p. 717.

―――. "John Chinaman in New York." *Galaxy*, September 1870, p. 426.

————. "Journalism in Tennessee." Buffalo *Express*, 4 September 1869.

————. "The Last Words of Great Men." Buffalo *Express*, 11 September 1869.

————. "The Latest Novelty." Buffalo *Express*, 2 October 1869.

————. "The Legend of the Capitoline Venus." Buffalo *Express*, 23 October 1869.

————. "Mark Twain: His Greeting to the California Pioneers of 1849." New York *Tribune*, 14 October 1869; reprinted in Buffalo *Express*, 19 October 1869.

————. "Mark Twain on Agriculture." Buffalo *Express*, 12 April 1870.

————. *Mark Twain's (Burlesque) Autobiography and First Romance*. New York: Sheldon, 1871.

————. "Mark Twain's Map of Paris." *Galaxy*, November 1870, pp. 723–25.

————. "A Memory." *Galaxy*, August 1870, pp. 286–87.

————. "More Byron Scandal." Buffalo *Express*, 7 September 1869.

————. "My Famous 'Bloody Massacre.'" *Galaxy*, June 1870, pp. 860–62.

————. "My First Literary Venture." *Galaxy*, April 1871, pp. 615–16.

————. "A Mysterious Visit." Buffalo *Express*, 19 March 1870.

————. "A Mystery." Cleveland *Herald*, 16 November 1868.

————. "The Noble Red Man." *Galaxy*, September 1870, pp. 426–29.

————. "Personal." Buffalo *Express*, 8–11 March 1870.

————. "Personal Habits of the Siamese Twins." *Packard's Monthly*, n.s. 1 (1869): 249–50.

————. "The Petrified Man." *Galaxy*, June 1870, pp. 858–60.

————. "Political Economy." *Galaxy*, September 1870, pp. 424–26.

————. "The Portrait." *Galaxy*, January 1871, pp. 150–52.

————. "Post-Mortem Poetry." *Galaxy*, June 1870, pp. 864–65.

————. "The 'Present' Nuisance." *Galaxy*, December 1870, pp. 880–81.

————. "A Protest." Holograph manuscript in MTP; to be published in *The Works of Mark Twain: Early Tales & Sketches*, Volume 4: *1869–1870*. Berkeley and Los Angeles: University of California Press, forthcoming, item 282.

————. "The Reception at the President's." *Galaxy*, October 1870, pp. 567–69.

————. "A Reminiscence of the Back Settlements." *Galaxy*, November 1870, pp. 731–32.

————. "Rev. H. W. Beecher: His Private Habits." Buffalo *Express*, 25 September 1869.

————. "Riley—Newspaper Correspondent." *Galaxy*, November 1870, pp. 726–27.

————. *Roughing It*. Hartford: American Publishing Company, 1872.

————. *Roughing It.* Edited by Franklin R. Rogers. Berkeley, Los Angeles, and London: University of California Press, 1972.

————. *Roughing It.* Edited by Hamlin Hill. New York: Penguin Books, 1981.

————. "A Royal Compliment." *Galaxy*, September 1870, pp. 429–30.

————. "Running for Governor." *Galaxy*, December 1870, pp. 878–80.

————. "A Sad, Sad Business." *Galaxy*, January 1871, pp. 158–59.

————. "Salutatory." Buffalo *Express*, 21 August 1869.

————. "Science vs. Luck." *Galaxy*, October 1870, pp. 574–75.

————. *Sketches, New and Old.* Hartford: American Publishing Company, 1875.

————. "The Story of the Good Little Boy Who Did Not Prosper." *Galaxy*, May 1870, pp. 724–26.

————. "The 'Tournament' in A.D. 1870." *Galaxy*, July 1870, pp. 135–36.

————. "Unburlesquable Things." *Galaxy*, July 1870, pp. 137–38.

————. "Valedictory." *Galaxy*, April 1871, p. 651.

————. "A Wail." Holograph manuscript in MTP; to be published in *The Works of Mark Twain: Early Tales & Sketches*, Volume 4: *1869–1870*. Berkeley and Los Angeles: University of California Press, forthcoming, item 283.

————. "The 'Wild Man' Interviewed." Buffalo *Express*, 18 September 1869.

————. "Wit-Inspirations of the 'Two-Year-Olds.'" *Galaxy*, June 1870, pp. 865–67.

Webster, Samuel Charles. *Mark Twain, Business Man.* Boston: Little, Brown, 1946.

Wecter, Dixon, ed. *The Love Letters of Mark Twain.* New York: Harper, 1949.

————. *Mark Twain to Mrs. Fairbanks.* San Marino, Calif.: Huntington Library, 1949.

Index

"About Smells," 102–3
Aldrich, Thomas Bailey, 194n.5
Alta California, 5, 34
American Indians, 125–26, 184
American Publisher, 144, 158, 160, 162–63, 165; Clemens's contributions to, 168–69, 182
American Publishing Company, xv, 31, 62, 121, 134, 144, 160, 169–70, 178–79, 182, 188. *See also* Bliss, Elisha
"Approaching Epidemic, The," 123
"Around the World" letters, 63–65, 84–87, 131
"Autobiographical Dictation," 165

"Bad Little Boy Who Did Not Come to Grief, The," 102, 200n.8
Beach, Emiline, xvii, 5
Beecher, Henry Ward, 197n.8
Beecher, Thomas K., 70, 114–15, 197n.8
Beecher family, 31
Benton, Joel, 81
Berry, Earl D., 60, 199n.5, 201n.13
Bliss, Elisha, 134, 188; and *American Publisher*, 158, 160, 168–69; Clemens on, 170, 203n.15; and *Innocents Abroad*, xv, 15, 36, 62; letters from, 132, 171, 178–79, 208n.14; letters to, 36–38, 43, 45, 53, 82, 99, 115, 117, 119, 120, 121, 127, 132, 133, 136, 140, 146, 148–49, 151, 164–65; and Mark Twain's reputation, 84, 170, 178–79; and Orion Clemens, 144–45, 160, 206n.13; and *Roughing It*, 115, 121–22, 132–34, 136, 140, 141, 144, 147, 148–49, 155–59, 166, 168–72, 180–82
"Blondes, The," 107–8

Bowen, Will, xv, 1, 79–80
Bowles, Samuel, 34–35, 195n.3
Branch, Edgar Marquess, 209n.11
Buffalo, New York, xvi, xvii, 20, 38–40; Clemens in, 23, 27–28, 40, 43, 44, 60, 61–62, 66–69, 139, 188, 201–2n.16; Clemenses' house in, 67–70, 73, 76, 77–81, 88–90; Clemenses in, 77–82, 94–95, 111, 143, 149, 202n.2; Clemens's work in, 172–73 (*see also* Buffalo *Express*); leaving, 95–96, 157, 164–66, 208n.12
Buffalo *Express*, 19; Clemens's financial interest in, 38–42, 45, 95, 157, 164, 208n.12; Clemens's work at, 22, 43, 44–47, 53, 58–60, 63–65, 67, 81–88, 91–92, 96–110, 116, 122, 147, 196n.6, 201n.13, 205–6n.8; Mark Twain at, 45, 47–59, 61–65, 77, 100, 109, 190, 196n.1, 199n.5
Byron scandal, 54, 57, 197n.8

California, 204–5n.2; Clemens in, 5, 16, 64–65, 131–35. See also *Roughing It*, California in
Chinese, treatment of, 102, 124–25, 129–30, 140
Church, Francis P., 99–100, 151–53, 200–201n.9, 207n.5; letters to, 81–82, 142, 151
Clemens, Jane Lampton, 145; letters to, xiv, 1, 18, 30, 33, 35, 38, 41, 132, 135, 202–3n.10
Clemens, John Marshall, 41, 120, 128, 203n.12
Clemens, Langdon, 143–45, 151, 156, 189

Clemens, Olivia Langdon. *See* Langdon (Clemens), Olivia

Clemens, Orion, 145, 201n.12; and American Publishing Company, 144–45, 160, 206n.13; letters to, 109, 122, 134–35, 136, 143, 151, 164, 170, 208n.12; and *Roughing It*, 134–36, 155, 158–63, 165, 169, 172–73, 177, 179–80, 182, 184, 185, 205n.6

Clemens, Samuel: as book writer, xvi (see also *Innocents Abroad*; *Roughing It*); in Buffalo (*see* Buffalo; Buffalo *Express*); and California (*see* California); diamond-prospecting book, idea of, 146–48; and eastern establishment, 16, 126; in Elmira (*see* Elmira); family of, 18, 30, 135, 145, 203n.10 (*see also* Clemens, Jane Lampton; Clemens, John Marshall; Clemens, Langdon; Clemens, Orion; Clemens, Susy; Langdon, Charles; Langdon, Jervis; Langdon (Clemens), Olivia; Langdon, Olivia Lewis; Moffett, Annie; Moffett, Pamela); as householder, 87–95, 204n.17; and Jervis Langdon, 41–43, 70–76, 116, 126–27, 170, 202n.9; as lecturer, xv, 15–17, 21, 27–28, 30, 45, 51–52, 59–63, 65–66, 82, 182, 190, 204–5n.2; and magazine writing, 99–102, 110, 162–63 (see also *Galaxy* magazine); and Mark Twain, 2, 15–19, 22, 56, 110, 172, 190; on marriage, 1–2, 23, 25, 28, 77–78; as moralist, 107, 112, 129; and newspaper editing, 27–40, 50, 53–60, 63, 81–88, 96–111, 118 (*see also* Buffalo *Express*); on newspaper writing, 55–58, 98–101; occupations of, 27, 201n.12; Olivia on, 94; at Philadelphia *Ledger*, 201n.12; as professional writer, 119–20, 183, 186–88; and public opinion, 163–64; publishers of (*see* Bliss, Elisha; Church, Francis P.; Sheldon, Isaac E.); reformation of, 2–7, 16–20, 194n.7; self-doubts of, xv, 154; travels of, 24, 27, 138; wedding of, 70–71, 78, 198n.10

— as Mark Twain, 11, 16; on American Indians, 125–26, 184; as book writer, 62–63, 154; at Buffalo *Express* (*see* Buffalo *Express*, Mark Twain at); characteristics of, xvi–xvii, 10, 18, 50, 82, 86–87, 92, 109, 129, 154, 176, 190; characters of, 176; and Clemens's reformation, 15–18; development of, xiii, xvi–xviii, 53, 64–65, 106–8, 110–12, 190; and domesticity, 91–92, 123–24, 174, 203–4n.17; in the east, 16–17; and Elisha Bliss (*see* Bliss, Elisha); as journalist, 116–17, 196–97n.3, 199n.5 (*see also* Buffalo *Express*); on married life, 174–75; moral humor of, 112, 129; popularity of, 79, 178–79; reputation of, 10–12, 15, 49, 62–63, 83, 107, 110, 121, 170, 182; social criticism by, 102–3, 107, 118, 125, 130

Clemens, Susy, 204n.22

Cleveland, 16, 20, 29, 33, 35, 38, 40, 41, 43

Cleveland *Herald*, 9, 10, 17, 29–31, 33, 35–38, 42, 45, 195n.5. *See also* Fairbanks, Abel; Fairbanks, Mary Mason

Colfax, Schuyler, 137–38, 206n.9

"Couple of Sad Experiences, A," 103–4

Cox, James M., 210n.15

Crane, Henry M., 45

Crane, Susan Langdon, 111, 114, 115, 119, 127, 168, 202n.2, 204n.22, 209n.8

Crane, Theodore, 114, 168

"Curious Dream," 110

"Dangers of Lying in Bed, The," 149

Day, Alice. *See* Hooker (Day), Alice

Day, Calvin, 31

"Day at Niagara, A," 48–50, 58, 107, 124

"Disgraceful Persecution of a Boy," 102–3, 125

"Dogberry in Washington," 142–43

Duncan, Capt. Charles C., 191

Duskis, Henry, 196n.1

Eastman, Max, 194n.7

"Editorial Office Bore, The," 105–6, 118

Elmira, New York, xvii, 31, 43; Clemens in, 6, 53, 60, 61, 63–66, 166–81, 188 (*see also* Quarry Farm); Clemenses in, 115, 119, 121, 122, 157, 166–68

"English Festivities," 49–50, 58–59, 107

"Facts in the Case of the Great Beef Contract, The," 102–3

"Facts in the Great Land Slide Case, The," 102, 205n.4

Fairbanks, Abel, 9, 29–31, 35–38, 40, 202n.2

Fairbanks, Mary Mason, xiv, xv, 3–5, 12, 29–30, 35, 78, 133, 194n.2; criticism by, 17, 50, 59; letters to, xiii, xvii–xviii, 2, 6, 7, 12, 14, 16, 17, 21, 27, 28, 29, 32, 33–34, 38, 39–40,

41, 43, 44, 50, 51–52, 59, 77–78, 81,
83, 88, 94, 99, 101, 118, 119, 132, 136,
141, 156, 164, 179, 183, 185,
195nn.5,8,13, 196n.7, 200–201n.9,
202n.5
Ferguson, DeLancey, 207–8n.7
Ford, Darius R., 63, 84–87, 119, 146
Fuller, Frank, xiv

Galaxy magazine, 99–107, 110; leaving,
164; "Memoranda" in, 102–6, 116–20,
122–27, 129–30, 135, 137, 140, 142,
145–49, 151–54, 162, 200–201n.9,
205n.4, 206n.14, 207n.5
Gibson, William M., 210n.15
"Goldsmith's Friend Abroad Again,"
129, 140
Goodman, Joe, 177, 209n.9, 210n.14
Grant, U. S., 121, 129
Gray, David, 111, 201–2n.16, 202n.18
Gray, Martha, 111
"Greeting to the California Pioneers,"
65, 131–32

Hank Morgan, 176
Harte, Bret, 113, 200n.8; and Clemens's
writing, 5–6, 194n.5; success of, 162–
64, 208n.13
Hartford, Connecticut, xvi, xvii, 20, 31–
35, 40, 41, 43, 68–70, 94; move to,
157, 160, 165, 188–89, 191–92
Hartford *Courant*, 31–35, 67–70
Hartford *Post*, 34
Hawley, Joseph, 31–32, 35, 70, 195n.3
Hill, Hamlin, 207n.6, 208n.14, 210n.15
Hine, Charles C., 82
Hirst, Robert H., 194n.5, 209n.11
"Hogwash," 104
Hooker (Day), Alice, 31, 94, 127, 167,
200n.2
Hooker, Isabella, 70, 188
Hooker, John, 188
Hosmer, Hezekiah L., 139–40, 161–62,
166
"How I Edited an Agricultural Paper
Once," 105, 118
Howells, William Dean, 63, 126, 204n.9
Huck Finn, xi, xiii, 65, 125, 176

Innocents Abroad, xiii, 28, 54, 90, 91, 105,
108, 157, 184, 194n.4; publication of,
31, 36–37, 188; reviews of, 63, 111;
sequel to, 115, 131–33, 164, 190 (see
also *Roughing It*); success of, xvi,
32, 62–63, 67, 79, 100, 101, 106, 111–
12, 121, 148, 178, 189; work on, 5–
6, 15, 19, 21

"John Chinaman in New York," 124–25
"Journalism in Tennessee," 55–58, 96

Kaplan, Justin, 72, 195n.1, 196n.2,
198n.9, 207n.7
Kennett, Thomas A., 196n.6

Langdon, Charles, 4, 44, 63, 84–87, 114,
119, 141
Langdon, Jervis, 39, 198nn.8,9,11; and
Clemens's business, 35–46, 72,
201n.15; and Clemenses' house, 66–
72; death of, 126–28, 135, 206n.9;
illness of, 114–20, 122, 202n.2;
influence of, on Clemens, 23, 68, 74–
76, 128–29, 157, 170; letters to, 14, 30,
37, 41, 95, 111, 117–18, 202n.9
Langdon, Olivia Lewis, 13–14, 16, 39,
42, 80–81, 111, 114, 116, 195n.13,
196n.7
Langdon (Clemens), Olivia: background
of, 25, 72, 126–27; in Buffalo (*see*
Buffalo, Clemenses in); Clemens on,
79, 82; courtship of, xvi, 1–2, 4, 6–12,
19–21, 42–43, 53, 67, 73, 194n.3;
engagement of, 11–12, 15, 29–30; and
Hartford, 31–32, 189; illness of, 145,
150, 151, 155, 157, 164; letters
from, 22, 67, 78, 88, 89, 94, 111, 113–
14, 127, 200n.2; letters to, 6–7, 9, 14,
15–16, 19, 20, 21, 23–24, 25, 27, 28,
30, 31, 34, 35, 40, 42, 44, 46–47, 50–
51, 52, 56, 62, 66, 67–68, 69–70,
72, 73, 89, 121, 149, 167, 185, 186,
192, 195n.3; and Mary Fairbanks,
195n.8
Langdon family, 9, 11, 13–15, 21, 30, 52;
home of, 24–26, 53, 60; letters to, 86,
87, 88, 89, 91, 100, 101, 115, 133
Larned, Josephus N., 50, 60, 196n.6,
205n.8
"Last Words of Great Men, The," 54,
197n.8
"Latest Novelty, The," 54, 63, 107, 108
"Legend of the Capitoline Venus,
The," 74–76

McElderry, Bruce R., Jr., 203n.12
"Map of Paris," 137–38, 140, 146, 205–
6n.8
Mark Twain. *See* Samuel Clemens, as
Mark Twain
"Mark Twain on Agriculture," 201n.10
*Mark Twain's (Burlesque) Autobiography
and First Romance*, 147, 152, 169–
71, 178–79, 209n.11

Mark Twain's Sketches, New and Old, 147–48

Massett, Steven, 200n.4

"Memoranda." See *Galaxy* magazine

"Memory, A," 119–20, 203n.12

Moffett, Annie, 72, 145, 198n.10

Moffett, Pamela, 198n.10, 202–3n.8; letters to, xiv, 1, 18, 21, 30, 33, 35, 36, 37, 41, 42, 45, 73–74, 118–19, 126, 132, 135, 136

"'Monopoly' Speaks, The," 46–47, 50

"My Famous 'Bloody Massacre,'" 104, 205n.4

"Mysterious Visit, A," 108–9, 204n.17

"Mystery, A," 9–12, 19, 20

Nasby, Petroleum V. *See* Petroleum Vesuvius Nasby

Nevada, 131; Clemens in, 5, 64, 177; and *Roughing It*, 87, 134–35, 173, 186. *See also* Virginia City, Nevada

"New Crime: Legislation Needed, The," 103, 110

"Noble Red Man, The," 125–26

Nye, Emma, 136–41

"Our Precious Lunatic," 103, 110

Paine, Albert Bigelow, 45, 196n.6, 196–97n.3, 198n.11, 203n.11, 209n.9, 210n.14

"Personal Habits of the Siamese Twins," 19–20

"Petrified Man, The," 103–4, 201n.11, 205n.4

Petroleum Vesuvius Nasby (David Ross Locke), 33, 45, 51, 63, 89, 199n.5

Piatt, Donn, 206n.8

"Political Economy," 123–24

"Post-Mortem Poetry," 104, 201n.12

"'Present' Nuisance, The," 142

"Protest, A," 98–99, 200n.6

Quaker City voyage, xiii–xvii, 2, 4, 91, 129, 191; correspondence from, 5, 28, 194n.4 (see also *Innocents Abroad*)

Quarry Farm, 166–68, 172–73, 175, 177, 181, 186, 209n.8

"Reception at the President's, The," 129

Redpath, James, 50–52, 192; letters to, 78, 113, 182, 204–5n.2

Regan, Robert, 194n.4

Reid, Whitelaw, 53, 62

"Reminiscence of the Back Settlements, A," 140–41

"Rev. H. W. Beecher: His Private Habits," 57, 197n.8

Riley, John Henry, 140, 146–48, 157, 158, 162, 171, 208n.12

Rogers, Franklin R., 207nn.6,7

Roughing It, 111, 210n.15; California in, 87, 131–35, 184–86; characters of, 141, 159–60; contract for, 121–22, 130, 134, 143–44, 157, 170, 203n.15; narrator of, 138, 159; Nevada in, 87, 134–35, 173, 186; pony-express episode in, 168–69, 180; revision of, 159, 161, 177, 180–81, 186; Sandwich Islands in, 184–86, 207n.6; Slade episode in, 140, 161–62, 169, 173–74; slowdown on, 141–43, 146–49, 155–56, 165; start of, 131–36, 138–40; the West in, 87, 134–35, 173–75, 183–86; writing of, xiii, 141–42, 158–61, 164, 169, 172–78, 180–86, 188, 190, 192, 207n.6, 207–8n.7

"Royal Compliment, A," 123

"Salutatory" (*Express*), 47–48, 53, 58, 100, 102

San Francisco, xv, 5, 16, 102

Sandwich Islands, 184–86, 205n.2, 207n.6

Selkirk, Col. George F., 196n.6

Severance, Emily, xiv, 4, 27

Sheldon, Isaac, 147, 148, 152–53, 170–71, 178

Slade. See *Roughing It*, Slade episode in

Slee, J. D. F., 39, 46, 67, 69–70, 114

Smith, Henry Nash, 194n.7, 201n.15, 207n.7, 210n.15

Spengemann, William C., 210n.15

Springfield *Republican*, 34

Stewart, William M., xiv

"Story of the Good Little Boy Who Did Not Prosper, The," 102–3

Stowe, Harriet Beecher, 197n.8

Tahoe, Lake, 174–75, 205n.2

Toledo *Blade*, 33, 51

Tom Sawyer, 176

Twain, Mark. *See* Samuel Clemens, as Mark Twain

Twichell, Harmony, 80, 101, 118

Twichell, Joseph, 14, 20–21, 31–32, 70, 80, 101, 118, 189, 195n.3

"Valedictory" (*Galaxy*), 153–54, 206n.14

Virginia City, Nevada, 140, 161–62; and *Territorial Enterprise*, 132–33, 177

"Wail, A," 96–99, 200n.4

Warner, Charles Dudley, 31–32, 34–35, 67–68, 70, 195n.3

Washington, D.C., xiv, xv, 120–22
Webb, Charles Henry, 145, 194n.5, 206n.14
Webster, Samuel Charles, 198n.10
Wecter, Dixon, 54, 194n.2, 197n.6, 202n.2

" 'Wild Man' Interviewed, The," 57–58, 197n.8
"Wit-Inspirations of the 'Two-Year-Olds,' " 104–5
Wolcott, Ella, 136

Young Satan, 176

Compositor:	Wilsted & Taylor
Text:	11/13 Bembo
Display:	Bembo
Printer:	Malloy Lithographing, Inc.
Binder:	John H. Dekker & Sons